QUALITY WITH SOUL

How Six Premier Colleges and Universities
Keep Faith with Their Religious Traditions

ROBERT BENNE

WILLIAM B. EERDMANS PUBLISHING COMPANY
GRAND RAPIDS, MICHIGAN / CAMBRIDGE, U.K.

Wm. B. Eerdmans Publishing Co.
2140 Oak Industrial Drive N.E., Grand Rapids, Michigan 49505 /
P.O. Box 163, Cambridge CB3 9PU U.K.

Printed in the United States of America

05 04 03 02 01   7 6 5 4 3 2 1

Library of Congress Cataloging-in-Publication Data

Benne, Robert.
    Quality with soul: how six premier colleges and universities
    keep faith with their religious traditions / Robert Benne.
        p.   cm.
    Includes bibliographical references.
    ISBN-10: 0-8028-4704-8 / ISBN-13: 978-0-8028-4704-1 (pbk.: alk. paper)
        1. Church colleges — United States — Case studies.
    2. Church and college — United States — Case studies.
    3. Secularism — United States — Case studies.   I. Title.

    LC427.B45   2001
    378'.071 — dc21

                                                    00-065423

www.eerdmans.com

For our grandchildren —
   in hopes that they might someday
      go to schools like those described herein.

Contents

Preface

I have always held the conviction that the Christian faith provides an account of *all* of life, not just of "private" or "spiritual" life. This belief has led to my interest — if not obsession — in relating Christianity to those many "non-religious" facets of human life — economic, political, social, and cultural. Sometimes such efforts seem futile, since much of the modern Western world's way of understanding and shaping those facets has little to do with the Christian account. Indeed, many of those understandings are intentionally neglectful or outrightly hostile to Christian accounts. Such attitudes, along with other powerful dynamics, have led to the widespread secularization of modern life, which I take to mean the gradual removal of religious control and influence from the sectors I mentioned above.

That secularization is most dramatic and shocking in the very institutions that churches created and shaped through direct control or pervasive influence. As churches tried to answer human needs according to their own vision of human flourishing, they established orphanages, hospitals, schools, colleges, seminaries, homes for the elderly, camps, and other social service agencies. At their founding and through their early lives, these church institutions were often controlled and almost always pervasively influenced by that Christian understanding of human flourishing.

But a strange thing happened on the way to the forum. Those institutions themselves have been gradually secularized, many fully and irretrievably so, some to a lesser degree, while a few have maintained a strong relation to their Christian heritage. Nowhere is this more evident and increasingly noticed than in the field of Christian education at the college and university level. An avalanche of books and articles has dissected the many instances of the secularization of church-related colleges and universities.

As a professor for the past eighteen years at a partly secularized church-related college, I have been acutely aware of the effects of that secularization.[1] Put simply, the Christian heritage in its intellectual and practical dimensions has been pushed to the margins of college life. Roanoke College has conformed to many of the dismal accounts of secularization offered by a number of scholars in the past few years, especially to that of James Burtchaell in his *The Dying of the Light: The Disengagement of Colleges and Universities from Their Christian Churches*.[2]

In telling us compellingly of what went wrong, Burtchaell's grim analysis implicitly points to what must be done in order to set things right. It is that latter task in which I am intensely interested. In this book I want to point clearly to things that have to be done for things to go right, for colleges and universities of the church to take seriously their Christian heritage, both intellectual and practical, in all aspects of their common life.

However, I do not want this exercise to be a purely theoretical one, though getting the theory straight is every bit as important as getting the analysis of secularization straight. I want the theory to rise not only from the analysis of schools that have been secularized (Burtchaell's work) but also from the current lives of Christian schools that have not. In this book, then, I will examine the success of schools that have maintained both quality and soul. I will elaborate why and how six schools from six religious traditions have kept their version of the Christian vision publicly relevant in all dimensions of the life and mission of their schools.

Such an effort is not without precedent. Richard Hughes and William Adrian edited a book with a title that could well serve as one for this volume: *Models for Christian Higher Education: Strategies for Success in the*

---

1. I have told the story of Roanoke College's secularization and subsequent efforts at reconnecting with its Lutheran heritage in "Recovering a Christian College," *Lutheran Forum 27* (Pentecost 1993): 58-66. My analysis of Lutheran colleges in general can be found in "Integrity and Fragmentation," *Intersections: Faith + Life + Learning* (Winter 2000): 4-10.

2. James T. Burtchaell, *The Dying of the Light: The Disengagement of Colleges and Universities from Their Christian Churches* (Grand Rapids: Eerdmans, 1998).

Twenty-First Century.[3] Judging from the attention the book has received, the book itself has been a great success. Many colleges are looking for ways to become "descript" rather than "nondescript," to use the words of Martin Marty. One way to do that is to reaffirm or reappropriate their religious connections.

This volume is different from that one in at least two significant ways. The various models in the Hughes and Adrian volume are described and interpreted by persons from the very schools that provided the models. While this approach does not automatically call into question the adequacy of the writers' portraits, it does not lend itself to objective critique. Indeed, the essays in that volume do not abound in self-criticism. As a sympathetic outsider, I hope in the following to make both appreciative *and* critical assessments of colleges that by all accounts have both quality and soul.

A second difference is this: I intend to derive from the empirical examples of the schools themselves a comprehensive and synthetic account of the qualities that make them successful. From the many portraits I hope to sketch a mosaic whose pieces, supplied by the various schools, make up a coherent and recognizable picture of a Christian college or university. Further, I hope to elaborate strategies that can insure that such qualities persist into the future.

A further intent of the book is to analyze in an appreciative way those kinds of colleges that can no longer be considered full-blown Christian colleges but still claim a church relationship. There is a full spectrum of these sorts of colleges, extending from those with a fairly rich connection to those with virtually none at all who nevertheless persist in claiming one. These mildly connected colleges no doubt represent the majority of private, church-related colleges and universities. It is important not to ignore them.

Indeed, I wish to spend some time elaborating a strategy for strengthening the connection of those sorts of colleges to their religious traditions, should they wish to do so. All of them can "profit," I believe, from such a connection. If I wrote above of Roanoke College's partial secularization, I can now also write of its partial reconnection with its Chris-

3. Richard T. Hughes and William B. Adrian, eds., *Models for Christian Higher Education: Strategies for Success in the Twenty-First Century* (Grand Rapids: Eerdmans, 1997).

tian heritage, which I believe has profited the school markedly. The strategies I write about come in some measure from my experience in helping the college reconnect.

I have many persons and institutions to be grateful to in this enterprise. I am indebted to Roanoke College for its sabbatical support for both this project and for the many efforts it has made to rejoin more robustly with its Lutheran heritage. Without support from and leadership by key administrative and faculty persons, I would have long ago given up hope for strengthening that connection.

I am deeply grateful to the Lilly Fellows Program in Humanities and the Arts, which has provided not only financial and institutional support for my project but also the ideal context for working it out. That program has allowed me to work on this project in close conversation with many persons who care deeply about my project's purpose, which is to forge stronger links between various Christian traditions and their colleges and universities. Among those have been Arlin Meyer and Mark Schwehn, directors of the program, as well as the five postdoctoral fellows — and their faculty mentors — who are preparing to teach in church-related colleges and universities. I believe it has been providential that I have been able to work with this program and these persons just at the time that plans for my project were coming to fruition.

Moreover, it is entirely felicitous that the Lilly Program is hosted by a Lutheran university, Valparaiso, that exemplifies many of the qualities that that program is trying to nurture. "Valpo" has provided a gracious and fruitful context for both the Lilly Fellows Program and my time as a Senior Lilly Fellow working on this project. Many friends and colleagues too numerous to mention have been gracious and helpful to me. For someone interested in such a project, this is indeed the "vale of paradise!"

The schools that I have studied have unfailingly offered me hospitality. Calvin, Wheaton, Valparaiso, Notre Dame, Baylor, and St. Olaf made literature available to me and arranged interviews for me that have proved invaluable in doing my work. Key persons from each institution provided essential insight, direction, and feedback, as well as cordial conversation. However, the interpretations of those schools in this book are finally my own, not those of any with whom I spoke.

I am also indebted to Eerdmans Publishing Company and its editor-in-chief, Jon Pott, for their willingness to publish this work. Christian colleges and universities themselves owe a great deal to this company that has published so much on the crucial subject of Christian higher education. I am delighted that Eerdmans is willing to give me a chance to go at it.

Finally, I wish to thank my wife, Joanna, for accompanying me not only on the journey to Valparaiso for this project, but for accompanying me on the journey of life. Without her presence I would easily lose my bearings. With it the world seems a far more habitable place.

ROBERT BENNE
Senior Fellow in the Lilly Program
  for Humanities and the Arts
Valparaiso University
Valparaiso, Indiana
May, 2000

PART ONE The Current Situation

This first part of the book is devoted to the analytical task of understanding the secularization process as it has affected church-related colleges and universities. The first chapter will deal with the "darkening trends" that have overtaken many church-related educational institutions. It will glean insights from the many studies of secularization that have appeared in the last several years. It will answer the question: "What have been the effects of secularization on church-related colleges and universities?"

The second chapter will get at the underlying factors in the secularization process. Many of these factors are implicit in the path-breaking studies of the secularization of church-related colleges and universities. I simply intend to make explicit what has been for the most part implicit. Here I will answer the question: "What are the underlying causes of the secularization process?"

The third chapter will be devoted to an examination of where church-related colleges and universities are situated on the continuum from "fully Christian" to completely secularized. As already mentioned, the greater share of church-related schools find themselves nearer the midpoint on the continuum than either pole. It will be helpful to develop analytic categories that will enable such institutions more fully to understand themselves. The third chapter will grapple with the question: "What are the defining characteristics of church-related schools at various places on the secularization scale?"

1

1 | *The Darkening Trends*

At the conclusion of James Burtchaell's massive study of the disengagement of colleges and universities from their churches, he makes this melancholy observation and judgment:

> Readers who have seen this story through thus far will naturally wonder whether this is the end: the end of Christian colleges and universities. . . . There was, in these stories told here, little learned rage against the dying of the light. . . . It is a shame that so much of yesterday's efforts has become compost for those of tomorrow.[1]

This magisterial work is an extended confirmation of Burtchaell's earlier article that helped to re-ignite the current conversation concerning religion's role in higher education.[2] It is not as though this conversation had not been going on; it had, especially in the boards of higher education of many of the churches, but it had not become a matter of public discussion taken up by many scholars independent of those churches and their schools.

Soon after Burtchaell's article, however, the role of religion in higher education became an important subject of wider public debate. George Marsden and Bradley Longfield edited a book, *The Secularization of the*

---

1. James Burtchaell, *The Dying of the Light: The Disengagement of Colleges and Universities from Their Christian Churches* (Grand Rapids, Eerdmans, 1998), p. 851.

2. James Burtchaell, "The Decline and Fall of the Christian College," *First Things,* April 1991, pp. 16-29.

Academy, in which a number of authors traced the waning strength of both Protestant and Catholic religious traditions within the universities and colleges they sponsored,[3] along with the same processes taking place among the colleges and universities of Canada and Great Britain. Mark Schwehn added his voice to the discussion by bringing out *Exiles from Eden: Religion and the Academic Vocation in America,* where he argues that liberal learning is dependent on the cultivation and practice of certain Christian virtues like humility and charity, and that liberal learning itself is in jeopardy as the religious traditions that sustain those virtues weaken in the liberal arts colleges.[4]

Marsden expanded his leading essay in *The Secularization of the Academy* into a major book, *The Soul of the American University: From Protestant Establishment to Established Nonbelief.* There Marsden traces how private and public colleges and universities were secularized.[5] In their early days the great private universities such as Harvard, Yale, Princeton, and Chicago were founded and shaped by church bodies. More surprisingly, the public colleges and land-grant universities were significantly imbued with the ideas and practices of the Protestant mainstream, even including mandatory chapel attendance in many cases. But all have gradually moved through several phases: first, making education "nonsectarian" by identifying with a general, generic Christianity; then by an appeal to spiritual and moral ideals of a vaguely religious or patriotic cast; and finally by the exclusion of specifically Christian religious values and practices in the name of allegedly universal intellectual, moral, and democratic qualities.

Appearing about the same time as Marsden's book, Douglas Sloan's *Faith and Knowledge: Mainline Protestantism and American Higher Education* outlined how a strong Protestant effort to reunite faith and knowledge on the basis of such powerful thinkers as Tillich and the Niebuhrs foundered in the late 1960s.[6] Instead, mainline institutions adopted a "two spheres" approach accepting the positivist assumptions of the academy.

3. George Marsden and Bradley Longfield, eds., *The Secularization of the Academy* (New York: Oxford University Press, 1992).

4. Mark Schwehn, *Exiles from Eden: Religion and the Academic Vocation in America* (New York: Oxford University Press, 1993).

5. George Marsden, *The Soul of the American University: From Protestant Establishment to Established Nonbelief* (New York: Oxford University Press, 1994).

6. Douglas Sloan, *Faith and Knowledge: Mainline Protestantism and American Higher Education* (Louisville: Westminster/John Knox, 1994).

According to this approach, "real" knowledge comes through experiment and verifiable experience, while faith is relegated to a private and subjective sphere. This gave over almost all fields of inquiry to pervasively secular methodologies.

Philip Gleason, in his *Contending with Modernity: Catholic Higher Education in the Twentieth Century,* traces a similarly damaging trajectory for Catholic universities and colleges.[7] After a period of self-confidence emerging from the Catholic intellectual renaissance of the 1930s and 1940s, genuinely Catholic education underwent a serious reversal from the 1960s onward. In order to receive federal funds and to garner the recognition of the academic elite, many Catholic colleges and universities rewrote their charters and laicized their boards. In the process they weakened these schools' commitment to Catholic identity. Many gradually became embarrassed by their Catholic identities, which to them meant mediocrity or worse.

With Burtchaell's *Dying of the Light* we have a massive documentation of the secularization of much of Christian higher education. The book contains the sad stories of sixteen representative schools from seven traditions in which he believes the light has gone out. One college for certain, and possibly two, measure up to his stringent standards. For the vast majority of colleges, he believes, the game is essentially over, though some new shoot of renewal may arise from the burnt-out stump. The book is inspired by Burtchaell's "belief that the ambition to unite 'faith and vital piety' is a wholesome and hopeful and stubborn one."[8]

I believe that Burtchaell's basic judgment is correct; most colleges have gone the way of all flesh. Later on, however, I will have the opportunity to qualify his thesis in two distinct ways. First, I will introduce some nuances into the messy scene of Christian higher education. There are, I will argue, a number of places on the continuum between a fully Christian college and a fully secularized one. More colleges find themselves in the gray areas between the brightness of the fully Christian college and the darkness of full secularization than find themselves on either pole. Burtchaell seems to have little more than scorn for those colleges that have not maintained the fullness of the light, and he shows little sympathy for

7. Philip Gleason, *Contending with Modernity: Catholic Higher Education in the Twentieth Century* (New York: Oxford University Press, 1996).

8. Burtchaell, *Dying of the Light,* p. 851.

those who struggle for small movements toward the light after having slid toward secularization. Those colleges have to be taken seriously, I think, and we will give them due attention in a typology that gets at the various places colleges find themselves on the continuum, and later in a proposal of strategies for making the relation to their sponsoring heritage stronger. Their sheer numbers make them a worthwhile subject for more scrutiny and, contrary to Burtchaell, I believe that colleges that are not totally secularized can, with the proper leadership, forge a more meaningful and genuine connection with their sponsoring traditions.

I will also qualify Burtchaell's argument by describing and analyzing colleges that have "kept the faith." It is interesting, to say the least, that he did not investigate a Calvin, a Wheaton, or a Baylor. In those examples of Christian higher education and others, it is clear that some schools have kept the Christian tradition publicly relevant to the pivotal dimensions of their life and mission. In Part Two I will describe six such schools and what they have done to maintain the light.

If full-blooded Christian colleges and universities are those in which the Christian heritage is publicly relevant to the central endeavors of the college, then colleges and universities in which secularization is occurring experience a waning of that public relevance, and find themselves less and less under the influence of the sponsoring tradition's vision and ethos. If the secularizing process is allowed to continue, that heritage will be increasingly marginalized and will disappear except for its mention in the historical account of the college's early life. In Burtchaell's terms, the light will die.

It seems that there are three components of the Christian tradition that must be publicly relevant: its vision, its ethos, and the Christian persons who bear that vision and ethos. The vision is Christianity's articulated account of reality. It is a comprehensive account encompassing all of life; it provides the umbrella of meaning under which all facets of life and learning are gathered and interpreted. Christianity's comprehensive account does not claim to have all the relevant data and knowledge about our life in this world, but it does claim to offer a paradigm in which those data and knowledge are organized, interpreted, and critiqued. Furthermore, the Christian vision is, for believing Christians at least, unsurpassable; it cannot be replaced by a better account, and therefore for believers its essential core persists through time. It claims to be the vehicle of ultimate truth, such that if another account of life surpasses the Christian story in the lives of believers, they no longer legitimately claim to be Christians. And finally, the Christian vision is central to life. It definitively addresses all the essential questions of life: meaning, purpose, and conduct.[9]

This Christian vision or account arises from the Christian narrative — the Bible and the long history of the Church. From that narrative emerged early on the apostolic or trinitarian faith, defined in the classic ecumenical creeds. Much theological reflection occurred throughout the history of the Church, and a Christian intellectual tradition took shape as a result. This intellectual tradition conveys a Christian view of the origin and destiny of the world, of nature and history, of human nature and its predicament, of human salvation and of a Christian way of life. It also contains a theory about how revelation and reason are related. As stated earlier, this intellectual tradition or account is comprehensive, unsurpassable, and central for Christians. In addition, each branch of Christianity has its own unique construal of that intellectual tradition. Catholics have their own interpretation of the intellectual tradition, as do Calvinists and Lutherans.

Christianity, however, is more than intellectual. The account it gives of reality is also lived, embodied, and expressed in an ethos, a way of life. And of course each specific Christian tradition conveys a specific ethos. First and foremost among those practices is worship — the public praise, reading, prayer, and sacramental acts performed in response to the actions of God recorded in the Christian narrative. Further, every Christian tradition has its heritage of music, both sung and played. Many traditions include observations of the liturgical year, holidays, and special commemorations of exemplary figures in those traditions.

An ethos certainly embodies patterns of moral action, and sometimes particular virtues such as humility or hospitality are deeply embedded in it. For many religious traditions the practice of vocation is central; all humans are called by God to exercise their gifts in service to others through specific roles. For most Christian colleges, of course, religious vocations were at one time highlighted. These schools were founded to help prepare pastors, priests, nuns, and other church leaders. The moral dimension of an ethos usually encompasses clear guidelines or rules about how

9. These characteristics are elaborated more fully by Paul Griffiths in his *Religious Reading: The Place of Reading in the Practice of Religion* (New York: Oxford University Press, 1999), pp. 3-13.

we should live together — rules governing issues of truthfulness, marriage and sexual life, dress, demeanor, and other matters of morality. Such an ethos is given public meaning and justification by the vision itself, which is articulated and taught by the leaders of the tradition. Conversely, a living and lively ethos stimulates reflection that further elaborates the vision.

Finally, the third necessary component of publicly relevant Christianity in higher education is the persons who understand and articulate the Christian vision and embody the ethos of that particular tradition. Without committed persons, a religious tradition is merely an historical artifact. Persons are the bearers of a living religious tradition as individuals and as participants in churches, church-related institutions, and associations of that tradition.

All three of these components of a religious tradition must be publicly relevant in the lives of colleges and universities if they are to be genuine Christian colleges and universities. The vision must be relevant in the intellectual life and give theoretical justification and guidance for the ethos. The ethos of the tradition must in some relevant way condition and affect the life of the college or university. And persons who bear the vision and the ethos must participate influentially in the life of the school. It is indeed possible for those who are not participants in the tradition to know it, respect it, and even further it, but it seems unlikely that they can embody it in a way that committed participants can.

The upshot of the many important studies I have mentioned above is that the Christian tradition as vision, ethos, and persons has gradually lost significance and influence in the majority of colleges related to the various specific traditions. Using the three components of a living tradition as an organizing schema, I will summarize the ways in which they have waned in importance in the church-related colleges and universities. In so doing I will be drawing on many studies as well as long personal experience in Christian higher education. However, for reasons that will become evident later, I will take them in reverse order.

Persons

The most dramatic and noticeable feature about the vast majority of church-related colleges and universities is that fewer and fewer persons of the parent heritage have occupied the student body, the faculty, administration, and boards of the schools. Burtchaell documents the slide in the percentages of such persons in each of the colleges he studies. Even Dordt College, the college in his sample that he finds most robustly connected to its religious heritage, has witnessed its percentage of Christian Reformed students slip from 95 percent in 1965 to 75 percent in the late 1990s.[10] The drop in other denominational colleges and universities has been much more precipitous, leading some not even to take any count of the number of students from their tradition. This is most true among schools of the Protestant mainstream, but many of Catholic heritage are in a similar position as well.

As the number of students from the sponsoring churches has declined to near zero, the students who inhabit these schools have increasingly seen the connection with the church as irrelevant. If it were important, more Lutherans or Baptists or Catholics would be there. So these students have been welcomed — and considered themselves welcomed — on secular grounds, and have resisted any appeal to the denominational tradition for ordering the life of the community.

While pressure to survive has driven many schools to recruit students from other denominations or from none at all, they also have undergone a less compelling but equally important diminution of their denominational faculty. Many church-related colleges and universities began with requirements that all faculty members be communicants of the sponsoring denomination. But in all the cases surveyed in the books above, such stringent requirements have long been relaxed. For a very few in the Protestant and Catholic mainstream, it is still important to keep key faculty positions occupied by communicants. For many, only a smattering of those representatives still remains. For some no records at all are kept; it no longer makes a difference.

The same trajectory can be traced for the administrative leadership of these schools. The partially secularized still maintain a president from the sponsoring denomination, while the more radically secularized no longer hold even that requirement. As one goes down the ladder of administrative leadership, denominational numbers have dwindled even farther. And the religious affiliation of departmental chairs, those crucial figures in the hiring and firing of faculty, has often been overlooked completely.

Boards of trustees have followed a similar pattern of declining de-

---

10. Burtchaell, *Dying of the Light*, p. 800.

nominational affiliation. By now, perhaps a bishop or judicatory president and one or two prestigious clergymen or clergywomen sit on the board by bylaw or custom. But the vast majority of trustees are there because they support the college with their worldly expertise, prestige, and wealth. They are often characterized by the common lay opinion that religion and education, like religion and business, do not mix well. From this perspective, it is bad form to bring up religious matters in the practical running of a school. Since most of them are Christians, these board members are not hostile to religion *per se*, but they nevertheless encourage only the mildest ornamental role for it in the life of the school.

Closely related to the issue of the makeup of the board of trustees is the governance question. A heavy majority of mainstream Protestant and Catholic schools were founded, funded, and controlled by the parent denomination or order. Each school was accountable in a decisive manner to the persons who formally represented the institutional church or order. These churches and orders in turn felt responsible to provide support, students, and guidance for their schools. But this too has passed for the vast majority of mainstream Protestant and Catholic colleges and universities. Formal governance links have often been severed, and the schools themselves, with their mostly self-perpetuating boards, have had to determine their own identity. And if the number of communicants of a specific tradition has waned dramatically, it is of course hard to muster any case for a robust relation to that tradition.

As secularization has proceeded, the number of persons — students, faculty, administration, and board members — identified with sponsoring traditions has receded. Along with them have gone the denominationally specific characteristics of ethos and thought. As the number of persons has waned, so has the importance of anything having to do with the parent tradition. Moreover, after a while, the relevance of the tradition has become first an ignored feature of public discussion and then an unwelcome one. It has become more and more difficult to bring up that relevance among people who no longer share any allegiance to it.

Interestingly, the early lives of Christian schools were thought primarily to be Christian — or more specifically Lutheran, Catholic, Presbyterian, etc. — because of the number of persons in them from their particular church. If a school's student body, faculty, and administration were, say, 90 percent Presbyterian, then how could it help but be Presbyterian? Young persons growing up in Presbyterian churches knew about the gathering of Presbyterians at such schools, and were inclined to join them. There they met people of similar affiliation in large numbers. Moreover, that kind of massive presence inevitably carried with it a distinct ethos, the subject to which we now turn.

Ethos

One of the most distinct features of the darkening trends in mainstream Protestant and Catholic schools has been the diminishing role of chapel. At the early stages of their lives, required chapel was nearly universal. A certain stretch of time every weekday and Sunday was set aside for worship. Chapel was a "public event" that defined the rhythm of life for the institution. Chapel was usually held in an imposing structure that dominated the landscape. Even if not everyone attended, there was a sense that the worship offered there was offered in behalf of the whole community. Important community events — sometimes of a tragic nature (the death of a member of the community) and sometimes of a celebratory nature — were enfolded into the daily worship rhythms of the school.

As secularization has progressed, the purpose and substance of chapel has metamorphosed. First, the "religious" content of the required period was mixed with more secular presentations. Then chapel attendance was required only for a portion of days during the week or term. Then it became voluntary, and with that was often dislodged from its "public" position. It became one event among others that persons could choose if they wished. Its time was no longer protected, and many other activities filled in the period once occupied by chapel. For many schools such an arrangement has become burdensome to sustain for the small number of attendees, and it has disappeared completely as a weekly event. It may live on as an ornament for important events, but it is no longer part of the collegiate way of life. In these attenuated chapel practices, the large religious structures that dominate so many academic landscapes have become an irritating reminder that the schools have shifted away from the purposes and practices of their founders.

There are other aspects of cultic life that have waned as secularization has proceeded. For schools of religious traditions that follow the liturgical year, the school year itself often was marked by the liturgical seasons, and for those of a less liturgical bent there was a strong affirmation of Sabbath-keeping. But for schools of both traditions, a more secular rhythm has ensued as secularization has increased. Fall and spring break became more important than pauses for Advent or Lent or Easter. Good Friday now often goes unnoticed. While Christmas break is still important, the concerts preceding Christmas have become less and less important, sometimes disappearing altogether. Baccalaureate, once a central religious event of graduation week, has gone from being a required on-campus event to a voluntary off-campus event, and in many cases simply to oblivion. Public prayer before faculty meetings and during commencement have become less frequent or disappeared. Sacred music concerts have turned from elegant events featured in chapels to more informal ensembles offering more contemporary music in venues other than chapels.

For most church-related colleges it used to be important to imprint their story on their students and faculty. The exemplary figures in that story — particularly the founders — were remembered and celebrated. Members of the academic community were part of an ongoing narrative that was sharply etched in communal memory. That narrative was rehearsed frequently and told in great detail in college histories that aimed at discerning the meaning of that narrative. As secularization has continued, the sense of being part of an ongoing communal history has waned. Few have "remembered Joseph" and, even more sadly, few now care if they do. Instead of being in a continuing common enterprise characterized by many covenantal elements, members of many schools now see themselves as individuals with their own academic purposes joined to the school by more of a contractual calculus than anything else. Such attitudes undercut the school's sense of tradition and community. Persons with these attitudes are unlikely to affirm and enjoy common worship, to see themselves as sons and daughters of a living tradition, to commit themselves to a common life with students and staff in which there are mutual affections and obligations, and above all to cherish the religious elements in the tradition, which more and more have come to look like arbitrary, irrational, bothersome demands, or even oppressive ones. Such attitudes often undercut not only religious traditions, but attempts at coherent liberal arts curricula as well.

Christian colleges and universities in their early years nurtured many sorts of religious and quasi-religious organizations. Among the most important of the religious sort were those devoted to cultivating pre-theological students, especially those headed for service in the sponsoring denomination. Among the quasi-religious organizations were the debating societies, which often discussed topics of an overtly religious character. At the mid-point of the history of American higher education, nondenominational organizations abounded, especially the YMCA and the YWCA. These associations promoted a general evangelical Christianity that most Protestants could share. Later, both denominational and non-denominational organizations waned in importance. Many hung on in a vastly diminished form or disappeared altogether, which then presented the opportunity for more energetic evangelical associations such as Young Life or InterVarsity to make their appearance on campus.

Another essential part of the ethos of the Christian college or university in its early stages was its willingness and confidence to take on the role of *in loco parentis*. And since the school was closely related to the religious tradition from which it sprang, it was insisted that the students learn religiously-grounded virtues and behavioral patterns along with other traits of civilized society. So, students were taught by faculty and staff — and by the older, more civilized students themselves — to be respectful of authority, to dress properly, to observe manners (including table manners), to work hard, to be honest and obedient. A major part of this communication process went beyond manners and mores to inculcate a sense of vocation, the sense that all humans were called by God to be of service to their fellow humans in their roles as family members, citizens, and workers. A great portion of the graduates of religious colleges went into teaching, social service, and, of course, the ordained ministry.

Church-related schools were also willing to promote a Christian sexual ethic. This meant that sexual intercourse was morally legitimate only within the marital covenant. Students were not to be tempted unduly by the mixing of the sexes in unsupervised college events or college accommodations. A double standard was often enforced — men were less supervised and limited in their campus lives than women — but all were watched over by an adult presence in their life together, especially in the residence halls. A morally upright student life in the dorms and at the colleges generally was seen to be the colleges' responsibility.

Certainly many students chafed under these limits, and many rebelled. But for the most part the rebellion took place off campus. Only the bravest or most foolhardy would violate a college's public standards with impunity. If they were caught in their errant behavior, they were chastised and sometimes expelled if the offense were serious enough.

Such an *in loco parentis* role reigned in state colleges and universities right along with church-run schools, often including the same religious elements, through the end of the 1950s. With the onslaught of the 1960s, however, state schools quickly abandoned this role, and mainline church colleges and universities quickly followed suit. Mainline Christian colleges and universities withdrew from many civilizing components of higher education. Student life on campus was set free from adult presence and supervision, often with disastrous results. The most devastating effects were excessive drinking and partying, but other facets of civilized life were also affected: respect for authority waned, manners declined, dress became completely a matter of choice, and honor codes were often discarded. While many students maintained the values and behavioral patterns they were brought up with, public legitimization was not offered to support them, while the unruly students were given much free rein to do as they willed.

Meanwhile, a whole profession — student affairs or student life or student services — emerged to fill the vacuum left by the departure of the faculty and staff from *in loco parentis* responsibilities. Trained in secular graduate schools, the student affairs officials adopted a utilitarian morality that we could call the "public health ethic," which tried to limit the gross effects of student behavior and tried to bend it toward more constructive ends.[11] External rules and regulations were used to guide behavior without the enculturation processes of the older ways. A sure sign of the shift was the absence of Christian rhetoric and justification for higher moral ideals, which were replaced by "consider the effects of your behavior" strategies. And as time went on, many of these efforts brought forth at least some fruit in the form of a more orderly and civil social life.

An important point must be made here. One dimension that the "new college," both religious and secular, has developed represents a real

11. An example of such utilitarian thinking combined with a flight from Christian morality was evidenced by a student affairs official at a Methodist college that one of my sons attended. A concerned parent asked about how the college handles situations in which a roommate brings back a date to the room in order to spend an overnight there, thus depriving the other roommate of lodging for the night. Instead of saying that the college as a Christian college prohibits such behavior on Christian ethical grounds, the official responded that the college does nothing if it is just for one night. If it amounts to more than that, the roommate is unduly deprived of a room for which she had already paid. Then, if the student complains, the college intervenes.

gain over the older forms. Almost every college or university now emphasizes "service" as a central part of campus life. A part of the vacuum caused by the withdrawal of religious ethos has been filled by the insistence that students — and in many cases, faculty — should be involved in organized service projects both near and far. These projects have come to be prized as a common enterprise of the school for both religious and secular members of the community. In order for that joint enjoyment to take place, however, religious justifications for involvement are often diminished or eliminated.

In the life of Christian colleges and universities up to World War II and into the 1950s, persons and ethos carried much of the institutional DNA. For some colleges whose religious traditions had no discernible intellectual tradition, persons and ethos were all they had. Many were unable to articulate a philosophy of education that flowed from their religious tradition, so when the great changes of the 1960s came they simply had no way to define themselves sharply enough to recruit faculty and staff consonant with their tradition. Absent a critical mass of persons who could bear the ethos of a specific tradition, whatever religious identity the school had quickly subsided. Others, however, could turn to a more articulated account of their religious tradition, which I am calling vision — the topic to which we now turn.

Vision

As I argued above, Christianity as a living tradition is an account of life that is comprehensive, unsurpassable, and central.[12] Theology gives an articulated account of that faith; it too aims to be comprehensive, unsurpassable, and central. One would think, then, that theology would be amply employed by Christian colleges and universities to articulate their identity and mission, to stipulate the relation of revelation and reason in their particular tradition, to gather a theology department in which its members would gladly carry that vision on behalf of the school and the faculty, to construct a curriculum, to elaborate a public justification for the school's ethos, and to provide a Christian intellectual tradition with which the whole school in its many departments could engage.

Sadly, however, this is where most schools historically have been the

12. See note 9 above for a full citation.

weakest. In the next chapter we will inquire as to why that has been the case. This weakness was particularly evident in the mainline Protestant colleges and universities; they were the ones most likely to have their character borne by a critical mass of persons and by their particular ethos. The fact that the vision was the weakest component in many schools' character is the reason I have placed it last in this discussion.

True enough, many of them in the early days of their lives articulated robust mission statements. They were "grounded in the Gospel," or were unabashedly "a Christian school." They were places where "Christianity in all its essential doctrines is fully and constantly taught." But, from the beginning, they seemed to shy away from their particular denominational construal of Christianity. They did not want to be "sectarian" or "denominational."[13] This led them to claim they represented a more generic form of Christianity. But this was not the "mere Christianity" of C. S. Lewis, wherein the essential Christian doctrines were sharply explicated and defended. Rather, this generic Christianity was liberal Christianity, slowly watered down to general theological themes like the "fatherhood of God and the brotherhood of man." This religious philosophy accentuated general ethical themes such as the sacredness of the individual, the importance of service, and the noble search for truth. It quickly amalgamated with broader American values and with the values of the ascending natural and social sciences. Indeed, many practitioners of this amalgamation thought they were opening Christian faith to the modern world, thereby keeping it relevant and vital.[14]

Rather than preserving vitality, however, they were evacuating the Christian account of reality from the intellectual enterprise. As secularization proceeded, they continued to whittle down the specifically Christian content of their mission statements. They often wound up with the assurance that they were "honoring their heritage" or performing their educational tasks in a "Christian atmosphere." But as the Christian personnel and ethos dramatically waned in these very schools, the heritage was hard to honor, and the atmosphere became almost impossible to maintain. The prevailing ethos was no longer publicly justified and shored up with Chris-

13. See Burtchaell, *Dying of the Light*, p. 830.
14. See, for example, the compelling story of Daniel Coit Gilman, the late nineteenth century President of Johns Hopkins, in Marsden and Longfield, *The Secularization of the Academy*, pp. 107-45.

tian rhetoric. Curricula were no longer shaped by religious concerns. Liberal arts programs were no longer grounded in Christian humanism. Required courses in religion were trimmed, and those that were required became choices among a variety of offerings. By and large, the "straight stuff" of Christian theology and ethics became hard to find, if indeed it ever had been there.

That last proviso — "if indeed it ever had been there" — is important. Since many schools rested their identity upon the overwhelming number of persons from their tradition at the college and upon the ethos they bore, they frequently did not offer courses specifically in their denomination's theology, church history, or ethics. Several courses in Bible were thought to suffice. Further, for reasons too numerous and complex to mention here, many schools fled the theological particularity of their own denominational tradition. In searching for something more generic or more acceptable to the emerging educational elite, they fled theology for general religious philosophies of an ever-thinner character. So as time went on, many Christian colleges and universities became increasingly unable or unwilling to articulate their identity and mission in substantive theological terms. When they seemed not to need such articulation because of the many denominational ethos-bearing persons on campus, their rhetoric struck only the few theological themes needed to identify them as Christian denominational schools. But when the massive influence of personnel diminished, the theological articulation of their identity and mission was far too flimsy to enable them to recruit new persons to continue their tradition.

This theological weakness was particularly destructive for the internal intellectual life of higher education. The many secular disciplines were becoming more and more autonomous as the century progressed, which generally meant more and more distance from a Christian frame of reference. They also became more specialized and demarcated from other disciplines. The "uni" in university became an impossible hope. Coherent liberal arts curricula fractured under the centrifugal force of the disciplines. In order for a Christian school to engage the secular disciplines, to strive for the convergence of truth, and to sustain an ordered ground for the liberal arts, it badly needed theological expertise. It needed a theological vision that was comprehensive, unsurpassable, and central. But for the many in need there was scarcely any solid sustenance. There was a failure of vision, at least of theological vision that proceeded from a living religious tradition.

With regard to vision, Catholic schools followed a somewhat different trajectory. Up until the 1960s they were able to draw upon the neo-Thomist vision that had provided the coherence for Catholic education for the greater part of the century. That vision ordered the liberal arts and offered a Christian perspective on many fields of inquiry. It also integrated powerfully with Catholic theology to provide a formidable intellectual tradition. But the post–World War II consensus gave way under a number of challenges. Most Catholic colleges quickly jettisoned their Catholic intellectual tradition and joined the Protestants in their drive for survival or "success."

The vast majority of mainline Protestant and Catholic schools have been caught up in the darkening trends; some have succumbed to those trends completely. In a moment we shall reflect on why so many schools were affected as they were. Before we conclude this chapter, however, it is important to note that submitting to secularization did not mean death for most of these schools. It did not even mean the complete severing of their relation to their sponsoring traditions. Many redefined themselves around other purposes than their traditional ones and maintained an ambivalent relation to their parent heritage. A number got involved in an array of professional and pre-professional schools, some very successfully. A few became excellent liberal arts colleges of a secular bent, while a larger number became generic, moderately successful liberal arts colleges with only traces of their tradition detectable. A sizeable number continued to adapt to market conditions for the sake of survival, which left them little sense of internal direction. But nearly all colleges were able to upgrade their faculty and become more professional in their various divisions. The country is dotted with these sorts of colleges that once were tightly connected to their religious tradition but now are going it on their own. Some have done away with their church ties; more have opted simply to loosen them.

2 | *Underlying Factors*

How did it come about that so many church-founded colleges and universities wound up with their sponsoring traditions playing such minor roles in their life and mission? What is the "story within the stories," as Burtchaell puts it?[1] A short and flippant answer to these questions is simply this: an adequate number of persons — board, administrators, faculty, and students — with a firm understanding of and commitment to the vision and ethos of each school's sponsoring heritage was not available to either school or church at the necessary times to translate that heritage into the school's life in a persuasive manner. Not enough committed and competent persons were present at crucial times to insist that the sponsoring heritage be publicly and fittingly relevant in all the facets of college life. That is the crux of the matter.

But such an answer begs the further question: Why did the school and the church not have these people ready at the proper time to meet the serious challenges faced by each generation? The set of answers to that question is complex and poignant, for many leaders of church-related colleges and universities did not intend their secularization. Some were not even aware of those processes going on; they were like the proverbial frog in the water slowly being brought to boil. Others faced intractable problems that led them to make dubious virtues out of sheer necessities. Still

---

1. James Burtchaell, *The Dying of the Light: The Disengagement of Colleges and Universities from Their Christian Churches* (Grand Rapids: Eerdmans, 1998), pp. 819-51.

others understood what was going on but were unable or unwilling to respond constructively.

There are two sets of factors of interest in this inquiry, one external and one internal, though finally it is impossible to keep the two completely separate. Indeed, colleges often internalized the external challenges they faced, making them part of the internal problem. Indeed, internal and external challenges to Christian higher education often have operated in something of a pincers movement encompassing every American college or university. They have been particularly daunting for church-related colleges and universities because they have challenged especially their "soul," the religious dimension of their life and mission. We do a disservice to both the history of these colleges and to the people who shaped them to underestimate the problems that they faced. Most succumbed to the forces of secularization precisely because it proved to be no puny combatant.

External Forces

Religious schools faced two enormous challenges from beyond their walls: the demands of survival in a constantly changing educational market and the dominance of the so-called "Enlightenment paradigm" in the world of American higher education, especially its graduate schools. Both presented enormously difficult challenges that would have demanded the most adept responses. Unfortunately, such responses were not available to many colleges and universities when they needed them most.

Educational Market

One of the most obvious characteristics of the colleges and universities that have moved toward pervasive secularization is their flight from what they called a "sectarian" identity and approach. Their fateful move toward openness in personnel, vision, and ethos was prompted by, among other things, a felt need to expand their appeal to many sorts of students. While some of the colleges began with large majorities from their own traditions, they in time noticed that they had competition for those students from many sources, not least of which were the public institutions of higher education. Many also decided that students from their own tradition alone could not long make for a viable enterprise in a competitive environment, so they opened themselves to all comers. Something similar could be said for the failure to recruit administrators and faculty of the sponsoring tradition, though that would have seemed a more feasible task.

Whether the judgment that they needed to "open up" was truly accurate is a provocative question. Perhaps there were more potential students and faculty interested in a more sharply defined religious identity, but institutional leaders thought not. At any rate, the movement toward inclusion and away from specificity of denominational identity was pronounced. It then became a self-fulfilling prophecy. The flight from specificity didn't leave enough definite appeal to those who had specific tastes, and they went elsewhere. Of course, the sponsoring churches were not without blame in this matter. Many did not support their colleges by supplying sufficient financial support and sending their sons and daughters to their own colleges.[2] Under such conditions, the schools thought they had to appeal to a broader market by playing down the specificity of their own tradition. Later, we will see that schools that have maintained a strong relation to their specific religious heritage have also been providentially and amply supplied students from that heritage.

Another contributing cause to the blurring of denominational control and specificity was the requirement by external agencies that such specificities be diminished in order to gain financial support for pension plans (the Carnegie Foundation) or, in New York, Bundy funding, which could be granted to a school only if it was not "primarily a religious institution." Efforts to acquire the latter were especially damaging to Catholic schools in New York.[3] Furthermore, some wealthy donors required that schools become less "sectarian" if they were to be beneficiaries of their largesse.

Catholic schools have followed a somewhat different timeline than mainline Protestant schools, but have ended up in more or less the same condition. Early on, Catholics constituted an outsider community that

---

2. This continues to be a serious problem for church-related colleges and universities. A major study prepared for the Lutheran Education Council of North America found that Lutheran colleges enroll only 5 percent of all Lutheran college-bound high school students. "Reclaiming Lutheran Students Project," report of Hardwick/Day Education Management for LECNA, 1999, p. 1.

3. Burtchaell, *Dying of the Light,* pp. 646-54.

wanted to maintain religious, and sometimes ethnic, identity in an over-whelmingly Protestant nation. They created a parallel elementary and sec-ondary educational system that fed students into Catholic colleges and universities, which then were characterized by very high percentages of Catholic young people. These schools had something of a protected mar-ket. But with the dramatic Americanization of the Catholic community since the early 1960s, Catholic schools have been subject to market dynam-ics similar to those faced by Protestant ones. Social changes since then have wiped out the market for all but a few Catholic women's colleges. Further, a very large number of Catholic students have been drawn to public and Protestant schools, often making them the largest denominational group at those institutions. And it is safe to say that few young Catholics were drawn to secularized Protestant colleges because they or the schools were seriously religious. Since the changes of the 1960s most Catholic colleges and universities have had to operate in an open market, subject to the same dynamics shaping Protestant schools.

Those schools that were already diluting their denominational iden-tity and that were also economically vulnerable were even more suscepti-ble to market forces than those who were reasonably strong. They had to get students in order to survive. One response to such a severe challenge was simply to cast about for educational programs that students wanted. A fairly common result of this search was to move into professional and pre-professional training, especially business, but also engineering, nursing, social work, law, and communications. Lately, programs in environmental studies and information science have come into favor. Each of these en-deavors, however, moves schools away from a liberal arts focus and thereby diminishes cohesion as academic communities. In these conditions, a liv-ing tradition of education — especially one religiously based — becomes difficult to maintain, particularly when each of these professional endeav-ors brings to the school a fairly autonomous and secular understanding of its particular field. Even religious people who participate in these endeav-ors as administrators, teachers, and students are expected to drop their re-ligious identities and see any religious thought patterns as irrelevant as they become immersed in the field.[4] And it becomes increasingly unlikely

4. I am reminded of how relieved the chair of Roanoke College's Business and Economics Department was when I gave up teaching business ethics. When I taught that course I tried to take seriously the religious motives and values that business-

that colleges will advertise themselves as seriously religious if they are try-ing to attract students to these sorts of programs. This reluctance further dilutes religious identity and mission.

An even more pervasive market reality is the adaptation of the no-tion of "consumer sovereignty" to education. In such a schema the pro-spective student is viewed as a customer and, as goes the conventional wis-dom, the customer is always right. So the whole offering of the school is aimed at responding to what students might want in their prospective school. Extensive research is done on what appeals to students. Is it the beauty of the campus, the friendliness of the students, the liveliness of the social life, the pleasantness of the dorms, the academic prestige of the fac-ulty, or the presence of some preferred major? And what is the overriding reason for coming to college? To enhance one's long-term standard of liv-ing seems to be the most dominant, particularly among those students who are likely to come to a college or university of low or moderate selec-tivity. Far down the list is the goal to develop a meaningful philosophy of life. A minuscule number expressly come to such colleges for religious rea-sons, partly because the college's religious aura is so weak it is barely dis-cernible. Seriously religious prospective students are likely to go to a col-lege with a stronger religious presentation of itself.[5]

So, as Robert Bellah has argued, colleges and universities have be-come places to "meet the pre-established needs of students."[6] And given the formation of many younger Americans in what he has called "expres-sive individualism" and "utilitarian individualism," schools simply will not risk presenting themselves as what Martin Marty calls "descript" institu-tions. And if it is dangerous to present the school as a strong and demand-

---

persons brought to their endeavors, but the chair thought it very unseemly that such concerns should intervene in this worldly field.

5. A humorous story is told about a student at the Roanoke College of the 1970s, when its religious connections had reached a historic low. It seems that a student had a powerful religious conversion in a local church and reported to his advisor that he was thinking of transferring to a religiously related college! He had not even perceived Roanoke College's connection to its Christian and specifically Lutheran heritage, such as it was.

6. Robert Bellah, "Freedom, Coercion, and Authority," *Bulletin of the Council of Societies for the Study of Religion* 28 (April 1999): 35-39. In this article Bellah argues that the market has become the dominant organizing paradigm for higher education and is thereby destroying the essential character of the university.

ing liberal arts college, just think of the danger in presenting the school as Christian or, worse, Lutheran or Catholic or Presbyterian. At least, so believe many of the marketers — the admissions directors and their consultants.

Interestingly, as schools reduce their "descriptness" to appeal to a larger network of prospective students, they strive to find some attractive and unique angle that will draw those students. In order to do that, they hire consultants who try to help them discern and arrange for those unique and attractive elements. The trouble is, the same coterie of consultants moves from school to school, giving out similar advice. Most are deaf and dumb to religious elements in the school's tradition. The schools then come up with very similar appeals to the same prospective students they all share. The trick is to stay one step ahead of your competitors. But soon those competitors also will have appeals to students about the "diversity of faculty and students," about "service to the community," about study abroad, about the "caring and intimate nature of student-faculty relationships" and about the opportunities for internships and student-faculty research. When schools have reached this level of market driven recruitment, they will rarely propose that students come to the college for engagement with the Christian tradition. That is far too distasteful or even offensive to what they think is their clientele; they prefer an approach that makes them ever more generic.[7]

It is easy to be scornful of what seems to be an appeasement of market dynamics. But is there any such thing as mere survival? When a college or university is in a fight for its life or even for its relatively good "market position," it responds to what the market demands and then tries to squeeze in its own specific contributions that may transcend those demands. It is a difficult balancing act. But if it accedes too easily to the former, it loses what made it distinctive in the first place — its soul.

Thus, the external demands of the market create an internal culture of caution about religious matters in those schools that already lack a strong identity and position in the market. A cycle of diminishment en-

---

7. Of course I disagree with this "genericizing" of church-related colleges and universities, even those that have gone far down the road to secularization. It seems to me that the right language can be composed to offer to students who are religiously interested — a not insignificant number in many places in the country — an opportunity to engage Christian thought and practices of both a general and particular sort.

sues. To then make a bold move in asserting one's religious identity entails either a traumatic crisis that forces a reassessment of the identity of the school or a charismatic leader who is able to bend dramatically the trajectory of the school. Sometimes both come together, as seems to have been the case with the Franciscan University of Stuebenville, Ohio, where a president has remade the university into a strongly Catholic institution.

The Enlightenment Paradigm

The early Enlightenment — especially in its moderate Scottish, English, and American manifestations — was not hostile to all Christian metaphysical and moral claims. Many of the great early Enlightenment figures, such as Sir Isaac Newton, thought they were doing natural theology. They believed in God and an orderly world of divine natural laws, which were ascertainable by the exercise of reason. They believed in a Judeo-Christian morality succinctly summarized in the Ten Commandments. They believed that Jesus was the supreme model of human piety and a sublime teacher of morality, though that religious piety and moral truth could be discerned by rational means. They held the fond hope that these religious and moral truths would guide the use of science and technology to untold progressive heights in this world. The Enlightenment could bring forth the "heavenly city" on this earth. Indeed, Carl Becker, that great interpreter of the Enlightenment, believed that these early representatives shared more with the preceding Christian centuries than we moderns would like to admit.[8]

That said, however, it is also clear that there were many divergences between the worldview of much of the early Enlightenment and classical Christianity, disagreements about the nature of God, history, and Christ and the church, to name a few. But perhaps the sharpest disagreement was epistemological, that is, how we know the religious and moral truths that guide us. The Enlightenment was adamant in claiming it had an alternate route to the Heavenly Throne; it was not through revelation that we know these divine things, but through reason and that lofty product of human reason — science. Revelation entailed a kind of supernaturalism many Enlightenment thinkers thought retrograde. If we can know ultimate truth by

8. Carl Becker, *The Heavenly World of the Eighteenth Century Philosophers* (New Haven: Yale University Press, 1921), p. ix.

the clear light of universal reason and science, why make an appeal to revelation, which is so encumbered by particularity that it seems parochial and
arbitrary, if not superstitious?[9]

It was with this moderate version of the Enlightenment faith that
many American religious leaders in higher education thought they could
enter into creative partnership. Nineteenth-century presidents of elite private institutions modulated classical Christianity into a liberal "nonsectarian" formulation that could more easily accommodate the Enlightenment faith. The Christian moral vision could guide the newly liberated
scientific enterprise to produce untold good for humankind. These liberal
leaders thought they were making non-dogmatic Christianity relevant to a
new world aborning. Christian and American moral idealism could combine with science to create a powerful progressive vision. As President
Eaton of Beloit College put it in 1886:

> This Christian education is not adequately given in forms of dogmatic
> assertion. The growing mind is sensitive and suspicious of mere author-
> ity. It dreads wearing a chain. . . . There is sometimes even an exalted
> feeling, as in the performance of high duty, when one abandons inher-
> ited convictions that seem to be invalidated by growth. . . . The hope of
> accomplishing this lies in cherishing a spirit of fearless investigation,
> teachers and taught seeking the truth in the love of truth; not paddling
> in the still water of tradition, but pushing out into the rapids of present
> thought.[10]

The Enlightenment trajectory, however, had not remained settled in
its "natural theology" mode. Hume and others quickly found the God-
hypothesis that had undergirded the older worldview not only to be in-
credible but also unnecessary. The orderly world of nature simply existed;
it didn't need a divine ground to guarantee it. Before long, evolutionary
views replaced more static ideas, and the world was seen to be developing
along purely naturalistic lines. No purpose was necessary. The old theological glue was gone, though it took some time for the news to spread to the
hinterlands of America.

In the elite graduate institutions, each field of inquiry developed in
its own autonomous way. As science and technology progressed, so did

9. Becker, *The Heavenly World*, pp. 28-31.
10. As cited by Burtchaell, *Dying of the Light*, p. 81.

their prestige and credibility. While practitioners in these new fields were still anchored in a basically Christian moral culture, the worldviews implicit or explicit in their fields were dominated by something quite different. Philosophical naturalism became the great framework of interpretation in the natural and social sciences. The tight chain of cause and effect replaced the divine will as the engine of reality. Only truths that were demonstrated by scientific experiment could claim to be valid. The humanities barely maintained their status through a continuing though waning confidence in reason's ability to discern the good, the true, and the beautiful. Theology, however, wedded as it was to discredited notions of revelation, was consigned to the dustbin of history.[11] This seemed particularly apt in view of theology's tendency to engage in intermittent warfare over issues that seemed quaint and irrelevant to the modern mind. In this new progressive world, religion was expected to follow theology to public insignificance. Was it not irrational and arbitrary, fit only for the inner recesses of the private life, where it could be treated more like a hobby than an ultimate concern?

Such attitudes rendered even the liberal versions of Christianity unfit for university life. John Dewey replaced them with his democratic common faith, while religious liberals genteelly applauded their own demise. The pale aura of Christianity that haunted the great universities soon departed under such an onslaught. Human learning was "liberated" from its Christian shackles.

I have compressed a long process into a brief capsule and no doubt have exaggerated the pervasiveness of the secularization process in our great universities, both public and private. It is important to note that universities vary in their degree of secularization. Some still hold to a closed

11. When theology was pushed outside the universities for the most part, "religious studies" sprang up to take its place. This allegedly scientific and neutral study of religion has generally become the only vehicle for the teaching of religion in the secular university. Even in this watered-down arrangement — religion is understood in categories foreign to itself but more congenial to enlightened prejudices — "religious studies" still fights for its legitimacy in the research university. While some doubt its legitimacy on intellectual grounds, others, like D. G. Hart, doubt its legitimacy on theological or religious grounds. Hart, in *The University Gets Religion: Religious Studies in American Higher Education* (Baltimore: Johns Hopkins University Press, 1999), argues that religious study that caters to the criteria set up by the public university cannot possibly have any religious authenticity or value.

version of the Enlightenment faith, while others have always been more open to religious claims. Still more are now being shaken by various strands of postmodern thinking, about which I will say more later.

The point I want to make here, however, is that Christian colleges and universities faced a gigantic challenge as the Enlightenment paradigm settled powerfully into both the prestigious research universities of America and the various accrediting agencies to which Christian schools were beholden. To the academic elite, these Christian enterprises seemed to be atavistic throwbacks to a bygone world. They seemed to be clinging to a way of understanding the world that had been surpassed by a new and more successful faith. It is little wonder that these Christian schools tried to maintain their respectability by soft-pedaling their Christian connections, or at least by relegating them to the "atmosphere" of the college or to the piety of the individuals who inhabited it. It took real courage and intellectual acumen to continue to claim that the Christian intellectual tradition was relevant to the central educational thrust of higher education when that tradition was ignored or held in contempt by the leading educational institutions of the land. It was a far easier path to accommodate to the secularization of higher learning while continuing to maintain nominal though affable relations with sponsoring churches.

This path of least resistance was even more understandable in light of the characteristics of the faculty being hired by these schools. The prospective faculty were being trained in the graduate schools that had imbibed heavily the Enlightenment faith. They were trained in the methodological atheism of the many fields in which they were getting their degrees, ignoring religion as an independent variable in any human action or endeavor. For most graduate students such training met little resistance, since few had been educated in their religious tradition beyond a Sunday school version of the faith. This meant that thousands lost their faith in graduate school. They said goodbye to what they thought was a childish vision of living in the world, some wistfully, others with good riddance. Many other faculty-to-be compartmentalized their lives into two different worlds: a workaday one in which their discipline held sway, and a private one in which their faith survived. Very few were able to integrate their faith and learning on the basis of a more sophisticated conversation between the two.

As graduate students left their Ph.D. work, they joined learned societies and guilds that became touchstones for the legitimization and assessment of their work. These societies reinforced and continued the secular outlooks of the research universities. They became arbiters of what was worthwhile and elicited the loyal consent of their members. They provided a powerful set of constraints on the identity and work of the faculty who wanted to be respectable members of their guilds.

Thus, faculty underwent a formation process in their universities and the learned societies they joined that made it unlikely that they would be able to hold up Christian intellectual criteria as they moved into their colleges. As the Enlightenment paradigm took powerful hold of the research universities after World War II, and as the colleges expanded in those same years, faculty were hired who were heavily socialized into the predominant beliefs operating in those universities. This process has continued throughout the decades to the present day. Unless administrators had unusual perceptiveness and courage, they took in faculty who were programmed to marginalize the religious heritage of the college they joined.

Once a critical mass of such faculty came aboard, it became increasingly difficult to assert any public relevance for the sponsoring religious heritage. Each generation's attempt to state the identity and mission of the college has been marked by an ever-thinner veneer of religious language. Burtchaell takes delight in tracing the movement in those mission statements from robust and particular claims to more general religious notions and finally to the generic language of "values."

Secularized faculty factions then guard the public educational space from incursion by those who attempt to bring religious perspectives to bear. Since few among them bother to examine more advanced versions of the Christian faith or to learn about schools which embody both faith and learning in a sophisticated way, they see every effort to connect with the sponsoring religious heritage as a coercive and repressive move. They interpret a move toward reconnection as an attempt to assert the fundamentalism of a Bob Jones University or a Liberty University. Even Christians among them don't quite see how faith in its intellectual forms can relate to different fields of secular learning, mainly because they see little or no intellectual content to the Christian faith. Even these Christians tend to see such religious claims as arbitrary and repressive.

Thus, the Enlightenment culture of the research universities became internalized among both non-believers and believers in these secularizing schools. What was an external challenge became a major internal block to taking religious heritage seriously. In such conditions, the few that believe that the religious heritage of a school should be intellectually relevant have a daunting task before them. They not only have to convince the "cultured despisers" of religion in their communities that religion is intellectually relevant, but they have to convince their own fellow believers that in fact religion can and ought to make public intellectual and moral claims in a Christian school. Add to such resistance the fears that such claims will frighten off prospective students, and we have a perfect formula for continuing secularization.

Again, as in our discussion of Catholic schools' relation to the educational market, a case can be made here for their exceptional status. The effects of the Enlightenment paradigm did not take hold on them as early as the Protestants, who had to weather Enlightenment claims for more than a century. Catholics had their own system held together by a neo-Thomist synthesis that in some schools achieved an extraordinary coherence and excellence. The 1960s brought many challenges to these schools and their Catholic educations, but not least among them was the charge that they were not living up to the acceptable standards of academic excellence maintained by the Enlightenment-oriented elite universities. A pivotal moment came when John Tracy Ellis, himself a Catholic, published his *American Catholics and the Intellectual Life,* which more or less argued that Catholics had no such life to speak of.[12] His thesis was widely accepted, and many Catholic colleges and universities threw themselves headlong into an effort to become like the elite. They accepted much of the Enlightenment ideology and quickly accommodated to it. For many this meant the upgrading of their academic offerings at the expense of their Catholic heritage.

It is true that the Enlightenment faith we have been talking about is breaking down, at least in the social sciences and the humanities. Some of the breakdown is attributable to the proliferation and specialization of knowledge. The various fields of inquiry simply move in their own direction according to their own lights. The Enlightenment vision can no longer hold the whole educational enterprise together. Add to this plight the highly pragmatic views of education that have sprung up with the various land grant universities and technical schools — what matters to them is

12. John Tracy Ellis, *American Catholics and the Intellectual Life* (Chicago: Heritage Foundation, 1956).

the technical competence necessary for a job or profession. Schools and departments go this way and that. A chaotic pluralism ensues, held together if at all by a successful football or basketball team. "Universities" are such only in name.

Such chaos quickly filters down to the liberal arts colleges, just as Enlightenment notions once did. Each department organizes itself according to the conventional knowledge of the day as defined by the large universities. Faculty in the departments take their cues from their professional societies. Few talk to each other across disciplinary lines. The colleges themselves break into fiefdoms ruled by department chairs.

Not only is the unity of the liberal arts college threatened by such a development, its connection to its religious heritage is even more endangered. Religious claims from outside the disciplinary knowledge are interpreted as alien and arbitrary. Even the attempt to organize the curriculum around a coherent Christian humanism is suspect, since by now few faculty understand or concede that Christian intellectual claims can have a comprehensive meaning and scope.

But another source of the demise of Enlightenment unity is the arrival of various forms of postmodern thinking and practice. Such approaches disdain the Enlightenment claims to universal reason and the high culture that allegedly emerged from it. They sharply challenge the Enlightenment meta-narrative of progress and all other comprehensive schemes of historical meaning. This reversion to particularity over universality is not only an intellectual movement; it is at least partially a reflection of the fracturing of our wider society's unity and coherence. Diversity is with us socially and therefore intellectually.

The most extreme forms of postmodern thinking deny any transpersonal objective knowledge at all, but most emphasize the perspective-based character of all knowing and accentuate the importance of one's "social and historical location" in shaping one's perspective. They challenge Enlightenment claims to the objectivity and universality of knowledge, opening the door to the "interested" perspectives of social traditions and groups, especially those who have been "made invisible" by the dominant way of looking at things. Feminist, Marxist, Native American, Africanist, and gay and lesbian perspectives have found their way into the offerings of colleges and universities. Indeed, the current emphasis on "diversity" and "tolerance" is at least partially fueled by ideological multiculturalists of a distinctly postmodern sort. They want the hegemony of dominant groups and viewpoints broken down — deconstructed, as it were.

In some research universities such postmodernism opens the door for Christian studies. After all, if feminists and Marxists can teach openly from their "interested" perspectives, why shouldn't Christians? But others remain hostile, partly because of alleged church-state constitutional questions, but mostly from a residual belief that Christian claims are arbitrary and hegemonic. Nevertheless, the arrival of postmodernism in the research university has on the whole meant, or at least promised, a more hospitable place for Christian perspectives.

But secular postmodernism does not operate in such a benign fashion in church-related colleges and universities. In such schools the overarching commitment to a Christian frame of reference, past or present, is enough to bring that frame of reference under suspicion. For many secular postmodernists in church-related institutions, the school's commitment to the Christian heritage is a commitment to a meta-narrative that is viewed as repressive of minority views. For some the Christian heritage becomes the totalizing and imperialistic bogeyman, analogous to the Enlightenment faith in the secular research universities. Of course there has been some alignment between a number of Christians and a moderate postmodernism that emphasizes the importance of discrete traditions in history, but more often postmodernism is used as a weapon against traditional Christianity rather than for it. Add to this the traditional individualism of highly educated people, and one finds little grounds for a common vision, especially a Christian one. Even though faculty members often talk of the need for community, they are typically the last to consent to a common vision that would make community possible.

In summary, great modern (Enlightenment) and postmodern intellectual movements have powerfully affected the destiny of Christian colleges and universities. The former has been an especially powerful engine of educational secularization, but the latter has proven to be a powerful centrifugal force as well. Not only have these intimidating external challenges discouraged Christian colleges from remaining Christian, they have also become internal challenges as administrators and faculty shaped by them move into the maws of the schools themselves.

Intellectual movements, as daunting as they were and are, however, still may not account for all the most powerful external secularizing influences. The need to compete for survival in a brawling educational market must certainly be added to the list. Almost from the beginning colleges blurred their specificity to appeal to a larger number of students and faculty, not only for survival's sake but for the "betterment" of their status in the larger world of academe. Once the identity and mission are bereft of vigorous and specific Christian notions, it is difficult to get them back in. There are simply too many worries that such specificity will put off the prospective student, the sovereign consumer. Taken together, these two external challenges have taken a devastating toll in the secularization of Christian colleges and universities.

Internal Factors

While it is true that Christian colleges and universities have faced daunting external challenges, which then often have become internal as they have been imported into the personnel of the schools in question, it is also true that the secularization process has been at least partially the making of the schools themselves. They were not fated to submit to secularization, as our examination of schools in Part Two will demonstrate. The secularized schools participated fully in the making of their own destiny.

Incapacity for Adequate Theological Articulation of Identity and Mission

1. CULTURAL ACCOMMODATION

For a myriad of Protestant and Catholic schools, the educational enterprise was for generations an unconscious ethno-religious undertaking. Certainly denominations founded colleges for religious purposes. Protestants wanted to provide for the undergraduate education of pastors and ministers. But because they needed more students than simply the pre-seminarians, they included the laity-to-be. They intended to encompass them with a Christian ethos that would be edifying. Catholics were more likely to found schools to provide an ethno-religious educational culture in contradistinction to the heavily Protestant society around them. As I mentioned in the first chapter, the ethos borne by a heavy majority of persons from the sponsoring tradition seemed to ensure that such-and-such was "our school." The schools, like their parent traditions, were fairly homogeneous enterprises that offered an immersion in the "atmosphere" of their ethno-religious culture.

From their inception until the 1960s, the predominance of persons from the sponsoring tradition fulfilled the claim that they were "Lutheran" or "Catholic" or "Methodist." If almost everyone at the college or university were Lutheran, how could it fail to be a Lutheran institution? Further, there were elements of ethos that attended the many persons from the denomination. Chapel, behavioral expectations, religion courses, and a generally supportive "Christian" leadership were all parts of the ethno-religious mix. Many faithful exemplary figures filled the colleges.

These pre-1960s church colleges and universities were part of an ecological system of Christian formation. Children were born into a church to which their forebears had belonged, perhaps for generations. They were brought up in a large and active Sunday school. Some Protestants and many Catholics were schooled in an elementary and secondary school sponsored by their church. Each church had an active youth ministry that took up where the Sunday school left off. There were summer camps for the whole family, with a particular focus on children and youth. Into this continuing formation process came the admissions counselor of the regional denominational college with the suggestion that the young people in the church seriously consider going to the church's school.

These religious sub-cultures were supported by the larger Protestant culture, what Martin Marty has called the *the* culture. This was the normative system of meanings and values that had been shaped over generations by the traditional mainstream Protestant groups — Presbyterians, Episcopalians, Congregationalists, and Methodists. This normative system set standards not only for religious institutions and persons, but also for the whole society. It shaped even the elite culture, which by the 1950s had generally jettisoned the religious roots of the system. It guided and restrained popular culture — movies, music, dress, and sexual and marital ethics. Indeed, it provided the moral compass for the whole society, so that even those who did not participate in churches were formed in the same socio-moral system as those who did. Since the *the* culture affirmed schooling within the Protestant, Catholic, or Jewish subcultures, the whole ecological system was encouraged and legitimated.

But such a comfortable and often unconscious accommodation to a larger cultural system had its dangers. The church colleges and universities rested amiably in the expectation that the formation system would go on by its own momentum forever. As they drifted into bland and generic religious patterns that were not markedly connected to their own specific denominational heritage, they felt no need for sharp articulations of the school's identity and mission. After all, the generally Protestant character of the larger culture formed young persons that easily fit into the identity and mission of the college, even if they weren't members of the school's sponsoring tradition. Everyone seemed to benefit from the cultural consensus that had emerged by the 1950s; even the Catholics, who were the odd man out, benefited from the settled conviction that, as President Eisenhower put it, participation in religious institutions — including schools — was a good thing.

Because there seemed to be little need for theological articulation of each college's identity and mission, there was little or none. Because there seemed little need for each denomination's specific tradition of thought to be taught, it wasn't. Because the basic moral meanings of the larger culture seemed to undergird what each college itself was attempting to do, little effort was made to project a specifically Christian moral vision that was more than a bit countercultural.

But then the changes came, changes that are both too many and too familiar to catalog here. Suffice it to say that the demographic and cultural shifts were pervasive and dramatic; they continue in accelerated form to the present day. Amid these ongoing changes, colleges and universities without an articulated theological vision of who they were and what they were doing simply did not have the standards to acquire the right kind of boards, administrations, faculties, and students to continue whatever religious identity was left in the old system. They simply were not ready for the external challenges outlined above.

By "not ready" I do not mean that the church-related colleges and universities simply collapsed — they did not. Many adapted to the changes. Some found new ways to define themselves. Not a few went for high quality and high selectivity in pre-professional education. But most became generic liberal arts colleges in which their religious heritage played a very small role — a flavor in the mix, a social ornament, or a fragile grace note. Most were not ready to retrieve or reassert their religious identities because they didn't have the theological resources to define themselves cogently as Christian enterprises in higher education. They had relied on cultural processes to carry the day.

2. PIETISM

If one major hazard was to rely on the regnant cultural system to carry the day, another came more directly from the religious traditions themselves. Like cultural accommodationism, pietism had an a-theological, if not anti-theological, quality about it. It did not have the capacities to articulate theologically the identity and mission of the college because it quite simply did not respect theology as a necessary means of offering a Christian account of reality that was comprehensive, unsurpassable, and central.

Burtchaell comes down heavily on pietism as a key element in the secularization of the colleges.[13] While he gives some due to positive elements in the pietist movements in Europe and the United States, he judges pietist traditions as clearly deficient, tending to degrade over time into a shallow theological liberalism or distaste for the church. An even greater challenge for colleges connected with pietist traditions, however, was pietism's focus "on the individual life of faith, as distinct from the shared labor of learning."[14]

Pietism emphasizes above all the interior life of faith, the religion of the warm heart, which can be sustained by worship and private devotion and renewed by revivals. It also emphasizes pure living according to the simple commandments of God. Reacting to the sclerotic and cold orthodoxy of many classic church traditions, pietism tries to avoid theological controversy by distilling the faith into a few simple affirmations. It shies away from the grander intellectual formulations of the faith. In part, however, pietism has also constituted a retreat to the inner life in the face of the Enlightenment's understanding and mastery of "external" life. Inward religious feeling and moral virtue could flourish even while the acids of scientific rationality secularized the external world.

This interiorizing of faith was and continues to be a fatal flaw. In this approach Christianity is not given intellectual content. Public life in the world is not beholden to Christian claims. It is unchecked by Christian critique because Christianity is not accorded an intellectual dimension. Christianity is only an affair of the heart, not the mind.

While this deformation of the Christian vision is a resource for individuals splitting their lives into Sunday (private, interior, and sacred) and

13. Burtchaell, *Dying of the Light,* p. 839.
14. Burtchaell, *Dying of the Light,* p. 842.

weekday (public, external, and secular), it is also a major reason for drastic weakening of Christian higher education.[15] If faith has no intellectual content of its own, how can it engage with secular learning? Education under such auspices, even if nominally Christian, will look like education anywhere else. Secular learning will have no sparring partner because its Christian counterpart has no intellectual punch.

If this weakness from within a religious tradition itself is combined with a militant Enlightenment challenge from without, it is painfully evident that the college's main task — its intellectual one — will be given over uncritically to whatever the "world" says it should be. And there will be little reason for the leadership of the school to select faculty on Christian intellectual grounds, since their Christianity is irrelevant to their intellectual quest.

To be fair to serious pietist colleges and universities, it must be acknowledged that they can maintain a "Christian atmosphere" even if the intellectual enterprise itself is secularized. Through the strong presence of Christian persons of a pietist bent and the ethos they carry, there can be colleges in which real Christian presence is "added on" to the main intellectual tasks. In worship, in personal relations, in extracurricular activities, in private devotional life, and in genuine communal solidarity such colleges can certainly claim the adjective "Christian." Faculty can certainly be selected to fit into and support such an ethos. But such an approach finally leaves students and faculty as "partial" Christians, for whom the intellectual side of life is not engaged by the Christian vision, and the two poles can be drawn so far apart that they contradict each other. Then participants in the educational process must choose between ignoring this con-

---

15. A classic case of this sequestering of religion from the practical activity of running a college was played out in a controversy at Roanoke College in the late 1980s. A businessman on the board felt strongly that Roanoke's tie to the Lutheran church was a hindrance to the college. The first thing that needed to be done, he thought, was to strike down the constitutional requirement that the president be a Lutheran. The requirement, it seemed, reflected some residual conviction that religious allegiance may have some effect on how and in what direction the president would lead the college. But the businessman would have none of this. As he put it in a letter to the rest of the board, "the board should have little concern about what the President does on his weekends." For the businessman, religion was simply a private hobby that was publicly irrelevant to the life and mission of the college. The majority of the board, perhaps influenced by pietist or secularist sensibilities, agreed with him.

tradiction and opting for one or the other of the poles as the real key to understanding life in this world.

3. INADEQUATE THEOLOGICAL RESPONSES

If the two internal weaknesses we have discussed above are basically a-theological, the three we will now discuss, while theological in character, have proven to be inadequate to carry forward a sharp sense of Christian identity and mission for colleges and universities related to religious traditions.

1. Liberal Theology The irony of much of liberal theology is that it set out to revise classic Christianity enough to make it credible and persuasive to a new generation but wound up allowing the new generation's criteria of credibility to supplant Christianity in favor of a rival view of the world. Its good intents to save by revision have transmuted into destructive effects, at least from a classical Christian point of view. Perhaps the essence of such liberal theology is its tendency to transform the biblical, doctrinal, and ecclesial sources of the Christian faith into a religious and moral philosophy decisively shaped by the leading philosophies of the day in both worldview and morality. Indeed, much of liberal theology is so overwhelmingly concerned with progressive moral imperatives that it is tempted to reduce religion to morality, especially social morality.

Such a paradigmatic trajectory is modeled in the life of John Dewey, whose early life was influenced by his mother's Calvinist faith and the liberal evangelicalism of his hometown Congregationalist church, where he became a member and taught Sunday school.[16] After college at the University of Vermont and graduate school at Johns Hopkins, he taught philosophy at the University of Michigan. Enthused by Hegelianism, Dewey believed it to be "in its broad and essential features identical with the theological teaching of the Christian faith."[17] In this period of his life he maintained church membership and became active in the Students' Chris-

16. Bradley J. Longfield, "From Evangelicalism to Liberalism: Public Midwestern Universities in Nineteenth-Century America," in George Marsden and Bradley Longfield, eds., *The Secularization of the Academy* (New York: Oxford University Press, 1994), pp. 62-64.

17. Longfield, "From Evangelicalism to Liberalism," p. 62.

tian Association. As his time at Michigan unfolded, however, he liberalized his Christianity further. In a sermon preached toward the end of his Michigan tenure, he disavowed Christianity's association with any particular theory, ritual, act, or institution. Rather, he saw Christianity as a spirit of inquiry fueled by the conviction that truth is one, just as God is one. Thus, Christianity was "the continuously unfolding, never ceasing discovery of the meaning of life."[18] Because truth could not be discovered individually, but rather cooperatively, Dewey identified Christianity with democracy. "It is in democracy that the incarnation of God in man becomes a living, present thing." As people practiced the democratic faith, it would enable "the spiritual unification of humanity, the realization of the brotherhood of man, all that Christ called the Kingdom of God."[19]

Later, when Dewey moved to the University of Chicago, he dropped his church membership as well as any supernatural vestiges remaining in his philosophy. The democratic faith as pragmatic problem solving supplanted whatever was left of his traditional Christian faith. In an effort to make Christianity credible and relevant to himself and his time, Dewey gradually jettisoned Christianity as a comprehensive, unsurpassable, and central account of things and developed his own constructive philosophy of life, which he believed was more adequate. And in a certain sense it was. Dewey's philosophy undoubtedly fit well with the Enlightenment ethos that dominated his era. Science, practical reason, and progressive idealism were the themes of the day and his philosophy fit them well. However, for those wanting to maintain any sort of Christian identity and mission for their university, Dewey's liberal theology-become-pragmatic-philosophy would not have been much help.

Similar, but less thorough, cases of liberalizing theology can be documented among many nineteenth- and twentieth-century leaders in higher education, particularly those of public universities. George Marsden traces the process of such leaders coming more and more to define Christianity as a "moral outlook."[20] D. G. Hart traces such a movement more specifically in the career of Daniel Coit Gilman, the president of Johns Hopkins University. Gilman's liberalizing faith was "essentially moralistic," writes

18. As cited by Longfield, "From Evangelicalism to Liberalism," p. 64.

19. As cited by Longfield, "From Evangelicalism to Liberalism," p. 64.

20. Marsden, "The Soul of the American University," in Marsden and Longfield, eds., *The Secularization of the Academy*, p. 27.

Hart, and it supplied "the ethical framework and meaningful direction to the emerging industrial and urban order."[21] Believing that Christianity and science both lead to the same truths, Gilman affirmed that together they enabled genuine progress in human history. In essence, however, there was little left of classic Christianity in Gilman's optimistic formulations. It had been reduced to a vague spiritual and moral outlook.

One can have some sympathy for such efforts, duplicated in the careers of many other educational leaders, for they were attempts to redefine Christianity for a new and enlightened age of science and progress. Many liberal efforts, however, crossed a line in which American or Enlightenment idealism replaced the Christian vision. When the Protestant religious hegemony ended in the American universities, there was little need to use Christianity to ground the educational enterprise — American idealism could suffice.

Similar liberalizing of Christian theology took place in many church-related colleges and universities as well; it is at least one factor in the flights from "sectarian" identity that Burtchaell documents so well. While such flights were also meant to broaden the appeal of these schools to many sorts of religious traditions, they were also intended to revise the Christian vision for more "enlightened" times. But as Christian intellectual content was evacuated from the guiding vision of the school, the specifically Christian mission in higher education became something else, an exercise in American idealism. It is not necessary to staff a college or university with confessing Christians to engage in such an exercise. Good, idealistic Americans will do.

Sadly enough, even American idealism, which in some ways seemed more solid and credible than Christianity, fell upon hard times with the traumas of the 1960s. While church-related colleges never backed completely away from their civic rhetoric, such a justification for identity and mission never again could rise to the levels of clarity and self-confidence it once had. Yet such liberal idealism is making a comeback in many schools, both public and private, in a rhetoric and practice of service. Casting about for a unifying theme beyond mere academic competence, these schools latch onto the ideal of service. Interestingly enough, though, secularized church-related schools cannot find the nerve to justify their service

21. D. G. Hart, "Faith and Learning in the Age of the University," in Marsden and Longfield, eds., *The Secularization of the Academy,* p. 128.

efforts in Christian terms, which would be embarrassingly narrow. So they again rely on more generic American ideals.

Other forms of liberal theology have come to the fore, however. In their continuing efforts to remain relevant, mainstream Protestants often lurch heavily toward recent intellectual and social currents, or what has come to be called "political correctness." Most of this lurching could perhaps best be interpreted as cultural accommodation rather than a self-conscious attempt at liberal theological construction. Following mainstream Protestant churches, many mainstream colleges commit themselves to diversity, inclusiveness, multiculturalism, ecological concerns, and feminist causes as correctives to, or sometimes surrogates for, the classical Christian vision. Having lost interest in communicating that Christian vision, they accommodate instead much more current elite liberal cultural imperatives. Unsurprisingly, the more militant adherents to these imperatives use them to subvert or marginalize the Christian vision itself. Catholic colleges take similar paths when they conflate liberal social and political causes with their traditional "peace and justice" concerns. The "proper" socio-political opinions and actions then take the place of Catholic formation.

2. "First Article" Theologies Liberal theologies made way for secularization by evacuating the substantive meaning of classical Christianity in their formulations and replacing it with the intellectual fashions of the day, be they philosophical or political in character. But there have been other, more traditional theologies put forward that have within them certain formulas for secularization. We might call these "first article" theologies. "First article" refers to the first article of the Apostles' Creed, in which the first person of the Trinity, God the creator and sustainer of all, is confessed: "We believe in God the Father, maker of heaven and earth."

This confession affirms that all reality is grounded in God the creator. All that is good, true, and beautiful is grounded in him. The creator has etched a design or pattern in creation that is discernible to reason. Further, the creator has given each creature a "law written on the heart," a moral conscience. Thus, God sustains and orders creation through both natural processes and human agents.

Lutherans have called this created realm the Order of Creation. It is governed by the law, the "left hand of God," which uses positive and negative power to sustain and order it. This realm is open to understanding by human reason and experiment. It is not necessary to be a Christian or to employ revealed knowledge to understand this created order. It is open to all genuine inquiry.[22]

In matters of salvation, however, this realm is useless. The law of creation cannot save. On the contrary, salvation is a gift of God in his gospel, the good news of Christ (the second article of the creed). This gospel, which is the revelation and saving power of God, frees us from the bondage of sin and death for loving service to our fellow human beings. This new life "in Christ" is fueled by the work of the Holy Spirit, who works in us to bring us to Christ and through us to serve the neighbor.

Flowing from these theological assertions, the Lutheran Church in America articulated a rationale for its involvement in colleges in a document entitled "The Basis for Partnership between Church and College" (1976). This rationale continues in force for the colleges of the LCA's successor church, the Evangelical Lutheran Church in America.

> This means that education in general, and the church-related college in particular, has an integrity and purpose grounded in the Creed's first

22. The first article rationale for Christian higher education extends far beyond the Lutheran colleges. The majority of Protestant colleges as a whole seem to proceed from first article assumptions, if they indeed put forward any theological rationale for their enterprise whatever. Merrimon Cuninggim, who played a very important role in shaping postwar Protestant approaches to Christian higher education, exemplifies this approach. The key academic values, he asserts, are truth, freedom, justice, and kinship. Since these are grounded in God the creator, any learning proceeding from a sincere commitment to them is pleasing to God and helpful to humanity. Church colleges, because of their roots in the Christian faith, may be more constant and firm in their commitment to these values. Indeed, such a commitment is the primary requirement that the church should make of its colleges in order to maintain a continuing relationship. Colleges do not need to justify publicly their commitment to those academic values from a Christian point of view, though they should not hide their historic relation to the church. This first article strategy requires no members of the sponsoring tradition to bear it, and it includes no demand that the Christian vision or ethos be publicly and directly relevant to the various facets of the college's life. In principle there would be little difference between a secular and a church-related college, if both were grounded in the academic values Cuninggim mentions. For him as well as for other such Protestant theorists, there really have not been any "darkening trends." Secularization, if it means the relinquishing of the desire for the Christian tradition to be publicly relevant, is a good thing. Sponsorship of essentially secular colleges is a legitimate role for the churches. It is their gift to the world. Cuninggim develops this theory of higher education in his book, *Uneasy Partners: The College and the Church* (Nashville: Abingdon, 1994).

Article, concerning Creation. The capacity to learn — to search into the secrets of nature and use its resources, and grandeur, to search into the riddle of history and be stalkers of meaning — is possible because of God's goodness. . . . Education is the gift of a loving Creator. Through it he would enhance and enrich people's lives. Through it he would inform, motivate, and equip them to make society what he intends it to be. Sound scholarship, careful research, and effective teaching do him honor and serve his cause.[23]

While this rationale has many strong points — it affords a high view of reason, affirms academic freedom, and gives ontological grounding to secular fields of learning — it also has serious defects that have contributed to the secularization of Lutheran colleges. Primary among them is that it gives no epistemological status to the claims of the Christian intellectual tradition. It leaves little if any room for a Christian account of reality. As a contemporary Lutheran college president has put it: "Church-related higher education is called to employ reason to pursue truth with all the intellectual rigor at its command. There should be in most cases no substantive difference between scholarship by Christians and by non-Christians."[24] Or, in the same article: "Christian substance appears in the Christian calling of faculty, staff and students and in the Christian context surrounding the academic enterprise — only rarely in the results of scholarly inquiry itself."[25]

Instead of providing room for a dialogue between the gospel (in its full trinitarian account of reality) and the law (the realm of secular learning), this faulty interpretation of the Lutheran teaching on the two ways that God reigns (law and gospel) robs the Christian account of any epistemological status. It does this by narrowly defining the gospel as the doctrine of justification, which is preached in the chapel and taught by the theology department. But the gospel is not the full-blown Christian account of reality explicit in the trinitarian faith. It does not have the intellectual content of the Christian account. Therefore, the gospel — in this fuller sense — cannot engage secular learning. In effect, the two ways of

---

23. As cited in "Statement of Partnership of Roanoke College and the Virginia Synod of the Evangelical Lutheran Church in America," 1989, p. 3.

24. Mark U. Edwards Jr., "Christian Colleges: A Dying Light or a New Refraction?" *Christian Century,* April 21-28, 1999, p. 461.

25. Edwards, "Christian Colleges," p. 463.

knowing — the Christian account given by revelation and the many accounts offered by secular reason — are kept apart.

As I argued earlier, one does not have to be a Lutheran to fall into this kind of separation, in which all substantive knowledge is given to autonomous reason while Christian accounts retreat to the margins of the college and university.[26] Douglas Sloan confirms my argument that is it is precisely this kind of split between faith (the gospel as a full Christian account) and knowledge (secular reason under the law) that led to the marginalization of Christian perspectives in the vast majority of mainline Protestant colleges and universities.[27]

Liberal and first article theologies were flawed theological attempts to accommodate to the great changes precipitated by the Enlightenment challenge. The former essentially replaced the Christian account of reality — and the intellectual tradition that sprang from it — with quite another account, one that often owed its substance to the Enlightenment account itself. The latter did the same thing for other reasons. It limited Christian claims either to the gospel of justification (the Lutheran approach) or to the ontological ground from which academic values arose (the general Protestant approach). In either case, first article theologies evacuated Christian intellectual claims from the educational process. Meanwhile, pietism did not press Christian intellectual claims because theological elaboration was not central to the pietist account of true religion.

3. Reactionary Theologies If the above theological rationales hastened the secularization of colleges and universities either by accommodating or side-stepping the intellectual challenges of the Enlightenment, another type of deficiency was manifested in reactionary theologies that found no place for change, experience, modernity, or intellectuality itself. Burtchaell recounts many instances of reactionary responses to the varied intellectual challenges precipitated by the Enlightenment. Sometimes, as with the case of President Bartlett of Dartmouth, they came from within the college or university itself; according to Burtchaell, "His stubborn and reactionary behavior as an administrator seemed all of a piece with his unbending religious orthodoxy."[28]

26. See note 22.
27. Sloan, *Faith and Knowledge.*
28. Burtchaell, *Dying of the Light,* p. 24.

More likely, in Burtchaell's account, reactionary protests came from hostile representatives of the churches on the school's governing board or from critics in church judicatories. Some of these were simply anti-intellectual screeds. Methodist Bishop Peirce attacked Vanderbilt's Divinity School with the following: "Give me the evangelist and the revivalist rather than the erudite brother who goes into the pulpit to interpret modern science instead of preaching repentance and faith. . . . It is my opinion that every dollar invested in a theological school will be a danger to Methodism."[29] Sometimes assertions are right for the wrong reasons.

Similar voices were lifted in the ongoing tension between the North Carolina Baptists and Wake Forest University. Constant bombardment of Wake Forest by fundamentalist preachers on issues of faith and morality led finally to complete severance with the North Carolina Baptist Convention. What seemed to be the ignorance and arrogance of unlettered "rednecks" led an administration and faculty, already disposed to distrust religious accounts of reality, to distance themselves further from the Baptist churches. Comparable cutting of ties is occurring among many Southern Baptist colleges as they face an increasingly fundamentalist Southern Baptist Convention.

Colleges of the Lutheran Church–Missouri Synod experienced a similar dynamic when that denomination was taken over by reactionary forces. But in that case the colleges were directly owned by the synod, so the reactionary pressure simply served to suppress biblical and theological scholarship within the schools. "As regards right doctrine (the Missouri obsession)," Burtchaell writes, "conformity was traded off heavily against energetic articulation or exploration, so although theology was the premier discipline at the colleges, it was not particularly biblical in its development or scholarly in its outcome."[30]

As we have seen, the great external challenges we elaborated above were often met with inadequate theological responses from within. These deficient responses not only prevented a fruitful dialogue between faith and learning on the campuses of the church-related colleges and universities, they also tended to undercut the confidence of the religious tradition to embed its ethos in the life of the college. Without a public theological

---

29. James Burtchaell, "The Decline and Fall of the Chrtistian College," *First Things,* April 1991, p. 18.

30. Burtchaell, *Dying of the Light,* p. 536.

rationale for the ongoing legitimacy of a religious way of life on campus, that way of life tends to diminish over time. Further, without such a rationale for a continuing critical mass of persons from the sponsoring religious tradition, that critical mass tends to shrink as well. In a curious way, then, both religious ethos and the persons necessary to bring that ethos to bear are dependent upon an adequate theological vision of a school's identity and mission.

Weak Mutual Accountability and Support

One of the darkening trends described in the first chapter was the gradual decline in the numbers of persons from the sponsoring religious tradition inhabiting the board, administration, faculty, and student body of each school in question. This decline had a number of underlying factors. Certainly one was the lack of church support in money and students. It was a rare church or order that supplied its college or university with ample financial support after the school's founding. It was only a bit less rare a church that supplied its school with high quality leadership and committed students. The histories of church-related colleges and universities are full of entreaties by the schools for more money and more students. However, many of the sponsoring churches and orders simply did not have the money to sustain their colleges in addition to other churchly expenses. But another reason lurking behind the lack of support was the set of deficient theological understandings mentioned above. When such inadequate theologies — or none at all — were held by church authorities and by ordinary pastors and laypersons, the schools simply did not appear to be a very important part of the mission of the church. For many, the schools were of second-order importance at best and could not command enthusiastic support. The pietists distrusted the life of the mind, as did the anti-intellectuals. The liberal and first article theologians did not see enough difference between church-related and public schools to warrant the kind of support church schools really needed.

The lack of success of these plaintive appeals to the churches led the schools to diminish their denominational identities in hopes of appealing to contributors and students from beyond their denominations. As they did that, it naturally seemed less important that the schools hire people from their traditions. Moreover, as colleges secularized, they seemed less interested in maintaining close ties with their sponsoring traditions, especially if those traditions accompanied their niggardly support with anti-intellectual sniping from their constituents. Not many colleges or universities wanted to maintain direct, or even indirect, accountability to a body that gave such little support. Add to this the lack of appreciation of the Christian intellectual tradition on the part of secularized faculties, and few grounds remained for a rich mutual relationship between church and school. Over the years, then, because of a mutual decline of support, the links between the two weakened.

What are we to make of all these core factors? What is the crucial issue that underlies them all? Why did the bulk of church-related colleges and universities finally disengage from their sponsoring traditions? Fundamentally, it seems to me, that disengagement took place because both parties, the school and the church, lost confidence in the Christian account of reality. At bottom this matter was a crisis of faith, or at least a crisis in faith's confidence in its own intellectual and moral potency. Deep down, both church leaders and faculty members no longer believed the Christian faith to be comprehensive, unsurpassable, and central. Other sources of inspiration, knowledge, and moral guidance slowly displaced Christianity. In that context, secularization was simply the natural next step.

3 | *Types of Church-Related Colleges*

Many colleges and universities find themselves somewhere between the poles of "fully Christian" on one side and complete secularization on the other; indeed, it is perhaps the case that most find themselves at midpoints on that continuum. Consigning these less-than-perfect examples to perdition would obliterate many important signs of religious influence, for many schools have meaningful and valuable connections to their heritage that should be admired and cherished. In the following chapter I will mark distinct places on the continuum and describe, according to an "ideal type" method, the characteristics of the colleges and universities that inhabit those places. It is my contention that these partially secularized schools are not fated to complete the process of secularization. Not only should we appreciate the schools that have not succumbed completely to secularization, we should find ways to strengthen the partial connections they have to their sponsoring traditions and to find new connections that have never existed before.

The following is a typology of church-related colleges. Those on the left side of the chart have the strongest connection to their religious heritage; those on the right side have the weakest. Like all typologies, this one cannot take many different nuances into account, and it forces each school into one category when in reality schools are frequently mixtures of the various types even though they might most resemble one. Nevertheless, the typology will be helpful in understanding the various stages in the secularization process.

Types of Church-Related Colleges

	Orthodox	Critical-Mass	Intentionally Pluralist	Accidentally Pluralist
Major divide:	the Christian vision as the organizing paradigm		*versus*	secular sources as the organizing paradigm
Public relevance of Christian vision:	Pervasive from a shared point of view	Privileged voice in an ongoing conversation	Assured voice in an ongoing conversation	Random or absent in an ongoing conversation
Public rhetoric:	Unabashed invitation for fellow believers to an intentionally Christian enterprise	Straightforward presentation as a Christian school but inclusive of others	Presentation as a liberal arts school with a Christian heritage	Presentation as a secular school with little or no allusion to Christian heritage
Membership requirements:	Near 100%, with orthodoxy tests	Critical mass in all facets	Intentional representation	Haphazard sprinkling
Religion/ theology department:	Large, with theology privileged	Large, with theology as flagship	Small, mixed department, some theology, but mostly religious studies	Small, exclusively religious studies
Religion/ theology required courses:	All courses affected by shared religious perspective	Two or three, with dialogical effort in many other courses	One course in general education	Choice in distribution or an elective
Chapel:	Required in large church at a protected time daily	Voluntary at high quality services in large nave at protected time daily	Voluntary at unprotected times, with low attendance	For few, on special occasions
Ethos:	Overt piety of sponsoring tradition	Dominant atmosphere of sponsoring tradition — rituals and habits	Open minority from sponsoring tradition finding private niche	Reclusive and unorganized minority from sponsoring tradition
			(Dominantly secular atmosphere)	
Support by church:	Indispensable financial support and majority of students from sponsoring tradition	Important direct and crucial indirect financial support; at least 50% of students	Important focused, indirect support; small minority of students	Token indirect support; student numbers no longer recorded
Governance:	Owned and governed by church or its official representatives	Majority of board from tradition, some official representatives	Minority of board from tradition by unofficial agreement	Token membership from tradition
			(College or university is autonomously owned and governed)	

While many of the depictions on the chart are self-explanatory, a number need further clarification. *Orthodox* schools want to assure that the Christian account of life and reality is publicly and comprehensively relevant to the life of the school by requiring that all adult members of the ongoing academic community subscribe to a statement of belief. They insist on proceeding from a common Christian commitment, meaning all the ongoing personnel are assumed to live out that commitment at the school. Sometimes students are required to subscribe to a statement of belief, but often they are not held to the same rigorous standards as the adults. This unanimous Christian commitment presumably ensures that the ethos of the college will be Christian. For some orthodox schools, the communication of an ethos is the main point. For others the ethos must be supplemented by employing vision (the intellectual articulation of the faith) in an engagement with secular learning.

Critical-mass colleges and universities do not insist that all members of the community be believers in their tradition or even believers in the Christian tradition, though they do insist that a critical mass of adherents from their tradition inhabit all the constituencies of the educational enterprise — board, administration, faculty, and student body. However, they define "critical mass" in different ways. For some it is three-fourths or more; for others it may be a bare majority, while for a few it may be a strong minority. But at any rate, the critical mass must be strong enough to define, shape, and maintain the public identity and mission of the college consonant with the sponsoring tradition. The insistence upon built-in pluralism of belief — or non-belief — is done for theological reasons. For some religious traditions, reason is respected enough that even non-believers can contribute genuinely to the quest for truth; reason and revelation need not conflict. Colleges and universities are, after all, places where people pursue the truth. For others, the belief that all human conceptions of truth are characterized by finitude and sin makes representation of a number of perspectives engaging together important in the quest for truth. Critical-mass schools are often committed to the proposition that there must be genuine alternative belief systems presented to students if their faith is to be genuine and strong. For them, operating from a solely Christian perspective leads to a certain kind of coercive smugness that is neither genuine nor strong. Nevertheless, these schools make clear that the Christian ethos and vision represented by the critical mass are "established." They constitute the normative stance of the college or university.

There is a major divide between the *orthodox* and *critical-mass* schools and the *intentionally pluralist* and *accidentally pluralist* categories. The former two hold the Christian vision and ethos as the organizing paradigm for the life of the college or university. They are convinced that the Christian religious account of life and reality is comprehensive, unsurpassable, and central. This does not mean that the Christian account is their only source of knowledge and wisdom, but it does mean that the Christian account provides the umbrella of meaning and value under which all other knowledge is organized and critiqued, or, alternatively, provides the prescribed conversation partner for all other perspectives. Schools that operate with a theological vision of their identity and mission must be willing to move "against the grain" of the larger American educational world, which operates from very different paradigms. As George Marsden has observed, schools that have maintained their religious identity are often sponsored by traditions that are not entirely comfortable and accepted in American life.[1] They are sufficiently in tension with the American educational mainstream that they feel obligated to define themselves differently than mainstream institutions, even if they might have to bear the ridicule or even contempt of that mainstream.

The intentionally pluralist and accidentally pluralist schools, on the other hand, proceed from quite different assumptions. Here the religious paradigm has been dethroned from its defining role by the secularization process. It is no longer "established" or normative; some other conception of the educational enterprise has taken its place. That conception may be the classical ideal of liberal education in which the rational process itself becomes the defining reality. Then Christian perspectives take their place in the rough and tumble of unfettered inquiry and debate. Alternatively, it may be a more contemporary postmodern framework in which any overarching paradigm is rejected, including that of reason. Then Christianity is one perspective among many others. Or, more realistically, that alternative conception may be a practical notion of the educational task that equips students for finding good jobs. In any case, a different organizing model for defining and shaping the identity and mission of the college has supplanted the religious one. There is still room for Christian perspectives in this case, but they must make their way among many different viewpoints.

The intentionally pluralist college or university respects its relation to

1. Marsden, "Dying Lights," *Christian Scholar's Review* 29 (Fall 1999): 180-81.

its sponsoring heritage enough that it intentionally places members of that heritage in important positions, starting with the president. There is a straightforward or tacit commitment to representation of the vision and ethos of the tradition here and there in the school's life. This approach does not establish or privilege the tradition as the guiding paradigm of the school, but does privilege it in the sense that persons from the sponsoring heritage are the ones who are intentionally and strategically placed around the school. For example, in this model a full-time chaplain from the sponsoring tradition is employed. Similarly, special attention is given to making sure that members of that sponsoring tradition are sprinkled through the faculty. This strategy is accommodated within a fundamentally secular model for defining the identity and mission of the college, but which often seems satisfactory to both school and sponsoring church. Christian presence, though very much disestablished, is nevertheless guaranteed in some form.

However, this strategy has a certain level of fragility. Sufficient numbers of persons in the educational community must continue to be convinced that representation of the sponsoring heritage is a good thing. Since a growing majority of persons in this undertaking are not part of the sponsoring tradition, it may become a "hard sell" to maintain even the modest representation of that heritage. Nevertheless, many schools cling to this strategy. For some schools there may be overt "payoffs" — indirect support, for example — for retaining this strategy, or there may be serious penalties for giving it up. Others may retain the intentionally pluralist strategy because key leaders in the college are simply committed to guaranteeing a voice for the sponsoring tradition in the life of the school.

The *accidentally pluralist* school does not have enough commitment to its sponsoring tradition to push for its representation in key facets of the school, though in many cases the president continues to be a member of that tradition. But he or she does not operate the college out of a religious vision, nor does he or she find it compelling to represent it in a disciplined way. Rather, the school leaves it largely to chance — or to providence — to maintain the presence of persons from the sponsoring tradition. Perhaps if the representation sinks to dangerously low levels a few strategic appointments may be made to maintain appearances. But other than that, members of the sponsoring tradition — and whatever ethos or vision they might bear — are in the community by chance. The makeup of the school may not include any more members of the sponsoring tradition than the local state college or university.

Obviously, such an approach indicates a low estimation of the continuing relevance of the tradition within the life of the college. It is difficult to see why the school and church would want to maintain a relationship under these conditions, but if both parties tacitly assume that the Christian account of life and reality is not comprehensive, unsurpassable, and central, then this mild and affable relation might continue indefinitely. On the other hand, if there is noticeable discomfort by either the church or the school with this mildly hypocritical arrangement, a decision may have to be made to push the school toward either a formal parting of the ways or a more intentional pluralism.

Public Relevance and Rhetoric

Because defining marks of the orthodox and critical-mass schools are closer to one another than to the pluralist schools — which also share defining characteristics — it is useful to work through the various categories in pairs. The orthodox and critical-mass schools insist on the public relevance of the Christian vision in all areas of the school's life. Indeed, they organize the school's life according to the Christian vision. But since the orthodox school insists on everyone consenting to a substantive set of Christian beliefs, it assures that relevance by virtue of the persons it hires. The relevance of the sponsoring tradition might be most noticeable in the ethos expressed by the overwhelming numbers of persons from that tradition. But increasingly the orthodox colleges want that relevance also to be intellectual, so that the religious account with which it is operating is indeed demonstrated to be comprehensive. They want the Christian account to address the mind as well as the heart.

These colleges do this partly by educating new faculty into the tradition's account and partly by replenishing knowledge of the tradition for the continuing faculty. Orthodox schools have extensive programs that socialize their faculty into their vision. They want to deepen and enrich their understanding and equip them to use it in their teaching and scholarship. These programs are generally required of all new faculty and advanced versions are strongly recommended for continuing faculty.

The *orthodox* college unabashedly presents itself in its publications as a Christian endeavor. It aspires to be inclusive of all sorts of persons as long as they agree upon common Christian belief. If a student is not a

Christian of the sort that sponsors the school, the school explicitly states its intentions to shape them in that direction. Its mission statement is straightforward about all these things. Because it is so straightforward, the statement is often quite brief and simple. If the identifying materials of the school are read at all, it should come as no surprise to persons joining the community as faculty or students what sort of community it is. Every publication of the school has direct marks of its Christian commitment. In the academic catalogue, each department's mission is spelled out in relation to the college's Christian commitment.

The *critical-mass* college or university manifests some important differences. While it is clear that the Christian vision is normative for the operation of the whole school, there may be many places in the school where a secular orientation is noticeable — for example, many academic departments may operate according to secular modes. But each endeavor of the school could be in principle and often is in fact brought into dialogue with the Christian vision of the sponsoring tradition. The Christian commitment of the college or university conditions everything that goes on there, not in the sense that it can simply trump secular learning but in the sense that it is the honored partner in an ongoing dialogue. One way that the critical-mass school compensates for its toleration of secularity in some areas is its elaboration of centers, institutes, journals, and programs that are explicitly anchored in the vision or ethos of the sponsoring tradition. Even so, serious problems may arise when secular learning and the Christian vision conflict. The orthodox school is clear about which voice wins out in such a conflict, but the critical-mass school is less clear, particularly in intellectual matters. It lives with serious ongoing tensions.

One of the tensions with which the critical-mass school lives is that between wanting the whole faculty to have an adequate grasp of the tradition's construal of the Christian vision and respecting the freedom of each participant. Most critical-mass schools have educational or mentoring programs that aim at introducing new faculty to the riches of the Christian intellectual tradition as it is borne by the specific parent religious body. But rarely are these required or rigorous. However, because the specific Christian account is "established" in the public life of the school, there are many opportunities for the newcomer to hear perspectives from that account. Meanwhile, an inner core of members of the tradition are expected to bear its vision, teach it to others, and connect that vision with all facets of the school's life.

The critical-mass school's public presentation of itself is unambiguous — it is unmistakably Catholic or Lutheran or Baptist — but because it posits a more complex and tense relation between faith and learning than the orthodox college, its mission statement is longer and more complex. Further, it often explicitly invites believers of other traditions and non-believers into the institution as administrators, faculty, and students. Because there are many secular domains in the school, many facets of the school's life are presented with a less Christian appearance. Academic departments will not necessarily relate their mission to the Christian commitments of the school itself. Persons of other beliefs can find space within such a school to live without feeling pressed. But they can also be attracted to the rich tradition of the school and therefore support and participate in it vigorously. On the other hand, they can move in the other direction; they can become resentful of the "established" character of the sponsoring tradition and work to undercut its strength.

The *intentionally pluralist* college or university sees the Christian account represented by its sponsoring tradition as publicly relevant as one voice in a larger discussion. That voice is not *the* honored partner in every major intellectual engagement; it is one voice among many. The school may not even ensure that that voice is heard in all or even the majority of scholarly conversations. But it does recognize it as an important perspective that should not be shut out of the ongoing life of the school. It should neither dominate nor disappear. The school is operating out of a different paradigm than the Christian story, but its continuing relation to a religious tradition reminds it that the tradition's perspective is legitimate and important. However, because another paradigm has replaced the religious tradition, many persons within the institution will pay little heed to that voice. Hiring, promotion, and tenure will generally have little to do with membership in the sponsoring tradition. It is not unusual for the administration in the intentionally pluralist school to intervene now and then in the hiring process to insist that a member of the parent heritage be hired. Indeed, this modest "affirmative action" of the intentionally pluralist model may cause resentment among those who see little relevance for the religious tradition. The secular domain of such a college is extensive and liable to increase. Thus, the college often establishes a center or institute to remind its religious constituency that the voice of faith has not been ignored completely. But by and large the school proceeds with the voice of faith audible only as one among many.

Since such a school does not privilege its own religious account, it has no real grounds for educating new faculty or staff into its religious tradition. Few schools of the intentionally pluralist stripe have mentoring or induction programs into the sponsoring religious tradition. But the sprinkling of voices from the tradition may at least serve as an invitation for other faculty to learn more about it. But in general the intentionally pluralist school as a whole knows little about the tradition. The students may not even be aware of any religious connection.

This unsurprising and unhappy fact results from presenting an institution as a secular liberal arts college. It has attracted its current market share of students and faculty on secular grounds, and it is reluctant to put forward a more "Christian" image. Its mission statement often claims "grounding" or "rootage" in the Christian heritage but this can mean as little as a few Christian voices sprinkled about or as much as a serious representation of the Christian voice in each of the school's endeavors. The statement often avoids a strong affirmation of any specific denominational heritage. However, the intentionally pluralist college will recruit students from its sponsoring denomination. It looks to the denomination as one of its promising recruitment fields because it still affirms its church connection and can with some integrity point to the places in the college where the tradition's presence and voice are represented. Frequently the minority of students from the sponsoring tradition makes contributions to the school far out of proportion to its numbers.

The *accidentally pluralist* school is not likely to be aware of such contributions, because it no longer keeps track of the number of students from its sponsoring denomination. Neither does it do so for its faculty, for it neither establishes nor assures the voice of its sponsoring tradition in the life of the school. The teaching and scholarship of the school proceed in a pervasively secular manner. But since there may be serious Christians on the faculty — even Christians from the sponsoring heritage — it is likely that Christian perspectives will surface now and then. The accidentally pluralist school does not discourage such phenomena; indeed, it welcomes them as evidence of its affable connection to its church. The college does not make any attempt to educate new faculty into its parent heritage. But the few members of that heritage yet remaining serve as colorful adornments to an otherwise secular community.

Obviously, the accidentally pluralist school will not present itself as a church-related college, let alone a Christian college of a specific denominational perspective. The prospective student or faculty member has to dig deeply into the school's history or its catalogue to find clues of a connection to a religious heritage. New students and new faculty do not expect to be met with any sort of religious pitch at such a school, and they don't. Religion is at best a grace note on a secular score.

Membership Requirements

I have already commented above about requirements for membership in the sponsoring tradition. However, it may be useful here to reflect briefly on the resistance exhibited by many academics concerning the use of any kind of religious membership requirement. A large proportion of the professorate react in horror to any kind of "religious test" required by colleges or universities. But such a reaction seems premature for a number of reasons. First, if the sponsors and leaders of the school really do believe that the Christian account of life and reality is comprehensive, unsurpassable, and central, it seems perfectly permissible that it would require its members to believe in that account. That requirement may lead to a heavy-handed conviction that the Christian account can simply trump or negate secular learning; such an attitude then would threaten the school's status as an academically respectable enterprise. But if the tradition and its school have a far more sophisticated conception of the relation of faith and secular learning, in which both are given due respect, then orthodox belief can indeed coexist fruitfully with secular learning. The "constraints" put upon the school's members might not seem in principle debilitating or oppressive in such a case. Indeed, critical-mass schools intentionally hire faculty from other or no religious traditions on theological and pedagogical grounds. For them the interaction between faith and secular learning takes place not only within Christian scholars, but also between believers and non-believers within Christian institutions. But maintaining a critical mass of believers is a necessary means to ensure that the Christian account is taken seriously.

Second, the claim that there are no constraints involved in the exercise of academic freedom in secular schools is a canard. Up until very recently, the constraints required by the Enlightenment paradigm were very strict indeed. They were nurtured and enforced by the major research institutions and reinforced by the learned societies to which faculty belong. The belief, for instance, that only knowledge acquired through scientific rationality is trustworthy was and is a powerful constraint that simply does not allow revelation — upon which great religious traditions are based — any space at all at the academic table. Further, every college or university has a mission that involves constraints upon how people are hired, promoted, and tenured. A research institution such as the Massachusetts Institute of Technology hires according to much different criteria than an undergraduate teaching institution. The government, too, with its many regulations and requirements, exercises constraints. But above all, the academy's culture — whose subtly but powerfully enforced canons have come to be an important part of a larger movement known as "political correctness" — places sharp limits and conditions on what faculty do or say or write. In the legions of schools dominated by a politically and culturally liberal atmosphere, a philosopher who wrote strongly and publicly against abortion would be subject to much disapproval, if not ostracism. In more politically conservative colleges — a far smaller category than the first — a public defense of strong affirmative action would make life uncomfortable for a professor. In such a welter of already extant constraints, why are religious ones particularly horrifying?

All of this does not mean that schools informed by a Christian account ought to ignore or throw over the basic standards of evidence and argument. The Enlightenment paradigm certainly should not be cast out; it has much that is valid in it and much that has its origin in Christian approaches to truth. But it does mean that the Enlightenment account of life and reality is a tradition too — one with its own limitations. While we should recognize and respect its constraints, we ought not absolutize them so that Christian accounts are simply pushed to the side. If a college or university is to remain Christian in some meaningful sense, it has the right and obligation to consider the accounts of life and reality to which its leadership and faculty subscribe. Since every school has its constraints, there are more serious questions to be asked. Which constraints are valid? From whence do they arise? How defensible are they? How are they administered? To what do they lead in the life of a school?

Theology — Departments and Courses

In both orthodox and critical-mass schools the theology departments are large and prestigious. In these schools theology is still "queen of the sciences." The departments are large because they have many required courses to teach and prestigious because they bear the prized Christian vision of the parent heritage in its most articulate and persuasive form. This latter function is essential to the entire project of the school and can be entrusted only to highly capable and faithful Christian intellectuals. The mission of the theology department in orthodox and critical-mass schools is to articulate accurately the tradition's theological account, to communicate it creatively to the rest of the school, to employ its theological vision in shaping the school's curriculum and in justifying its ethos, to use that vision constructively in grappling with new issues of faith and morality, and above all to provide a general or specific Christian intellectual tradition that can engage secular learning across the board.

These are "theology" rather than "religious studies" departments because they stand confessionally and normatively in a religious tradition. They study and present theology on behalf of the tradition and the school so that the school can maintain a substantive religious direction. Such departments are not detached or neutral. They speak *for* the tradition that sponsors the school, not simply *about* it. This is certainly not to say that other theological or religious traditions — including other world religions — are not presented accurately or fairly in such schools; good scholars can always present fairly what the world looks like from points of view other than their own.

Orthodox colleges typically insist that their entire theology departments be communicants of the sponsoring tradition, while critical-mass schools allow more diversity in terms of both belief and orientation toward the mission of the department. Critical-mass schools intentionally hire persons from other faith traditions and employ specialist scholars who cannot or will not participate directly in the mission-based functions listed above, but who are nevertheless expected to support the overall mission of the department. Such diversity can be the source of creative dialogue, but it also can be the occasion for endless bickering in the theology departments of critical-mass schools.

The theology departments of orthodox colleges teach a required battery of courses. These schools believe that students simply must encounter the normative claims of the Christian tradition as it is taught in their college. That encounter is the most important thing that goes on at the college, since the Christian account is held to be comprehensive, unsurpassable, and central. Those qualities of the faith are so important that most, if not all, courses taught in other areas of the curriculum are affected by the Christian account shared by the faculty who teach them. Orthodox schools aim at an *integration* of the Christian account and secular learning on terms set by the Christian account. This integration may in some cases mean a heavy-handed "trumping" of secular learning by Christian faith, but that need not be the case. These institutions simply claim that the Christian account is unsurpassable, so other sources of knowledge must be brought into harmony with it.

Critical-mass colleges or universities typically require two to four courses in theology, but there are usually a number of choices for students. Given the diversity in both the faculty and the student body, those choices allow students to follow their own preferences more freely than they could in orthodox schools. The critical-mass schools also attempt to foster dialogue between the Christian vision and secular learning; they are likely to aim at an *engagement* of the Christian account with secular learning rather than an *integration* of the two. They are usually willing to live with more ongoing uncertainties than orthodox schools are. They tend to strive for a mutually probing dialogue, which is also nurtured by the institutes and centers they typically foster. Like orthodox institutions, the critical-mass school intends that all students seriously encounter Christian moral and intellectual claims somewhere along their journey, but in a more open-ended way.

An intentionally pluralist college or university typically has one required course in religion or philosophy where Christian claims are presented, perhaps in the general education curriculum, where those claims are mixed with other religious and philosophical claims. While there may be one or two "confessional" theologians in a small religion department, the department itself is more aptly characterized as a "religious studies" department in which scholarly detachment is cultivated. There tend to be far more courses in other traditions and religions than in the specific tradition that has sponsored the school. Courses in that tradition usually consist of one or two electives. The faculty of an intentionally pluralist school is often reluctant to see the sponsoring tradition "established" in any way, so its specific tradition of thought is allowed to be only one option among many.

The accidentally pluralist school also has a small, religious-studies-oriented department. There may be no representative of the sponsoring tradition in the department and therefore no courses in the thought or history of that tradition. Indeed, it is unlikely that the general Christian account is normatively taught at all. It is more likely that trendy courses on New Age religion or the search for spirituality are offered to entice students to take courses in religion, since none are required in the regular curriculum. Religion courses are options in a distribution system or simply electives. This reflects the deeper fact that the Christian account is no longer publicly relevant in the educational life of the school.

Chapel and Ethos

Orthodox and critical-mass schools have "public" chapels in imposing buildings. They are public in the sense that the worship they sponsor is held at times set aside for chapel services, during which other educational functions of the schools are supposed to be closed down. They are also public in the sense that they are officially sanctioned and encouraged events in the institutional life. High-quality worship is planned and led by a staff of clergy and student assistants. It is held from three to five times a week. Chapel is one of the institutional habits of such schools. Even though only a portion of the academic community usually attends, worship is felt to be an event offered on behalf of the whole community. Both orthodox and critical-mass schools place chaplains in visible and important roles, often as members of the governing cabinet. Orthodox schools are more likely to require worship, while critical-mass schools rarely do. Even if not required, chapel attendance at orthodox schools is likely to be higher than at critical-mass colleges and universities.

Both types of schools supplement the religious formation offered by chapel activities with large networks of Bible and religious study/devotion groups in dorms. Such networks are officially endorsed and often organized and encouraged by the chaplain's office. They also often connect to service activities that are usually intense and widespread in these schools.

Orthodox colleges exhibit the piety of their sponsoring tradition. The language and practices of the sponsoring tradition are evident in the life of both students and faculty. Christian personal moral ideals are articulated and rehearsed repeatedly. These schools are willing to take the *in loco parentis* role with regard to the formation of their students. They are so public and enthused about their religious and moral vision that they often stimulate pockets of rebellion among students who consider their atmosphere oppressive or hypocritical or both. Critical-mass colleges are more secular in tone, although the language and practices of the sponsoring tradition are publicly and unapologetically present. Since there is room for dissent and variance, the atmosphere of such a college is more inattentive than rebellious with regard to its ethos. Its moral vision is oriented more to social rather than personal morality. It is less willing to take a strong *in loco parentis* role.

Chapel at intentionally pluralist schools is absolutely voluntary. The chaplain must search for convenient times to have worship services because there is no set-aside time for one common chapel program. This generally means that there are a variety of services tailored for specific groups. The worship practices of the sponsoring tradition are represented, but only as one among a number of options. Worship often takes place in the small chapels or alcoves of a large worship facility left over from the days when worship was more central to the institution. Only a very small percentage of the student body and faculty attend. Worship is not a public habit of the institution. There may be some student religious organizations sponsored by mainstream Protestant or Catholic traditions, but interdenominational groups like InterVarsity or Fellowship of Christian Athletes provide much of the Bible study, devotions, and worship activities. The ethos of the intentionally pluralist college is definitely secular, but there are pockets of piety on campus. There may in fact be a strong network of Bible study and prayer groups springing out of the interdenominational ministries, but they are not a result of the official strategy of the school. Service activities may well be organized and encouraged by the school, but their justification rarely comes in Christian terms.

Accidentally pluralist schools are easy to describe with regard to chapel and ethos. They often have chapels that are used for other purposes along with worship. Public worship, if there is any, is held only on special occasions and then is intended to be "inclusive" of many religious traditions. Chaplains, who may or may not be from the schools' sponsoring traditions and who may or may not be full-time, are definitely peripheral to the life of these colleges. The ethos of such schools is pervasively secular and may in fact be hostile to publicly devout Christians. Only the interdenominational groups seem to survive and perhaps thrive in such an atmosphere.

Church Support and Governance

The orthodox college or university is dependent upon its sponsoring religious tradition for both financial support and an ample supply of students from that tradition. Significant direct financial support from religious organizations (churches, judicatories, individual congregations) and even more significant indirect support from wealthy persons of the sponsoring tradition provide the orthodox college with a reliable financial base. Perhaps even more important for tuition-dependent schools is the supply of students from the sponsoring tradition. If an orthodox school is to be viable it has to have available ample numbers of committed students and faculty from its sponsoring tradition.

Because of such significant support by committed churchly institutions and wealthy individuals, and because the school itself has obligated itself to transmit the vision and ethos of the sponsoring tradition, there is a strong bond of accountability between the school and the sponsoring tradition. Sometimes the school is owned by the church and therefore is directly accountable to the church. But the more likely link of accountability is the board. An orthodox college has a board composed solely of communicants of the sponsoring tradition, many of them elected to serve on the board by the church itself. Some members of the board may be wealthy and successful, but the main mark of the orthodox college board member is that he or she is a faithful and significant participant in the parent religious tradition. Indeed, orthodox board members understand the religious vision of the tradition and can often articulate it well. They know it well enough to hold the president of the college and the college itself accountable to the vision. The president, being a faithful communicant of and an articulate spokesperson for the tradition, is responsible for assembling the leadership that will hold the college or university to its stated mission as an arm of the tradition.

The critical-mass college or university is far less dependent than orthodox schools on direct support from church organizations, though indirect support from wealthy individuals in the sponsoring tradition is very important. A critical-mass school is also dependent on its parent religious body for supplying the critical mass of students it needs to maintain its specific identity. The governing board of such a school is often made up of a preponderant majority of communicants of the sponsoring tradition. A significant percentage of board members are alumni of the school. A smaller number are official representatives of the sponsoring religious body. Board members are not expected to be as articulate about the religious vision of the school as those of an orthodox school. Even though the board is knowledgeable enough of the tradition to hold the administration accountable in a general sense, the religious direction of the school is more dependent upon the leadership of the president and provost. So while the links of accountability are not as strong as those of orthodox schools, they can and often do provide reliable guidance for the identity and mission of the school.

The intentionally pluralist school continues a relation to its sponsoring tradition by eliciting targeted support for the religious dimensions of the school's life. For example, an endowed professorship reserved for a scholar from the sponsoring communion might be established by the school and funded by the church or one of its wealthy members, or a similar arrangement might be made for a chaplain from that tradition. But otherwise there is minimal direct support from the church. The school continues to recruit among the communicants of its tradition, but only a minority portion of the student body come from that tradition — perhaps 10 to 20 percent. The board of the intentionally pluralist school will insist on continuing representation of the parent body among its numbers, but often only by tacit agreement or custom. Still, that small representation can stimulate the college to continue to provide a voice for the tradition within the school.

The accidentally pluralist college or university often continues to receive indirect support from members of its sponsoring communion long after its connection to that communion has weakened, but most of the direct and indirect support from the tradition is in the past and may linger on only in the names of buildings and programs. Likewise, students from the tradition continue to be present but no special effort is made to recruit them. They are small in number. The board contains only a token representation from the tradition, and those who represent it are trusted not to raise uncomfortable questions about the religious identity of the school.

◆   ◆   ◆

Tracing the various stages on the continuum from maximal to minimal connection of schools and their religious heritage provokes a number of challenging questions. Are colleges and universities destined to move across the chart from left to right as the forces of secularization gradually press in upon them? Will they slowly but inexorably secularize as they seek acceptance by and approval from the educational establishment? Must colleges therefore seek quality by neglecting soul? Is movement only possible in one direction — from left to right on the chart, from less secularization to more?

James Burtchaell strongly suggests an affirmative answer to each of the questions above, but such an answer is not wholly satisfactory. In the following chapters I intend to examine quality colleges in which the Christian light has not died. While nothing in the future is certain, I will also argue that those colleges and universities that have maintained a robust relation to their religious heritage have a fighting chance to maintain it, and perhaps even to strengthen it, in the future. Moreover, I believe that many of the colleges and universities that have moved in a secular direction have the chance to recover a more meaningful relation to their sponsoring heritage than they have had in the recent past. The future does not have to be as dark as it may seem.

PART TWO Six Ventures in
Christian Humanism

This second part of the book gets at the heart of the task before us. In it I will describe and analyze church-related colleges and universities that have not succumbed to the secularization process. Of course all have been challenged by it, but in some cases that has served only to strengthen the resolve to make the Christian account of reality publicly relevant to all of life. In other cases the secularization process has produced some darkening effects — certainly not extensive enough to destroy these schools' character as Christian institutions, yet they may be at risk over the long run.

Before I move to a consideration of vision and ethos, I will provide a brief sketch of each religious tradition included in this study and its school. Certainly the sponsoring churches are important to know about, since they supply the persons, ethos, and vision that are needed to the shape the identity of the school and guide its mission. Indeed, it is the strength of the religious tradition that makes possible its translation into a robust religious identity and mission for a school. Without a strong religious tradition — usually a church — behind it, a college can have great difficulty maintaining its religious identity and mission. I have selected six schools from six strong traditions: a Reformed college (Calvin) sponsored by the Christian Reformed Church; an evangelical college (Wheaton) sponsored by a number of churches, persons, and organizations belonging to the evangelical tradition; two Lutheran schools (St. Olaf and Valparaiso) historically associated with two different Lutheran churches; a Catholic university (Notre Dame) sponsored by the Congregation of the Holy Cross; and a Baptist university (Baylor) associated with the Southern Baptist Convention.

Chapters Five and Six are the key chapters of the book. They will get at why and how these schools have maintained a robust relation with their religious traditions. They will attempt to get at the crucial elements in maintaining a strong connection to a sponsoring religious heritage. Chapter Five will attend especially to the animating vision — the theological rationale — of each religious tradition and the college or university it sponsors. That theological vision will spell out that tradition's perspective on the relation of revelation and reason — faith and secular learning — and thereby give not only a rationale for its existence as a college of the church but also a vision for justifying the ethos of the school, for shaping its curriculum, for building and preserving the kind of theology department it needs, and for providing an intellectual tradition to engage various fields of secular learning. Chapter Six will deal with the ethos of each school — the non-curricular facets that add significant elements to its soul. In that chapter I will examine the role of chapel in each school, the additional ways in which the school engages in the religious formation of its students, the ways it orders its moral life, its involvement in service, and the special non-academic programs and events that give religious texture to its life.

4 | *The Traditions and Their Schools*

The Christian Reformed Church and Calvin College

It is hard to imagine a more religiously intense and theologically literate —
or perhaps religiously literate and theologically intense — church tradition
than that of the Christian Reformed Church. A powerful system of religious
formation in tightly knit and highly disciplined churches and in a system of
elementary and secondary schools produced a people with a clear and solid
identity. The key to that identity was Reformed theology, in which even immigrant Dutch farmers of the CRC were versed enough to discuss and debate with other laity and to challenge their local clergy. Such theological literacy lives on in the board of trustees of Calvin College, which examines for
theological orthodoxy not only the president of the college, but every new
faculty member hired and every applicant for tenure.

Such religious and theological formation has provided fertile soil for
the nurturing (and sometimes the rebellion) of many noted writers, poets,
philosophers, theologians, professors, politicians, and teachers.[1] Much of

---

1. James D. Bratt elaborates an intriguing picture of these sons and daughters of
the church in his lively history of several Dutch Calvinist traditions in America in his
Dutch Calvinism in Modern America: A History of a Conservative Subculture (Grand
Rapids: Eerdmans, 1984), especially Chapter 11, where he describes four renegade nov-
elists from that subculture.

the fabric of society and culture in its principal areas of settlement is decisively conditioned by the Christian Reformed tradition. Bright and aspiring sons and daughters of the tradition are proven successes in every walk of life. The phenomenon is perfectly amazing. With its emphases on the importance of education, cultural formation and preservation, and even covenant theology, the Christian Reformed subculture is arguably Protestantism's counterpart to Judaism.

The animating vision of this church is Reformed theology, stressing the sovereignty of God over all things, the total fallenness of humanity and the creation in all its facets, the election of the saved, the central drama of salvation in Christ, and a strong doctrine of sanctification that leads to transformation of persons and society. Indeed, the Reformed vision has been so defining for the Christian Reformed Church that it has been more compelling than ethnicity in bringing and keeping its members together. As other ethno-religious subcultures have declined or assimilated in America, this one has held together remarkably well because of its theological identity.

Reformed theology has been given additional specification in this tradition by one of its leading thinkers, Abraham Kuyper (1837-1920), the Dutch theologian, activist, university founder, and statesman. Kuyper's theology, it seems, enabled the smallish band of Christian Reformed adherents in America to transcend a natural sectarian inclination to withdraw from society (because of their size and ethnic isolation) for a firm commitment in principle to transform everything around them, beginning with the thought patterns of America and the modern world. Such a commitment was inspired by the belief that, in Kuyper's words, "There is not a square inch on the whole plain of human existence over which Christ, who is Lord over all, does not proclaim: 'This is mine!'"[2] While there were countervailing voices within the Christian Reformed Church — the "Seceders" wanted to withdraw from American society — and within the Kuyperian party itself — the "Antitheticals" intended to build a religious outlook completely separate from American society — the "positive" Kuyperians won out.[3]

---

2. Quoted by James D. Bratt and Ronald A. Wells in "Piety and Progress: A History of Calvin College," in Richard T. Hughes and William B. Adrian, eds., *Models for Christian Higher Education: Strategies for Success in the Twenty-First Century* (Grand Rapids: Eerdmans, 1997), p. 143.

3. Bratt, *Dutch Calvinism*, pp. 48-54.

They took up the challenge to Christianize all the sectors of American society of which they were a part, beginning with themselves and the institutions they developed.

The contention within the denomination suggested above is illustrative of the theological strife in Dutch Calvinism's history. Such intense attention to theology inevitably leads to disagreements over its finer points. After many splits and secessions, the Christian Reformed Church was established by that name in 1890. It grew from very modest beginnings to its present size of about 295,000.[4] Fully a third of its base is in Michigan, gathered around its headquarters in Grand Rapids. It operates an extensive network of elementary and secondary schools in the areas in which it is strong.

While the church has tried mightily to break out of its Dutch ethnic confines, it remains heavily Dutch in composition. Yet, the Christian Reformed Church is no unconscious and uncritical blend of ethnicity and religion. The religious vision predominates, and has given the church and its people the tools for a critical engagement with American society and culture that will remain long after the ethnic factor fades away. As one of its premier journals once put it: "We are not a pretty piece of paper upon which America can write whatever it pleases."[5] Americanization of the community has come at least partly on the church's terms.

So it is also with the Christian Reformed Church's premier educational institution, Calvin College. Its requirement that all administration and faculty be members of the church or one of its confessional partners assures a common theological vision that not only enables it to form its students strongly, but to encourage a kind of intellectual confrontation with modernity that simply doesn't happen in many schools. This common theological vision shaped by Kuyper's neo-Calvinism possesses a number of qualities that are manifested in Calvin College's life. First, the life of the mind is crucial for Christian living. If Christ claims all of our life and being, the mind is certainly part of that. This means that it has to be educated in the liberal arts but even more importantly trained in a theology that will equip Christians to live as whole Christians in the world. Calvin stresses that Christian claims cannot simply remain in the heart; they

---

4. J. Gordon Melton, ed., *Encyclopedia of American Religions,* 5th ed. (Detroit: Gale, 1996), p. 302.

5. Bratt, *Dutch Calvinism,* p. 113.

must also be active in the intellectual processes of the mind. Thus, the college classroom at Calvin has been a kind of chapel. Its own college chapel was built late in the life of the college, since there has long been a conviction that, in the educational domain, the classroom is an even more fitting place of kingdom service than the chapel.

Another characteristic of the Kuyperian construal of Calvinism is its emphasis on integrity and wholeness. It emphasizes that truth according to secular learning simply cannot conflict with God's truth as it is given in revelation. Thus, one of the main thrusts of a Calvin education is to integrate faith (revelation) and learning (reason and experience). In the next chapters we will get into the details of this integration process. Here it is important to note it as one of the ongoing characteristics the college inherited from its sponsoring church. Finally, another Kuyperian emphasis that has been communicated from church to school is an insistence on transformation of the person and, through him or her, the surrounding society. The college's motto, "I offer my heart to you, Lord, promptly and sincerely," illustrates the starting point of transformation. The college "educates for shalom," both within the person and within society, because persons and society must be reclaimed for the dominion of Christ.

Calvin College occupies a large tract of recently developed land in Grand Rapids, Michigan. It moved from an inner-city location to its present site in the early 1960s, an important move presided over by its strong and storied former president William Spoelhof. Its 230 faculty and 4,000 undergraduates — it intentionally remains a college — occupy a striking campus designed by a disciple of Frank Lloyd Wright. Calvin began as a theological seminary in 1876, developed into a junior college at the turn of the century, and became a four-year college in 1920.

The well-known *U.S. News and World Report* college rankings list Calvin as eleventh among regional Midwestern universities and third among its "best buys."[6] The *Templeton Guide,* which honors colleges for character development, has included Calvin in its top one hundred colleges for eight consecutive years.[7] Calvin is also included in *The National Review College Guide,* the *Fiske Guide,* and *Barron's Best Buys in College Education.*[8]

But these secular indices of assessment cannot approximate the es-

---

6. *U.S. News and World Report* rankings for 2000, available at www.usnews.com.

7. Calvin College Web site, www.calvin.edu.

8. *Peterson's Four Year Colleges* (Princeton: Peterson's, 1998), p. 627.

teem in which Calvin is held by Christian intellectuals of many traditions. Calvin is honored among them for its rigorous intellectual life. It produces many young people who go on to success in the arts, sciences, humanities, and business. Further, Calvin is honored for its commitment to Christian learning and scholarship, what it calls the "integration of faith and learning." For many years Calvin has had a solid and systematic approach to Christian learning that has been a source of inspiration and a model for many schools. Out of this commitment to Christian learning have come many luminaries who have carried the flag of Christian scholarship into many fields — Alvin Plantinga in philosophy, Nicholas Wolterstorff in philosophy of religion, George Marsden in history, and Richard Mouw in theological ethics, to name only a few. The college holds a range of summer institutes in Christian scholarship, at which many Calvin luminaries teach. American colleges and universities are sprinkled with Calvin graduates who both model and support the integration of faith and learning. Calvin College is admired widely by those who care about Christian higher education.

The Evangelical Tradition and Wheaton College

Since evangelicalism is a tradition of many churches and movements and not one church, it is far more difficult to describe than the Christian Reformed Church. Evangelicalism is made up of a myriad of small churches on the one hand and enormous denominations like the Southern Baptist or the National Baptist Convention on the other. Moreover, there are many para-church organizations and movements within evangelicalism, even in some cases reaching into traditionally mainstream Protestant churches. These many entities hold different theologies, worship in strikingly different ways, and promote different versions of the Christian way of life. Together they make up a massive portion of the American population — roughly 25-30 percent, totaling about sixty million adherents. The evangelical movement is estimated to be growing at three and one-half times the rate of world population growth, making it the fastest-growing major religious group and the only one growing significantly through conversion.[9]

9. U.S. Center for World Mission, reported on www.religiontoday.com for February 14, 2000. The same report indicates there are 645 million evangelicals in the

Roughly the size of the American Roman Catholic population and quite a bit larger than that of mainstream Protestantism (20 percent of the population), the American evangelical movement seems to possess a greater portion of members who practice their faith more intensely than either the Catholic or mainstream Protestant churches.[10]

Despite this diversity of churches and agencies, they can be designated as a tradition because they share some very distinct characteristics, though the very identification of those characteristics is itself the subject of continuous debate. I shall follow Mark Noll, a major historian of evangelicalism, who in turn takes his set of characteristics from a British author, David Bebbington. These authors agree that evangelicalism as a tradition derives from the renewal movements led by figures such as George Whitefield, John Wesley, Jonathan Edwards, and Nicholas von Zinzendorf. The common impulses in these movements, as cited by Noll and Bebbington, were conversionism (an emphasis on "new birth" as a life-changing religious experience), biblicism (a reliance on the Bible as ultimate religious authority), activism (a concern for sharing the faith), and crucicentrism (a focus on Christ's redeeming work on the cross).[11]

In the eighteenth and nineteenth centuries the evangelical movement in North America did in fact shape and bear an intellectual tradition. Indeed, Noll claims that early evangelicalism forged a Christian-cultural synthesis that included a republican theory of politics, a democratic understanding of society, and a liberal view of the economy.[12] But, according to Noll and others, the great social and intellectual changes of the latter part of the nineteenth century and early part of the twentieth century presented a daunting challenge to that tradition. Instead of facing the challenge with renewed theological creativity, evangelicalism largely transformed itself into the ambiguous movement called "fundamentalism."[13]

---

world today, about 11 percent of the world's population. It adds that Pentecostal and charismatic churches are growing even faster, at 4.5 times the growth of the world population.

10. Mark A. Noll, *The Scandal of the Evangelical Mind* (Grand Rapids: Eerdmans, 1994), p. 9.

11. Noll, *Scandal*, p. 8.

12. Noll, *Scandal*, pp. 59-76.

13. The challenges to the Christian communities were broad and complex, as were the responses on the part of those communities. Noll has a detailed account of both the challenges and the responses; see *Scandal*, pp. 115ff.

While it maintained orthodox Christianity in the face of a rising secularization of American life and culture, fundamentalism did so by turning its version of Christianity into an anti-intellectual and defensive caricature of the faith. In fact, Noll calls the effects of this turn the "intellectual disaster of fundamentalism."[14]

Since the late 1950s, however, fundamentalism itself has divided into two streams. The separatist party can still be called "fundamentalist," while the more open and engaged party has adopted the name "evangelical."[15] There is, of course, much overlap between these two parties within denominations as well as great tension between them, as evidenced in the power struggle within the Southern Baptist Convention. Therefore, it is very important to note that evangelicalism and fundamentalism cannot be used as interchangeable terms, as so much of the "elite" culture of America tends to do. Both of these discrete though closely affiliated wings of conservative Protestantism continue to grow in strength and numbers.

For much of its early history Wheaton College was firmly entrenched in the fundamentalist camp, though its first president, Jonathan Blanchard, did not share the separatist bent that would characterize the movement in later years. On the contrary, his particular brand of postmillennial perfectionism led him and the college into strong abolitionist activities. Under the leadership of his son Charles, however, Wheaton did move toward separatist fundamentalism, where the college remained until the late 1950s.[16] Even so, Wheaton was able to maintain a high standard of liberal arts education, albeit by largely separating faith and learning.

After the conflict-laden administration of President J. Oliver Buswell, who was fired by Wheaton's trustees in 1940, the college moved into a period of transition that gradually took it out of the fundamentalist camp into the more broadly evangelical one. A crucial figure in this move was Billy Graham, who graduated Wheaton in 1943. In many ways, Wheaton has paralleled the trajectory of Graham as he moved from an anti-intellectual, dispensationalist, premillennialist, sectarian, and fundamentalist orientation to one far more appreciative of the intellectual quest, more classically Protestant, more ecumenical, and more open to modern thought.

---

14. Noll, *Scandal*, pp. 109ff.

15. Michael S. Hamilton and James A. Mathisen, "Faith and Learning at Wheaton College," in *Models for Christian Higher Education*, p. 263.

16. Hamilton and Mathisen, "Faith and Learning," p. 264.

Noll, a member of Wheaton's faculty, has argued that Graham's moves have both led and legitimated Wheaton's because so many members of the board of trustees are admirers of Graham. Certainly the large and well-funded Billy Graham Center, which includes a number of evangelical institutes along with a museum dedicated to evangelism, attests to the affection and honor with which Graham is held in Wheaton circles. Noll worries that Wheaton will lose an important guiding and legitimating light when Graham passes.[17]

As an interdenominational college, Wheaton encompasses many varieties of evangelicals on its board, its faculty, and in its student body. While its requirement that all administrators and faculty sign its Statement of Faith and Statement of Responsibilities gives it an appearance of uniformity from the outside, such an appearance must be sharply qualified when viewed from the inside. For there are as many evangelical traditions and persuasions in the Wheaton community as there are in the broader world of evangelicalism, and these various persuasions often do not fit easily together. There are even vestiges of the old fundamentalism, as evidenced by the trustees' addition of a biblically literalistic human origins clause to the Statement of Faith in 1961.[18]

In terms of philosophies of Christian higher education, Wheaton in its more recent evangelical incarnation has witnessed two different approaches over time — what Michael Hamilton and James Mathisen call the "value-added" and the "integration" models.[19] The earlier value-added model was carried by the more pietist and Holiness elements in the Wheaton tradition. (It has also been called the "add-on" or "two-spheres" model.) In this model, excellent classroom teaching and learning went on largely as they would in any liberal arts school; Christian teaching and ethos were added outside the classroom in faculty-student relationships, revivals, Bible study, worship, and music programs, as well as "ministry" and social service activities in the larger community.

In recent decades, however, the "integration" approach has become dominant. A good deal of the integration model has been imported, with some modifications, from the Reformed approach most fully worked out at Calvin. Arthur Holmes, who became one of the most influential faculty

17. Interview with Mark Noll at the Wheaton campus, November 11, 1999.
18. Hamilton and Mathisen, "Faith and Learning," p. 277.
19. Hamilton and Mathisen, "Faith and Learning," pp. 270-71.

members at Wheaton, had strong contacts with Calvin philosophers, while Noll, also an enormously influential professor and scholar, has had close associations with Calvin historians. Hamilton and Mathisen offer a very helpful articulation of the Wheaton appropriation of the Calvin model:

> The distinguishing feature of integration is the belief that systems of discovered (secular) and revealed knowledge are, by themselves, incomplete. They are both needed for full understanding; they have areas of overlap and are each informed by the other. The mix, however, is a volatile one. When Christian knowledge and natural knowledge conflict, one must be revised to conform to the other. This keeps proponents of integration continually subject to criticism from both defenders of the divine prerogatives and the defenders of the discipline's prerogatives. The distinguishing feature of the integration model is the conviction that Christian scholarship differs from non-Christian scholarship in fundamental ways because it begins at a different starting place. Philosophy, sociology, literature, history, and perhaps even physics and mathematics will be done differently if undertaken with Christian presuppositions.[20]

This approach to connecting faith and learning is now deeply embedded in Wheaton's faculty, in part because of a seminar in faith, thinking, and teaching that has been going on since 1969.[21] But this approach — distilled in the formula "All Truth is God's Truth" — would not get very far without sufficient numbers of students to respond enthusiastically to it. And Wheaton has such students aplenty. Because it is a national beacon of evangelical learning, bright and motivated evangelical students come from all fifty states and a dozen foreign countries. It is a highly selective institution.[22] The student body of 2,400 is leavened by 150 young persons of missionary families and a contingent of graduate students in a limited number of areas. It is listed at number fifty among national liberal arts colleges by *U.S. News and World Report* for the year 2000. Moreover, it enrolls more National Merit Scholars and sends more students to prestigious Ph.D. programs than all but a handful of the very best liberal arts col-

---

20. Hamilton and Mathisen, "Faith and Learning," p. 271.
21. Hamilton and Mathisen, "Faith and Learning," p. 279.
22. *Peterson's Four Year Colleges*, p. 470.

leges.[23] Its most popular majors are English, music, biology, and biblical studies. It even has 107 philosophy majors! As its reputation for intellectual rigor and Christian commitment has grown, Wheaton has attracted increasing numbers of young people from mainstream Protestant denominations. Even a few Catholic and Orthodox students are appearing.

Wheaton's curricular purpose is the "development of whole and effective Christians through excellence in programs of higher education." The college, built in neo-colonial architecture, occupies eighty acres of land in Wheaton, Illinois, a once rural town that is now very much embedded in the vast western suburbs of Chicago. It has 165 full-time faculty members. It has a relatively new (1993) president, Duane Litfin, who is only the seventh president in 140 years.

The Southern Baptist Convention and Baylor University

It would seem an easier task to describe the Southern Baptist Convention, one church in the general evangelical tradition, than to describe that general tradition itself. But that would be a wrong impression, for there is almost as much complexity within the Southern Baptist Convention as there is within evangelicalism itself. Baptists as a group have a dynamic and complex history partly because of their own specific doctrinal emphases — the radical autonomy of the local congregation and the freedom of the individual conscience, to name but two. From the beginning of their history in England in the sixteenth (the Separatist wing) and seventeenth (the Particular wing) centuries to the present-day struggles for control of the convention, the Baptist journey has been lively and unpredictable. From a small minority of persecuted Christians in colonial America, Baptists in their various churches have become the largest Protestant family of believers in America. The Southern Baptist Convention is, at 16 million members, by far the largest church among the many Baptist churches. Indeed, it is the largest Protestant communion in America. Because of its numbers

---

23. The ranking comes from the *U.S. News and World Report* Web site, www.usnews.com; the National Merit scholarship data comes from the National Merit Scholarship Corporation Annual Report (1993-94); and the data about the origin of Ph.D.s comes from Franklin and Marshall College, *Baccalaureate Origins of Doctorate Recipients*, 7th ed. (Lancaster: Franklin and Marshall, 1993), p. 7.

and influence, the convention has become almost an established religion in a number of states in the South. The Baptist General Convention of Texas itself numbers 3.2 million self-reported members and 2.5 million fully recorded members.[24]

Baptists share certain views about the nature and practice of the Christian faith, including a high view of the authority of Scripture (often but not necessarily literalist), the autonomy of the local church, the liberty of the individual conscience, the priesthood of all believers, a regenerate church membership, ordinances of immersion baptism and the Lord's Supper, and a free church in a free state.[25] Baptists also share with other evangelicals a zeal for evangelistic activities; they have evangelized millions of persons at home and abroad and exhibit few signs of losing enthusiasm for missions. They continue to show significant growth.

However, Baptists are not a unified group, as even a cursory glance at the nation's religious news pages makes clear. Baptists in general and Southern Baptists in particular have always contested issues of faith and practice. Their history is anything but placid or harmonious.

While it is far too large a task to trace historically the religious eddies of the vast Southern Baptist river, the story can be simplified by referring to three groups that are currently contending for the allegiance and control of the state conventions, churches, and institutions — especially the colleges and seminaries — of the Southern Baptist Convention. One author has labeled these three groups the liberal-progressives, conservative-fundamentalists, and centrist-denominationalists.[26] The conservative-fundamentalists have taken control of most of the official machinery of the convention at the national level. One of their primary goals has been to purge the national-level bureaucracy and Southern Baptist schools of the liberal-progressives, who the fundamentalists believe are capitulating to secularizing tendencies. The liberal-progressives — one wing of the so-called "moderates" that are under great pressure from the fundamentalists — are more likely than the centrists to leave the Southern Baptist Convention and establish new institutions under their control. The other wing of the "moderates" — the centrist-denominationalists — are more likely

24. Listed for 1998 at www.adherents.com.

25. Bill J. Leonard, "What Can the Baptist Tradition Contribute to Christian Higher Education?" in *Models for Christian Higher Education*, p. 372.

26. Leonard, "Baptist Tradition," p. 374.

than the progressives to stay within the convention, especially if they can garner specific state conventions for their party. Baylor University is aligned with this centrist group, which is not fundamentalist yet is strongly loyal to the Southern Baptist tradition. The centrists have control of the largest state convention, the Baptist General Convention of Texas. It is instructive that Baylor named its new seminary after a revered centrist figure, George W. Truett.

An excellent way to begin the depiction of Baylor as a Baptist university is to note its motto: *Pro Ecclesia, Pro Texana* — for church, for Texas. Baylor was founded in 1845 by Baptist Judge R. E. B. Baylor and two Baptist ministers, when Texas was still a sovereign republic. The school intended to produce clergy and laity for the building up of both the Baptist churches in Texas and the young society around it. Though Baylor diminished its formal connections with the Baptist General Convention of Texas in the midst of worries about a fundamentalist takeover in the early 1990s, it has always had and continues to have a very strong relationship with it. Virtually the whole administration and many faculty members are active participants in Texas Baptist churches and in the Baptist General Convention of Texas. Some have argued that Baylor's involvement in the state convention kept it from capture by the fundamentalists. Moreover, the Baptist General Convention of Texas elects one-fourth of the board, while three-fourths of the board is self-perpetuating. As a result, the board is solidly centrist.

Baylor, like many church-related colleges and universities, began as a classic liberal arts college. An old-fashioned curriculum emphasizing math, classical languages, philosophy, and literature, and a senior course on moral philosophy taught by the president was the order of the day, and the ethos of the college was characterized by many Christian practices. However, toward the end of the nineteenth century that cozy combination of liberal arts and Christian teaching was shattered by the rise of two new models of the university — the land grant university, dedicated to technical and practical learning, and the research university, devoted to the building up of scientific knowledge. Neither one of these models had much curricular space for Christian teachings.

While all universities and colleges were faced with the challenge of these two emerging models of higher education (see Chapter Two), Baylor was particularly provoked. The head of the faculty of the blossoming state university in Austin, Leslie Waggener, precipitated in 1890 what Michael

Beaty and Todd Buras call an "academic shoot-out: Texas style."[27] Waggener, himself oddly enough a Baptist, publicly denounced denominational schools and called for their disbanding. He asserted that education under religious auspices could only be a pious fraud. Now that the state had the matter in hand and was setting up both technical and research institutions, he argued, the church-related schools should simply "retire to innocuous desuetude."[28]

This provoked much soul-searching among the Baylor leaders. Intimidated by the Enlightenment consensus that was building, they argued that church-related schools like Baylor did much the same thing in the classroom and laboratory as their fellow state institutions; they just added on a Christian atmosphere within which young Christians could be nurtured as they pursued their programs of learning. For many years, then, Baylor, like many other Christian schools, pursued what we earlier called a "two-spheres" or "add-on" model of Christian higher education. The Enlightenment model of scientific rationality could dominate classrooms while Christian activities provided a supporting ethos for students as they studied at the university. Following from this, Baylor has for many years required that its faculty and administration be observant Christians or Jews. When one applies for a faculty or administrative position at Baylor, one is required to list one's religious affiliation and current participation in a church, parish, or synagogue. Active religious persons would provide the kind of ethos Baylor needed to continue its mission as a Christian university.

In the last decade, however, a fresh vision of Christian higher education has fueled Baylor's intentions to become a unique and distinguished Baptist university. Embraced by an influential group of leaders, including the president and the provost, this vision is much indebted to the Calvin College model of the integration of faith and learning. That is, the Christian intellectual account of reality and life — especially in its Baptist construal — ought to be relevant within classroom teaching itself. The Christian account ought to move beyond the religion curriculum to engage and affect secular teaching and learning. As hiring has proceeded under this new regime, not only are the religious affiliation and participation

27. Michael Beaty and Todd Buras, "Pro Ecclesia, Pro Texana," *Journal of Texas Baptist History* 16 (1996): 9.

28. Beaty and Buras, "Pro Ecclesia, Pro Texana," p. 10.

of applicants checked out, but also their interest in the engagement of faith and learning. Further, there is a target that 50 percent of new hires be Baptist, though that is not a scrupulously preserved quota. It is more important that each person hired be a Christian who is committed to the conversation between faith and learning.

This new approach has not been uncontroversial, as one might expect. There is resistance to it in the faculty and among alumni and the surrounding community. While 58 percent of the faculty reject a compartmentalization of faith and learning, 56 percent do not feel capable of adding a faith-related perspective to their students' understanding of the courses they teach and therefore feel unable to do what they support.[29] So the new approach is not understood enough to be embedded deeply in the faculty. But Baylor is working on educating the faculty in this approach. Because it is supported by a Baptist population that has now achieved both wealth and power, Baylor has many tools available to get the job done.

Baylor has created a number of centers and institutes that will help faculty understand the integration of faith and learning. It is in the process of establishing twenty endowed professorships among whose major identifying marks will be a concern for faith and learning. It is developing a mentoring program for new faculty. And the persons hired in the last decade are more likely to be supporters of the new approach. The Baylor leadership believes the school does not have to choose between maintaining its religious identity and vigorous moves toward excellence; it is confident that it is doing both.

The university has plans to expand its doctoral programs so that it can move from a Doctoral Level II designation by the Carnegie Classification to Level I. While Baylor is ranked seventy-first among national universities by *U.S. News and World Report,* its leaders fully believe it can move into the top fifty in relatively short order.[30] It has an ample endowment of over $650 million, and the number of National Merit Scholars enrolled at Baylor places the university in the top 1 percent among higher education institutions. It has a Phi Beta Kappa chapter. Its leadership has a

29. Larry Lyon and Michael Beaty, "Integration, Secularization, and the Two-Spheres View of Religious Colleges: Comparing Baylor University with the University of Notre Dame and Georgetown College," *Christian Scholar's Review* 29 (Fall 1999): 84.

30. See www.usnews.com/usnews/edu/college/rankings/natunivs/natu_2.htm.

clear notion of what must be done to move forward and is committed to implementing that notion.

Baylor has approximately 11,500 undergraduate and 2,000 graduate students. Over 10,000 of the total are from Texas, though students come from all fifty states and eighty-five foreign countries. Over 6,000 of the students are Baptist, while 1,600 are Catholic and 1,200 are Methodist. Roughly 1,000 students are of Hispanic background. Its faculty of 650 includes 70 Methodists and 45 Catholics along with 315 Baptists. It is located in Waco, Texas — a community of 200,000 people — on a 432-acre campus on the banks of the Brazos River.[31]

The Catholic Church and the University of Notre Dame

When one looks up the worldwide Roman Catholic Church on adherents.com, a Web site devoted to statistics on religious belief, the electronic pages on Catholic national and regional churches go on for so long that it would take hours to reach the end where the totals are found. That's what it means to be a church of a billion members. The pages are slightly more manageable for the United States, where the Catholic community stands at about 60 million adherents and growing. Catholicism is a big tent indeed.

The Catholic Church, of course, is the church of churches. Truly catholic in time and space, it is the main bearer of the Christian mission in world history. It is spread so widely that it is dangerous to make too many generalizations about its nature and direction. Living in the United States or Europe, it is easy to get the impression that Pope John Paul II and his emphases are not taken all that seriously by the bulk of Catholics. There are a fair number of "cafeteria Catholics" in these areas who take what they like and discard what they don't. But when one looks more broadly at world Catholicism, the picture seems distinctly different. The great effort of the pope to re-center the church on its classic heritage and to engage in vigorous evangelization from there is taken with great seriousness by the larger share of Catholics around the world, particularly in regions where Catholicism is growing rapidly.

31. This data is provided by Baylor's Office of Institutional Research and Testing and is available at www.baylor.edu/about/facts.

At the same time that Pope John Paul II seems to be vigorously conserving that classic core — so much so that many Catholic intellectuals in the West consistently define themselves over against him — he is engaging the liberal heritage of the West in a critically positive way. Through his encyclicals and public actions he has led the church to a critical appreciation of democracy, market economic arrangements, religious liberty, and social pluralism. At the same time he has not hesitated to criticize them on the basis of the Catholic social teachings he has inherited and extended. He is taken so seriously as a public figure because he operates from a long and deep Catholic religious, intellectual, and moral tradition, not from the ideological fads of the day.

In his call to re-evangelize the West, he puts high on the list of priorities the Catholic engagement with culture — the meanings and values that guide societies. Among the key cultural institutions of every civilization are its colleges and universities, which the pope believes are crucial instruments in the re-evangelization of culture. The Catholic Church has had an intimate relationship with universities throughout its history, establishing the first universities and later planting many schools of all types. However, these schools have been as susceptible to secularization as their Protestant counterparts, as the pope himself has observed. In an attempt to retrieve them for the church and its vision of truth, he has promulgated a much-discussed letter, *Ex Corde Ecclesiae* ("From the Heart of the Church"). In that document he summons Catholic universities and colleges to re-establish close relationships with the church, even to the point of juridical accountability. As one might guess, such a call is very controversial on the American scene, with its strong commitment to academic freedom and institutional autonomy. Indeed, Notre Dame, like many of its sister Catholic schools, has an ambivalent posture toward the pope's call. We will explore Notre Dame's response to *Ex Corde* later.

In contrast to the Protestant pattern of the church itself founding colleges, Catholic universities and colleges have generally been established by various orders — Jesuit, Dominican, Franciscan, etc. Over the centuries each order has emphasized certain aspects of higher education. One such prominent order is the Congregation of the Holy Cross, the founding order of the University of Notre Dame. Dan G. Danner spells out the particular character of the order's colleges and universities this way:

At the heart of the Holy Cross mission in higher education is the study of theology, philosophy, and the liberal arts, seen as fully consistent with pre-professional programs in business, engineering, nursing, mass communications, and criminal justice. As this mission is etched out in the lives of individual students, Holy Cross believes it will bear fruit by contributing to aesthetic sensitivities, passion for justice, and compassion for the poor. Students' privacy and autonomy are to be respected, and student development programs such as campus ministry and residence life are designed to make known Holy Cross' concern for the welfare of students.[32]

Notre Dame is a university of the Congregation of the Holy Cross, but with a difference. Unlike many Holy Cross schools, Notre Dame aspires to be a great research university. It was founded in 1842 on the site of an old Catholic missionary outpost by a small band of impoverished French and Irish brothers led by Rev. Edward F. Sorin, C.S.C. By force of will and character Father Sorin developed in the early Notre Dame a reputation that inspired Catholics across the whole country. And as European Catholics immigrated to America by the millions in the late nineteenth and early twentieth centuries, Notre Dame became a beacon of hope and pride for them, making it one of the most famous universities in America. Certainly the growing pride in Notre Dame cannot be accounted for without reference to football; legendary figures like Knute Rockne made Notre Dame into a football power that soon surpassed the elite private universities with which it aspired to compete. Indeed, one way of understanding the current Notre Dame is to view it as another exercise in Catholic pride, this time matching and surpassing those same elite private universities — Harvard, Yale, Chicago, Princeton — in academic rather than athletic prowess.

There is little doubt that Notre Dame is making a concerted effort to join those elite few at the top of the educational heap. Currently ranked nineteenth among national universities by *U.S. News and World Report*,[33] it shows up in many indices of excellence as an up-and-coming research institution. If Catholics, like Baptists, were once toward the bottom of the socio-economic scale, that is certainly no longer the case. Wealthy Catho-

32. Dan G. Danner, "The University of Portland: Center of Christian Humanism," in *Models for Christian Higher Education,* p. 48.

33. See www.usnews.com/usnews/edu/college/rankings/natunivs/natu_a2.htm.

lics are making enough money available for faculty salaries, endowment, buildings, institutes and centers, endowed professorships, and research to make plausible Notre Dame's ambition to become a great research institution. Meanwhile, its undergraduate efforts continue to flourish. Eighty-five percent of the undergraduates accepted into the university are in the top 10 percent of their high school classes, while only 50 percent of all applicants are accepted, making Notre Dame one of only eight universities that admit fewer than half their applicants. Ninety-six percent stay at Notre Dame after their freshman year at an institution where 56 percent are studying more than five hundred miles from home. This high quality student input results in a high quality output: medical school acceptance of Notre Dame graduates is at 70 percent, and the university ranks eighteenth among private universities (first among Catholic schools) in the number of doctorates earned by its undergraduate alumni.[34]

Much of this great progress was initiated during the thirty-five-year tenure of its charismatic president, Theodore Hesburgh, who must be the best known of all recent presidents of American colleges and universities — a truly national figure. In this extended ascent Notre Dame has certainly not lost the public image of an intensely Catholic university, though a number of critics believe that its headlong pursuit of reputation indicates a "willingness to weaken or even betray the ideals of a Catholic college in the hope of being accepted by those who do not share those ideals."[35] But the public rhetoric is certainly there. Notre Dame's mission boldly declares that it is a "Catholic academic community of higher learning, animated from its origins by the Congregation of Holy Cross." Further, "As a Catholic university one of its distinctive goals is to provide a forum where through free inquiry and open discussion the various lines of Catholic thought may intersect with all forms of knowledge found in the arts, sciences, professions, and every other area of human scholarship and creativity."[36] There is little doubt that currently the university lends credibility to its mission claims. It has gathered a wide array of Catholic and non-Catholic Christian intellectuals who make an impact not only on the

34. Available at www.nd.edu/aboutnd/indicators/index.shtml.

35. Ralph McInerney, "Losing for the Gipper," *The Weekly Standard,* October 11, 1999, p. 38.

36. Notre Dame Mission Statement, available at www.nd.edu/aboutnd/about/mission/mission_statement.shtml.

university but also the wider culture. It attempts to hire not only fine teachers, researchers, and citizens of the university, but also those who will "contribute to the Catholic character of the university."[37] Its economic strength has also enabled it to deploy a significant number of institutes, centers, and journals that express and engage Catholic themes.

While a lay board of trustees has governed Notre Dame since 1967, the preponderance of board members remains Catholic. The trustees of the university are approved by the Fellows, a kind of cabinet composed equally of laity and Holy Cross fathers who have an advisory capacity as well as veto authority over the trustees. The president must be a member of the Congregation of the Holy Cross and many Holy Cross fathers are involved in the dorm as well as the academic life of the university.

Notre Dame occupies a 1,250-acre campus just north of the city of South Bend, Indiana, and is part of a metropolitan population of more than 250,000. Its faculty numbers 1,044, with an additional 336 professional specialists. Approximately 40 percent of faculty members are Catholic. Undergraduate enrollment is roughly 7,800, of which about 85 percent are Catholic students. Around 1,400 students are enrolled in graduate programs, and another 1,100 are in the Law School and MBA program. The university is residential (80 percent of its students live in its twenty-seven dorms), national (56 percent of the students are more than 500 miles from home), and international (700 students from seventy foreign countries).[38] Its campus is dotted with new buildings of a very substantial character.

The Evangelical Lutheran Church in America and St. Olaf College

The Lutheran Reformation of the sixteenth century began at a university with the instigation of a theological professor, Martin Luther. From the beginning that reformation included a strong intellectual element along with the religious, aesthetic, and practical. In its decisive break with Rome, the Lutheran movement articulated its faith in a refined and systematic theo-

37. Mark W. Roche, Dean of the Faculty of Arts and Letters, interview with the author, Dec. 9, 1999.

38. "About the University of Notre Dame," 1999-2000 fact sheet made available to campus visitors.

logical confession, the Book of Concord. As it developed it paid strong attention to the education of its clergy into this confessional tradition. Its clergy were academically trained in university faculties. This emphasis on an educated clergy is one of the defining themes of Lutheran identity. A second theme is the calling or vocation of all Christians. Christians are to act on behalf of their neighbors with faith, love, and hope in the specific worldly roles they have been given. But they are also to act with competence. This means provision for the education of the laity as well as the clergy, an education that extends from elementary through university education. A third theme in Lutheran theology is a high evaluation of human reason as a guide to earthly, civil life; in the words of Luther, "How dare you not know what can be known!" Lutheranism teaches that while reason cannot achieve saving knowledge of God, it can reach trustworthy knowledge of our world.

These three themes combined in Lutheran lands to encourage the development of high-quality universities. The calling of the professor became revered in those countries, as were the schools in which they served. Lutheran universities became great engines of knowledge both secular and theological. However, with the coming of the Enlightenment they were susceptible to the same kinds of secularization pressures that we recounted earlier in this book. Moreover, the church itself has had a tendency to ossify into dry orthodoxies against which many renewal movements have protested.

Among the great waves of Northern European immigrants who came to America between the mid-nineteenth century and World War I were many Lutherans from different nations. While generally pietist in orientation, they were not anti-intellectual. They had the three themes we described above deeply engrained in their minds and hearts.

When they arrived on these shores, Lutheran immigrants immediately established churches and schools — academies, colleges, and seminaries. The Norwegians of the upper Midwest followed paths similar to those of other Lutheran ethnic groups. The early days featured many scrambles over church alignments. Theological and ethnic differences created a fluid church scene. But by 1917 most Norwegians wound up in the Evangelical Lutheran Church, which persisted until its merger in 1960 into the American Lutheran Church, combining both German and Norwegian groups. Finally, the American Lutheran Church merged in 1988 with the Lutheran Church in America, which included a large wing of colonial

Lutheranism and the Augustana Lutheran Church, a church of Swedish heritage. This new denomination became the Evangelical Lutheran Church in America (ELCA), a body of about 5.2 million Lutherans with headquarters in Chicago. These many mergers reflected both the acculturation of ethnic Lutherans into American life and their theological commonalities.

In 1874 a Norwegian Lutheran pastor, the Rev. Bernt Julius Muus, established an academy in Northfield, Minnesota, called St. Olaf's School. Interestingly enough, it was coeducational from the beginning and stressed lay rather than clerical education in the liberal arts and the Christian faith. St. Olaf added a college program in 1886. Negotiating its way through many church-political squabbles in its early years, St. Olaf finally became in 1899 the approved college of the United Norwegian Lutheran Church, the predecessor body to the Evangelical Lutheran Church. Its strong bond with this church was crucial for its flourishing from the turn of the century through the 1960s.[39] The Norwegian love of literature, language, music, the Lutheran faith, and foreign missions was embedded in the life of the college through the many Lutheran Norwegians who taught at and attended the college.

It was under Rev. L. W. Boe (1918-1942), its energetic fourth president, that St. Olaf developed into a quality liberal arts college. He provided the context for two giants of Norwegian immigrant culture, O. E. Rolvaag and F. Melius Christiansen, to give St. Olaf national prominence in literature and choral music, respectively. The college achieved academic luster enough to be granted a Phi Beta Kappa chapter soon after his regime. The Christian character of the college was rich and unabashed, though mostly in an "add-on" context. Faculty and students from a strong Norwegian Lutheran church life lived out their academic lives at St. Olaf ensconced in a religious atmosphere.

In the post World War II years, the intellectual challenge of relating faith to learning came to the fore. Using the opportunity of a mid-1950s self-study and then later the occasion of its centennial, St. Olaf engaged in very sophisticated reflection about the nature of a Christian liberal arts college. The writing of two important documents in the life of the school,

39. See the fine historical account of St. Olaf by Mark Granquist, "Religious Vision and Academic Quest at St. Olaf College," in *Models for Christian Higher Education,* pp. 82-96.

Integration in the Christian Liberal Arts College (1956) and *Identity and Mission in a Changing Context* (1974), was strongly influenced by Harold Ditmanson, a theologian who gave his life's energies to the college. These documents lay out a Lutheran version of the engagement of faith and learning. The first document encourages an integration of all liberal arts learning through a framework provided by theology and philosophy and enjoins a "critical participation" of the faithful church in its cultural context.[40] The second, written two decades later, calls for a "Christian context" or framework of meaning for the liberal arts at St. Olaf. "Christian context" means giving equal weight to theological and rationalistic approaches to reality, encouraging a dialogue about the vocation of the Christian teacher and probing "the relevance of Christian faith for the academic disciplines."[41]

For years the college enjoyed a steady supply of faculty and students from the Norwegian Lutheran tradition, but that began to change in the 1970s and accelerated thereafter. St. Olaf became a genuinely national liberal arts college as its reputation grew. But with that came a newly diverse student body and faculty that no longer automatically shared the assumptions of earlier generations. In the past decade the college has held vigorous — and sometimes contentious — discussions on its identity and mission, particularly as they are embodied in its curriculum. It has used the occasion of its 125th anniversary to produce a fine celebrative and reflective volume entitled *Called to Serve: St. Olaf and the Vocation of a Church College.*[42] Its mission statement also expresses a forthright intention to make the Christian faith in its Lutheran construal publicly relevant to all the facets of the college's ongoing life:

> St. Olaf College, a four-year college of the Evangelical Lutheran Church in America, provides an education committed to the liberal arts, rooted in the Christian Gospel, and incorporating a global perspective.... It offers opportunities for encounter with the Christian Gospel and God's call to faith. The college intends that its graduates combine academic ex-

40. *Integration in the Christian Liberal Arts College,* ed. Howard Hong (Northfield, MN: St. Olaf College Press, 1956), pp. 65-69.

41. Harold Ditmanson, *Identity and Mission in a Changing Context* (Northfield, MN: St. Olaf College Press, 1974), p. 19.

42. Pamela Schwandt, ed., *Called to Serve: St. Olaf and the Vocation of a Church College* (Northfield, MN: St. Olaf College Press, 1999).

cellence and theological literacy with a commitment to life-long learning. . . .[43]

St. Olaf enjoys an administration of theologically literate Lutherans. Its
board — 60 percent ELCA Lutheran, including two bishops and a pastor — is
chaired by renowned Lutheran church historian Martin Marty. Its programs
in the arts — particularly Christian choral music — are nationally known
and appreciated. It has had a significant Lutheran momentum that has kept it
a seriously Christian college until the present day. Indeed, James Burtchaell
found it to be one of the most attractively Christian colleges he examined
among the seventeen he visited: "Clearly a Lutheran identity was more purposefully claimed, a lamination of scholarship with piety and theology more
bindingly achieved, an institutional integrity with responsiveness to the
church more amiably combined, and secularization much longer staved off,
at St. Olaf than at Gettysburg."[44] Though he voices doubts about its future,
Burtchaell gives a rare bow of appreciation to St. Olaf's accomplishments.

St. Olaf enrolls about 3,000 undergraduates on its solidly built campus that occupies a remarkable hill above the flat and fertile Minnesota
farm plains. It is a very selective school that maintains about a 50 percent
Lutheran student body. Its ample faculty of 347 (275 full-time) constitutes
a very low student/faculty ratio that has led to two painful retrenchments
in the past decade. Somewhere between 30-40 percent of its faculty is Lutheran. St. Olaf is ranked forty-fifth among national liberal arts colleges by
U.S. News and World Report and ranks in the top 5 percent among colleges
in the country whose graduates earn doctorates in all fields. Its most popular majors currently are biology, economics, and English. Fully 40 percent
of its student body participates in its music programs.[45]

The Lutheran Church–Missouri Synod and Valparaiso University

In contrast to the ELCA, the Lutheran Church–Missouri Synod is the only
major Lutheran body in the United States that has not experienced a

43. *St. Olaf College 1995-96 Academic Catalog*, p. 27.
44. James Burtchaell, *The Dying of the Light: The Disengagement of Colleges and Universities from Their Christian Churches* (Grand Rapids: Eerdmans, 1998), p. 518.
45. St. Olaf Web site, www.stolaf.edu.

merger. It has developed a reputation for uncompromising and combative defense of Lutheran orthodoxy. The church was founded in 1847 by two separate groups of German Lutheran immigrants — one group from Saxony under the theological leadership of C. F. W. Walther and one from Franconia under the sponsorship of the influential German theologian Wilhelm Loehe. It has grown from its initial twelve congregations and twenty-two pastors to a church of 2.6 million. Early on the church strove to remain German in its American environment and vigorously evangelized new German immigrants into its German Lutheran cocoon. In order to remain German and orthodox, it established a large network of parochial schools.[46] Its clergy were trained in a traditional German way — they went off to prep schools for a classical education, then to a senior college for a liberal arts education, and finally to the seminary in St. Louis for a confessional Lutheran theological education. This educational formula produced a large number of well-educated clergy, among them Lutheran intellectuals such as Jaroslav Pelikan, Martin Marty, Robert Wilken, Richard John Neuhaus, and Gilbert Meilaender. Indeed, "Missouri" at its best has been a theologically disciplined church that has shaped intensely loyal clergy and lay people. It has had a sharp and clear identity and sense of mission that has made it a strong tradition even after it shed some of its strong German ethnicity.

However, as the church acculturated to American society and its educational institutions — especially Concordia Seminary in St. Louis — moderated their defensive confessionalism, serious rifts appeared in the church. A reactionary quasi-fundamentalist movement emerged in the late 1960s that led to a deep and painful split in the church in the mid-1970s. In a pattern similar to what happened later in the Southern Baptist Convention, the denominational bureaucracy was taken over by the successful quasi-fundamentalist movement. That bureaucracy then purged the churches and schools of outspoken dissenters, who moved to a splinter church called the Association of Evangelical Lutheran Churches, which then merged in 1988 into the Evangelical Lutheran Church in America.

While these church troubles affected Valparaiso deeply, and continue to do so, they have not enveloped the governance procedures of the university. This was because Valparaiso University always was and continues to

46. Arthur Carl Piepkorn, *Profiles in Belief: The Religious Bodies of the United States and Canada* (New York: Harper & Row, 1977), pp. 114-16.

be an independent Lutheran institution. The university was founded in 1859 by Methodists as a co-educational college, but it had to close in 1871. Two years later it opened as the Northern Indiana Normal School, becoming Valparaiso College in 1900 and Valparaiso University in 1906. The second incarnation of the school also fell upon hard times, and a group of Missouri Synod Lutheran laity and clergy — the Lutheran University Association — bought the school in 1925 with the dream of making it into a Lutheran university. Oddly enough, the Missouri Synod itself was not enamored of the idea. It had other organizational interests of higher priority, and it had its own system of prep schools, senior colleges, teachers' colleges, and seminaries over which it had direct control, so it did not feel a need for an expensive university that might move in unpredictable and uncontrollable directions.[47]

But founded Valparaiso was. Unfortunately, the great dreams of being a national university foundered in the difficult economic times of the 1930s. In 1940, however, the association enlisted a man with a strong vision to restart the university. The Rev. O. P. Kretzmann, son of a famous Missouri Synod family, stepped forward and set the university in a new and vigorous trajectory with a rousing speech at his installation entitled "The Destiny of a Christian University in the Modern World."[48] Never one to dream small dreams, Kretzmann set about gathering a faculty of Lutheran professors and students who would make Valparaiso into a national Lutheran university. In his twenty-eight years as president he did much to reach that goal.

One of his grand dreams was to build a chapel commensurate with the kind of university he had envisaged. In 1959 the magnificent Chapel of the Resurrection was completed. Holding nearly three thousand persons in its huge nave, it stands astride the campus reminding the university of its life's center, as Kretzmann hoped it would. In it there are not only daily and Sunday services, but concerts, lectures, and celebratory events. Its great lantern-like tower seems to give off light to the rest of the university, giving architectural resonance to the university's motto: "In Thy Light We See Light."

---

47. Richard Baepler, "Flame of Faith, Lamp of Learning" (unpublished manuscript), Ch. 5, pp. 17ff.

48. O. P. Kretzmann, "The Destiny of a Christian University in the Modern World," in *The Lutheran Reader*, ed. Paul J. Contino and David Morgan (Valparaiso, IN: Valparaiso University Press, 1999), p. 109.

Never having the resources of a Baylor or a Notre Dame to become a research university, Kretzmann and his successors nevertheless have built the school into an excellent liberal arts college with a law school and several master's programs. As the sole comprehensive university for Missouri Synod Lutherans, it has attracted many bright students who have flourished in a free and creative atmosphere. Valparaiso, reflecting the beloved and charismatic Kretzmann, became an unusual combination of the parochial and the cosmopolitan. The school of a small, insular German-American church, it nevertheless constantly reminds itself that it stands at the juncture of Athens and Jerusalem. Its academic programs and non-curricular offerings in music and the arts aim at a certain transparency to Christian claims. It has constantly discussed what it means to be a Christian university in the Lutheran tradition down to the present day, now celebrating its seventy-fifth anniversary as a Lutheran school. In honor of that occasion it has produced a fine book entitled *The Lutheran Reader,* which is not only an account of Valparaiso's history as a Lutheran school but also a set of reflections about the nature of the faith-learning engagement. The authors' contributions in the book indicate a sophisticated commitment to the engagement of faith and learning at a level the earlier Valparaiso could not have achieved. Its academic reputation has risen even as it struggles to maintain its Lutheran Christian character.

The university walks a fine line in relation to its Missouri Synod constituency. A number of faculty left the synod after its 1970s conflict and have very ambivalent relations to it. The denomination itself often views the university skeptically. Yet, the university desires to keep its connections — it has a Missouri Synod clergyman as president, a number of its top administrators and most of its board are Missouri Synod, and it continues to draw about a fifth of its students from that church. It has reached out to other Lutheran bodies as well, with the result that another fifth of its students come from those traditions. But among the six schools we are examining, Valparaiso has the most unusual and tenuous relation to its parent church.

Valparaiso is ranked fourth among Midwestern comprehensive universities and fourth among "best buys" by *U.S. News and World Report.* Its College of Engineering is ranked among the top twenty undergraduate-only engineering schools by the same publication. Valparaiso publishes an excellent magazine of public affairs and the arts, *The Cresset,* and hosts a number of externally-funded programs relevant to its concerns as a Christian university, including the Lilly Fellows Program in Humanities and the Arts, of which this research project is a part. The quality of worship and music in the Chapel of the Resurrection would be difficult to surpass at any college or university. Its 310-acre campus hosts about 3,600 students, roughly 3,000 of them at the undergraduate level. They come from most states and forty different countries. Valparaiso is located in the small town of Valparaiso, Indiana, near the sand dunes of the southern end of Lake Michigan.[49]

◆　　◆　　◆

It would be safe to say that, were one to spend several days at any of these six schools, two things would become apparent. First, these schools are academically excellent according to any ranking system, secular or religious. Their curricula are well thought out and challenging, with excellent teaching by front-rank faculty and a good deal of impressive research and publication. The students are bright and engaged, and they often go on to successful careers. But a second thing would also become evident: the Christian account of life and reality made visible and relevant in all facets of each school's activities — academic, extra-curricular, music and the arts, worship, atmosphere, and self-definition. In other words, the schools have both quality and soul, bound up together. The next task is to try to understand why and how they have been able to maintain and combine those two qualities where so many others have failed.

49. Valparaiso University Web site, www.valpo.edu.

5 | *Vision*

Now that I have provided sketches of the six schools and their sponsoring traditions, it is time to move to the heart of the matter: Why and how do these colleges and universities maintain their soul? Why and how do they keep their Christian convictions publicly relevant to the identity and mission of their schools? I will proceed through the two chapters according to the categories of vision and ethos, discussing the third category, "persons," along the way. While these categories obviously overlap, they are nevertheless useful for getting at important factors in the lives of these schools.

Implied in the argument thus far are two interlocking claims. The first is the rather obvious claim that a thriving Christian college has a strong connection with the religious heritage of its sponsoring church or tradition. This connection is made concrete in the vision, ethos, and persons of the tradition that inhabit the ongoing life of the college or university. Without faithful persons from a thriving tradition who bear the vision and ethos of that tradition, a school simply cannot communicate them to students. The students themselves must be receptive to what the college offers, so it is important that its sponsoring tradition supply a goodly number of students to the school. My second claim is that the Christian account given by the religious tradition should constitute the organizing principle for the identity and mission of the college. The Christian story as a comprehensive, unsurpassable, and central account of reality must be held strongly and confidently enough to shape the life of the college decisively in all its facets. Again, the school is dependent on the sponsoring tradition to supply the persons who bear that strength and confidence.

Thus, there is a short answer to why these six colleges have maintained their religious identity in face of powerful secularizing forces. The persons responsible for them — their sponsoring churches, their boards, their administrations, and their faculties — have had enough confidence in the Christian account of life and reality to insist that it be the organizing paradigm for the identity and mission of the college. They have decided that the revelation of God in its full trinitarian scope is pervasively relevant to the life of the college or university. Their version of the Christian account may not always have been carefully thought through or articulated in a theological sense, but it has been decisively present in the strong background convictions of those responsible for each school. And in recent times, because of the challenge of secularization, each of these schools has had to sharpen its articulation of the Christian account.

Calvin College

It is appropriate to begin with Calvin College because Calvin has operated with the most articulate and systematic vision of all the surveyed schools. Certainly this articulateness has to do with its Reformed heritage, which has had a penchant for theological precision. Further, because of the Reformed emphasis on the sovereignty of God over all of life, Calvin has viewed the development of the intellect along Christian lines as being of paramount importance. It has never retreated into pietist simplicities. Its emphasis on an integral approach has meant that God's revelation must be integrated with all human knowing and doing. Human knowledge and action must be transformed by God's revealed will so that, as Kuyper put it, not one square inch of our world remains unclaimed by Christ.

The Reformed vision prevails at Calvin because a strong and disciplined Christian Reformed Church provides a board of trustees for Calvin College that is sophisticated enough theologically to monitor both Calvin's administration and faculty for theological orthodoxy and for skill in relating faith and learning. The church and the college also have brought forth a series of committed presidents who not only have understood the Reformed theological vision, but have also insisted that the college follow it in shaping its identity and mission. But above all, the church and the college have raised up young persons to be the philosophers and theologians who have articulated the vision in highly persuasive ways. They have sounded the clear notes to guide faculty members already committed to making the Reformed version of the Christian account pervasively relevant.

But what is the content of the vision? As mentioned in the preceding chapter, the Calvin College construal of the Reformed vision is indebted to the seminal work of Abraham Kuyper, the Dutch theologian, churchman, journalist, and politician. Though there were internecine struggles within the college between two wings of Kuyperian thought, the "progressive" or "positive" interpretation largely won out.[1] This has meant an outward thrust in which the Christian worldview engages the various secular fields of learning with the intent of transforming them into agents of Christian renewal.

The Reformed contention is that all human faculties — including reason — are affected by the fall. While non-Christian learning can indeed contain truths about the world, there is also a strong tendency for that learning to be distorted by human fallibility and sin. Therefore, it cannot be taught without Christian critique to young Christians in the educational process. It is assumed in this "Reformed epistemology" that the biblical worldview, interpreted by Reformed theology, is true. That worldview's perspective on the nature of creation and history, of human nature and its predicament, of human salvation, and of human conduct in the world is the starting point for all Christian scholars. When there are conflicts between secular learning and the Christian worldview, there must be faulty worldview assumptions in the secular approach (or perhaps culturally conditioned assumptions in an interpretation of the Christian approach) that must be teased out, analyzed, and critiqued by the Christian perspective. In principle then, such knowledge, critiqued and then "redeemed" by Christian scholarship, is claimed for Christ and integrated into the Christian worldview. In fact, however, Calvin College scholars readily admit that many attempts at integration are not immediately successful. There are many loose ends. Nevertheless, each field of learning can

1. Bratt and Wells, "Piety and Progress: A History of Calvin College," in Richard T. Hughes and William B. Adrian, eds., *Models for Christian Higher Education: Strategies for Success in the Twenty-First Century* (Grand Rapids: Eerdmans, 1997), p. 157. The following exposition of the Calvin "perspectivalist" approach to the integration of faith and learning is indebted to the fine lectures by Nicholas Wolterstorff entitled *Keeping the Faith: Talks for New Faculty at Calvin College* (Grand Rapids: Calvin College, 1989).

in theory be transformed into genuine Christian knowledge; there can be a Christian sociology or Christian economics.[2]

Worldview analysis and critique go on in classrooms across the disciplines at Calvin College. While this kind of analysis does not always come to the fore — there are many other things to communicate in the classroom — the professor is expected to demonstrate his or her own integration of faith and learning. Further, the prospective professor is expected to elaborate his or her own approach to faith and learning upon taking a tenure-track position at Calvin. That approach is then expected to be refined by the time the professor applies for tenure. The professor's approach is scrutinized not only by the department chair, appropriate faculty committee, provost, and president, but also by the board of trustees. In addition, Calvin puts a strong emphasis on Christian scholarship, expecting its faculty to contribute to the store of Christian knowledge in all fields. The college stimulates this Reformed approach to Christian scholarship in many summer institutes sponsored by its Center for Christian Scholarship — one powerful means for spreading the Calvin model for integrating faith and learning.

What would such worldview analysis look like? Let's take modern psychology as an example. Much of modern psychology operates from certain worldview assumptions that are usually implicit in the discipline. Most modern psychologies — behaviorist or evolutionary/biological — are based on the deterministic assumptions of philosophical naturalism. (Interestingly, many psychological scientists are not aware of or straightforward about such assumptions, so they propose their assumption-laden theories as scientific fact.) Their naturalistic assumptions lead them to

2. Calvin College puts out occasional scholarly booklets by its faculty on Christian approaches to economics, psychology, evolution, etc. Such efforts at integration are not always without controversy. One professor of physics, Howard Van Till, wrote one such booklet entitled *The Cosmos: Nature or Creation?* in which he argued for an integration of Christian faith and cosmology which allowed for a strictly naturalistic account of evolution, with the proviso that an omniscient God programmed into evolution from the very beginning all the elements necessary for the unfolding of the creation as we know it. In that booklet, and in a larger book entitled *The Fourth Day*, he allowed no supernatural interventions into the natural process. This of course upset many, and Van Till was criticized sharply. Yet not only did the college support him in his efforts, it finally awarded him its 1999 Faith and Learning Award. This award was reported in Calvin's alumni magazine, *The Spark* (Spring 1999), p. 25.

view humans as caught up in a nexus of cause and effect — either external or internal, depending on the school of psychology — that allows no space for human freedom. Thus, humans can neither be praised nor blamed for their actions. A small wing of psychology, humanistic psychology, may not operate from naturalistic assumptions that deny freedom, but rather move from optimistic assumptions that humans can complete themselves — "realize themselves" — by proper exercises of their will or therapeutic expertise.

The Christian worldview — in this case its anthropology — would directly clash with these approaches. Given the Kuyperian approach, there must be faulty notions of human nature in those psychologies. Such assumptions must be critically evaluated before any psychology can be "claimed for Christ" and become useful for Christians in their attempts to understand human nature in general as well as individual psychological problems and solutions.

A similar process can go on in every field of human learning. Far from being intimidated by the claims of secular learning and acquiescing to those claims, Calvin professors submit them to Christian analysis and critique. As students are initiated into this kind of sophisticated analysis of fundamental assumptions, they become critical of worldly claims to knowledge and refuse to let them overrun their Christian convictions. Instead, they attempt, as their mentors have shown them, to integrate their Christian convictions with their worldly fields of knowledge and activity so that they might live as whole Christians in the world, not as persons bifurcated between Christian and secular claims. Calvin graduates often survive graduate school with their Christian convictions intact and with a critical appropriation of their graduate school learning. Many go on to become excellent contributors to the quest for a Christian place in the intellectual world and to church-related colleges and universities that need every bit of help they can get to combat secularization.

This philosophical/theological vision shapes everything at Calvin. It shaped its current curriculum, the "Christian academic-discipline model," which "introduces students to the academic disciplines and equips some of them to work creatively in the disciplines themselves, all the while struggling to integrate the discipline in question with one's own Christian faith."[3] It will shape its new curriculum, to be introduced in 2001, in which

3. Wolterstorff, *Keeping the Faith*, p. 37.

there will be more emphasis on the needed virtues and skills of the Christian life, not only those needed for Christian thought. This theological/philosophical vision shapes its mission statement, which is omnipresent at the college: "Calvin College is a comprehensive liberal arts college in the Reformed tradition of historic Christianity. Through our learning, we seek to be agents of renewal in the academy, church, and society. We pledge fidelity to Jesus Christ, offering our hearts and lives to do God's work in God's world."[4] It shapes its moral outlook, which is explicitly commended to students in the student handbook. Instead of lapsing into a secular "public health ethic," the handbook asserts that community life at Calvin is intended "to shape hearts and minds through higher learning for Christian living" so that they might be "conformed more and more to the likeness of God incarnate."[5] Further, the Kuyperian vision affords a sharp critique of Western materialism and individualism. The "transformation" rhetoric employed by Calvin applies to social as well as personal dimensions. Prevailing American values are criticized along with secular approaches to learning.

Rarely has a college thought out and applied its vision in as much detail and with as much care as Calvin. The college has had the additional advantage of having first-rate minds involved in spelling out the vision, communicating it to others, and applying it to various tasks. Among the many that could be mentioned is Nicholas Wolterstorff, who has contributed so much to those activities. However, it is intriguing that Calvin College is not dependent upon such virtuosi. The vision is so deeply embedded in the faculty and administration as a whole that the Calvin approach would go on even without its brightest stars.

Calvin embeds its vision in several ways. First, in keeping with our categorization of an "orthodox" school, it insists that administrators and tenured faculty be communicant members of the Christian Reformed Church or one of its confessional partners. Second, administrators and permanent faculty must sign the Form of Subscription, which commits them to "apply the principles of God's Word as interpreted by our Reformed standards in the teaching of the subjects assigned to us."[6] This

---

4. Calvin College Viewbook for 1999, p. 2. The viewbook invites students to come to Calvin to "be transformed."

5. *Calvin College Student Handbook for 1989/99*, p. 1.

6. David J. Diephouse, Calvin's academic dean, quoting the Form of Subscrip-

form not only sets dogmatic boundaries but also delineates a particular way of thinking and seeing. It situates members of Calvin College in a "coherent confessional and intellectual tradition."[7] Further, as I have already mentioned, faculty on the tenure track must work out their own faith and learning approach for submission to various college authorities at several points in their academic journey.

Another powerful instrument for embedding the vision is the Kuiper Seminar — named not for the famous Abraham but for a more recent Calvin professor with a slightly different spelling of the name — which exists "to ensure that every tenure-track appointee to the faculty of Calvin College has a thorough encounter, through reading Christian theological texts, with the historic Calvinist theology and world view, and the particular Calvinist intellectual heritage that has shaped Calvin College and the Christian Reformed Church."[8] This intensive seminar, for which participant faculty are given a reduced teaching load, takes up fifteen full January days of reading, lecture, and discussion. It provides an intellectual encounter ample enough to equip all faculty members with a basic understanding of Reformed theology and the Kuyperian approach to Christian learning and scholarship. Calvin takes the time to enable its entire faculty to become theologically literate. As an added benefit, Calvin has the advantage of having presidents and deans who are thoroughly educated in the vision and can articulate it in the various contexts in which they hold forth. They do not have to play an outsider or amateur role in relation to the faculty's insider and professional knowledge of the tradition.

The Reformed/Kuyperian theological vision is the fundamental unifying element in the general education program. It also provides the Christian perspective that challenges and integrates other disciplinary approaches to knowledge in the major areas of concentration. Further, students must take Religion 103, which is a basic Bible course unified by a theological account of the history of creation, fall, and redemption, and Religion 201, Basic Christian Theology, which introduces the student to a

---

tion in his address to the annual meeting of the American Association of Colleges and Universities, Washington, DC, on January 15, 1998. The unpublished manuscript is entitled "Signing the Form: Religious Affiliation and Institutional Identity at Calvin College."

7. Diephouse, "Signing the Form," p. 2.

8. Appendix B of the Calvin College Faculty Handbook, "The Mandates of the Kuiper Seminar."

systematic elaboration of classical and Reformed Christian doctrine. In addition, students are required to take Philosophy 153, which "aims to give the student a Christian philosophical framework, along with awareness of important alternative philosophical perspectives."[9] Beyond those three required courses in philosophy and religion, two more electives from religion, philosophy, or history are required.

The Religion and Theology Department includes about a dozen faculty members, while the Philosophy Department has a few more. Both are strong and distinguished departments whose members share equally in their basic teaching tasks. Obviously, neither department takes a detached or pluralistic approach to their subject matters. Both operate from a shared theological/philosophical consensus that they employ both analytically and constructively. Even though the direct teaching of theology and philosophy is extensive, the indirect engagement of Christian perspectives with disciplinary approaches is even more extensive. It could be argued that the whole curriculum is an exercise in theological reflection.

What to make of all this? Certainly many, if not most, American academics would disdain this unified approach to learning. Not only would they find the church membership and confessional requirements for faculty outrageous, but they would also believe that such a strong commitment to one theological/philosophical viewpoint would fetter the free exercise of the intellect. Even many persons committed to Christian higher education believe that the Calvin model is too unified and constrictive. They would want to inject greater pluralism of viewpoints into the mix on theological and pedagogical grounds. Calvin, however, has resisted such an approach, arguing that its stance contributes to a genuine pluralism in higher education. Why must every school build pluralism into its outlook, which runs the danger of reducing education either to relativism or to the lowest common denominator? Further, it is inaccurate to suggest that agreement at the level of fundamental perspective cuts off disagreement and pluralism at other levels of interpretation and application. There is room aplenty for difference and disagreement, to which the college's history attests.

It would be hard to argue that Calvin's approach is uncreative or unsophisticated — it is far from that. Its scholars have contributed first-rate work to all kinds of scholarship, not just Christian, and the kind of critical

9. *Calvin College Catalog 1997-98*, p. 215.

reflection it provokes in almost every classroom in almost every student is certainly not simple-minded. Moreover, if one agrees that reason is fallen and finite, it makes sense to see reason as a handmaiden of faith rather than the other way around. Certainly Calvin holds to the Christian account as comprehensive, unsurpassable, and central. Its courage and clarity in doing so have earned it a place of high honor among Christian schools.

Yet it would seem that Calvin could open itself a bit more to risk. It could start with incorporating a minority of Christians from other traditions into its faculty. Such intra-Christian debate might well bring an even higher level of Christian intellectual excitement to the campus. Further, the Calvin model could take on the risk of making intellectual engagement as dangerous as it actually is; the privileged nature of the Christian worldview on campus gives it too easy an advantage over contrary claims. Christian interpretations of God's revelation are themselves fragmented and tainted by sin, just as worldly approaches are. Perhaps one could commend on theological grounds more tentativeness in the integration of faith and learning. But with all this said, it may well be far preferable to err in the direction of boldness than in supineness in the engagement of faith and learning. Such boldness has not been an overriding virtue at the vast majority of church-related colleges the way it has at Calvin.

Wheaton College

Wheaton College is appropriately the next object of attention, for it shares many characteristics with Calvin. It, too, is an "orthodox" college. All administrators and faculty must sign both the Statement of Faith and the Statement of Responsibilities.[10] These statements are not theological in

10. Both the Statement of Faith and the Statement of Responsibilities can be viewed in their entirety on the Wheaton College Web site, www.wheaton.edu. In addition to signing these statements, the prospective faculty member must write essays on his or her understanding of the liberal arts and how Christian faith relates to them, on his or her understanding of the relationship of the Christian faith to his or her discipline, and on her or his commitment to Christ, including reflections on spiritual growth and the expression of his or her faith in the life of the church (Faculty Application Form of Wheaton College).

character, as are Calvin's, but rather creedal and behavioral. Wheaton, like Calvin, is willing to speak of Christian learning and Christian liberal arts. It also has the courage to demand high religious and moral standards of participants in its community. It, too, defines itself with a measure of "over-againstness" toward American society. Above all, the two schools share a commitment to base the life of their college on the Christian account of life and reality. These two academic communities come together with confidence that the Christian account is comprehensive, unsurpassable, and central, and thereby crucially relevant to their educational enterprises.

Yet there are many differences between them as well. Wheaton does not operate from a shared, highly defined theological/philosophical perspective, as does Calvin. It is more evangelical in the classical American sense than Calvin — it is more shaped by a "born-again" religious orientation, it is more activist in evangelism, it is more likely to talk of biblical perspectives than theological ones, and it still has elements of biblical literalism and moral perfectionism in its tradition. It has few dominant ethnic characteristics and is related to a tradition, not to a specific church. So, in spite of many similarities to Calvin, Wheaton is very much a distinctive institution.

Wheaton's earlier history as a fundamentalist school dictated that it bore its Christian character in a particular way. While it taught mostly Bible courses for its religion offerings, its liberal arts course of study, though of high quality, generally ran along the lines of the classical liberal arts curriculum. Its Christian "freight" was carried by a plethora of Christian practices — prayer before classes, Bible study and devotional groups operating in the dorms, godly faculty modeling Christian behavior, required chapel, revivals, ministry activities of both an evangelistic and charitable nature, Christian counseling, and a strong dose of foreign missionary presence and activity. This was the classic "add-on" approach followed by many Christian colleges. It did not demand much theological reflection or faith/learning engagement, if any. Its Christian message to students was in its piety.

But that began to change in the 1960s with the important influence of Arthur Holmes, whose book, *The Idea of a Christian College*, articulated themes that he and others were working into the life of Wheaton. Reacting to the anti-intellectualism of the revivalist/fundamentalist approach that had led to what Noll has called the "scandal of the evangelical mind,"

Holmes drew upon his connections with professors from Calvin College to provide Wheaton with a different approach. As head of the philosophy department and presider over Wheaton's ongoing seminar on faith and learning, Holmes exercised enormous influence on the college's development from fundamentalist dispensationalism to an evangelical version of the Reformed approach. He wielded tacit authority over who was hired or promoted. The Reformed element in his approach is indicated by the titles of several of his other books — *Faith Seeking Understanding, All Truth is God's Truth,* and *Contours of a World View.*[11]

However, Holmes's perspective was not simply an imitation of the Calvin approach. He had drunk deeply of other approaches to faith and learning, and his book provides a capacious view of that task. In it he distinguishes four approaches: the attitudinal, in which Christian faith shapes the motivation and posture toward inquiry into any field of endeavor; the ethical, which brings Christian moral values to bear on the human issues that arise in the many disciplines; the foundational, which probes the deep historical roots and philosophical assumptions of academic disciplines; and the worldview, which engages the implicit worldviews in those disciplines with the comprehensive worldview given by Christian biblical theism.[12] Because of the variety of approaches proposed by Holmes and the different theologies that exist within the evangelical creedal consensus of the Wheaton community, the Kuyperian worldview approach so dominant at Calvin College is less dominant at Wheaton. Nevertheless, it seems to be a consensus that the Reformed approach is becoming the reigning model and is providing Wheaton with the coherent approach to faith and learning that it lacked earlier.

Wheaton, then, seems to proceed in its educational task on two levels. It establishes a baseline of creedal unanimity through its Statement of Faith, which assures solid Christian belief in the community as much as humanly possible. Beyond that, however, those that sign the statement hold a number of different theologies, practice different pieties and worship styles, and approach the faith and learning relationship in various ways. Indeed, if the Reformed approach seems to be in ascendance in the intellectual realm, "high-church" liturgical and sacramental practices seem

11. Arthur Holmes, *The Idea of a Christian College* (Grand Rapids: Eerdmans, 1987). The other titles are listed on the jacket of that volume.

12. Holmes, *The Idea of a Christian College,* pp. 45-60.

to be in ascendance in the realm of worship.[13] Wheaton is not nearly as uniform as one might think.

With its evangelical tradition of activism, Wheaton is not content with imparting knowledge and integrating faith and learning on the theoretical level; it also intends to form its students deeply so that they will affect the world. Its vision is incarnated in its mission statement and motto: "Wheaton College exists to help build the church and improve society worldwide by promoting the development of whole and effective Christians through excellence in programs of Christian higher education. This mission expresses our commitment to do all things 'For Christ and His Kingdom.'"[14]

Wheaton has had little trouble finding bright evangelical students to respond to its mission. Further, it appeals to conservative students from mainline Protestant traditions who find their own denominational schools less than fully committed to the Christian account. It is also now appealing to small groups of Christian Reformed, Catholic, and Orthodox students.

The college takes great care to assure its evangelical orientation in its key constituencies. The board of trustees is made up of twenty persons who are all evangelical Christians. It is chaired by Thomas Pratt, head of Prison Fellowship. The trustees have the obligation to make sure that the administration and faculty are in line with the evangelical vision of the college. They oversee the college closely, sometimes exercising their right to assess faculty essays on faith and learning as they come up for tenure. The current president, Duane Litfin, possesses two Ph.D.s, one in communications from Purdue and one in New Testament from Oxford. He is sophisticated and articulate about Christian philosophies of higher education. He distinguishes Wheaton from Calvin by suggesting the former is more directly biblical while the latter more theological in its approach to faith and learning. Neither fundamentalist nor dispensationalist, Litfin intends to honor the Reformed approach in ascendance at Wheaton but not allow it to exclude the other approaches of different faith traditions that are represented at Wheaton.

13. Roger Lundin, "An Evangelical Model for Christian Higher Education: Theory and Practice at Wheaton College" (unpublished manuscript written for the Erasmus Institute at the University of Notre Dame), pp. 2-5.

14. *Bulletin of Wheaton College 1999-2000*, p. 4.

The Reformed approach is increasingly visible in the education of faculty as they enter Wheaton. The earlier forms of faculty education were fairly relaxed. From 1969 on, and later under Holmes's direction, they ordinarily were held for several weeks in the summer. As the Reformed influence has increased, however, more funds and energy have been devoted to faculty formation. The Wheaton College Faculty Seminar in Faith and Learning now comprises ten sessions during the new faculty members' first year. The seminar includes introductory readings in the history of the college and issues of faith and learning as well as more practical matters. Things really get underway in the second year when all new tenure-track faculty attend a weekly seminar organized around challenging papers on the following topics: the biblical and theological foundations of the Christian account; Christianity and the liberal arts; forms and problems of knowledge; ethics; and exercises in integrating the Christian vision with various disciplines.[15] The Center for Faith and Learning makes funds available to Wheaton faculty to take courses in theology, to construct interdisciplinary courses that incorporate the Christian vision, and to invite off-campus scholars to lead faith and learning colloquia at Wheaton.

Besides these formal instruments of faculty formation, new faculty members are given mentors who help them work into Wheaton's life. One of the major requirements they must fulfill as they seek tenure and promotion to associate professor is to write a faith and learning paper, which is assessed by the coordinator of the Faith and Learning Seminar.[16] The faculty mentor helps them in this task, as does the ongoing seminar. The dean, provost, and president are also involved in this process of assessment. But it is not just faculty aiming at promotion and tenure who are held accountable to the faith/learning task — the whole faculty is. The

15. *Wheaton College Faculty Faith and Learning Seminar 1999-2000* (Wheaton, IL: Wheaton College, 1999), Essays I and II.

16. The task in this paper is stated in the college's Application for Promotion/ Tenure: "Please provide a statement in which you describe the ways in which you seek to incorporate Spiritual Modeling and Nurturing into your teaching ministry at Wheaton College. You should give attention to your own maturing walk with Christ, your development of the integration of faith and learning in teaching, advising and mentoring, your specific support of the chapel program, and other appropriate evidences and outcomes as suggested in the Faculty Handbook." One can see in this requirement the continuing emphasis on piety and modeling a holy life as well as on the intellectual challenge of relating faith and learning.

course and teacher evaluation forms, which naturally ask about general excellence, also ask students to judge how successfully a professor integrates the subject matter with the Christian faith and with other academic disciplines. Further, since one of the college's principal purposes is "to prepare students to think and behave redemptively as Christians within this world,"[17] faculty are expected to build up the students' faith in the classroom. The evaluation questionnaire asks how well "the course encouraged your growth as a Christian."[18]

The twin purposes of nurturing Christian belief and piety and of integrating faith and reason are thoroughly embodied in the general education requirements, which are called "Essentials of a Christian Worldview."[19] Students must take a course entitled "Theology of Culture," which is basically an introduction to the Christian faith. Then, besides many other requirements in the sciences and humanities, students must either pass competencies in Old and New Testament or take courses in each of them. Later on in their college careers they take twelve to sixteen hours of instruction in the area called "Faith and Reason." Each student takes two higher-level courses in Bible, an introductory course in philosophy entitled "Issues and World Views in Philosophy," and finally an upper-level course entitled "Christian Thought," which is a systematic encounter with Christian theology taught by a distinguished philosophy department (which also educates more than a hundred majors). Further, courses in "non-religious" disciplines provide occasions for faculty and students to inquire into how those disciplines relate to the claims of the Christian faith.

As one might guess, it takes a large theology department to carry the load of all those courses. At Wheaton the department of about twenty professors is called "Biblical and Theological Studies, Archaeology and World Religions." It has an impressive 180 majors. The department has carefully thought out its approach to the Bible and, following from that, the Bible's role with regard to other disciplines. Since Wheaton tends to rely directly on biblical knowledge as the partner in the faith and learning dialogue, it is important for students to know the Bible thoroughly. The department is of

---

17. *Bulletin of Wheaton College 1999-2000*, p. 4.

18. "Course and Instruction Evaluation Questionnaire," one of three different forms used for student evaluation of professors at Wheaton College.

19. *Bulletin of Wheaton College 1999-2000*, p. 33.

course committed to a high view of biblical authority, even to affirming "verbal inspiration" and "inerrancy." But the department qualifies these affirmations a bit by saying that it is the *original* text that is verbally inspired, and that "inerrancy" refers to what the Bible addresses, not to what it does not. Nevertheless, a "complete commitment to the Bible's authority seeks to evaluate the presuppositions, theories, goals, and methods of each discipline, and indeed of all life's activities, by the revelation of God's truth as found in Scripture."[20] Needless to say, the department is thoroughly committed to the mission of the college and is willing to bear the biblical vision on behalf of the whole enterprise.

As with Calvin, there is much to admire about Wheaton's guiding vision. First, it has allowed Wheaton to lift its quality as a rigorous liberal arts college without losing its soul. Because this vision has drawn bright evangelical students over many years, Wheaton has produced many impressive Christian intellectuals not only for itself but also for many other institutions. Perhaps more importantly, its vision of developing whole Christians has produced Christian lay people whose faith is not compartmentalized from their thinking and acting as they go out into the world. Wheaton's vision has enabled it to successfully meld faith and learning, faith and action, through a unique blend of lively evangelical piety and rigorous Christian intellectuality that is actively modeled by its faculty and absorbed by many of its students. Moreover, the quality of scholarship generated by many Wheaton faculty members is impressive indeed. Wheaton's top faculty — Mark Noll, Roger Lundin, Alan Jacobs, and Robert Roberts, to name but a few — would be top faculty anywhere. They are key figures in the emerging evangelical intellectual renaissance. Wheaton is a crucial center for giving intellectual muscle to the moderate evangelicalism that is such a promising development in American Christianity.

Yet, it is interesting that the very quality upon which its vision is founded — unanimity in the evangelical faith — is also the quality that is problematic. Though the college says it does not "exist to shelter students from a world hostile to faith in Jesus Christ,"[21] it generally does just that. Like Calvin, it is a fairly safe place. Everyone is a confessing evangelical Christian. Non-evangelical Christian views are not allowed to be expressed

20. Wheaton College Department of Biblical, Theological, and Archaeological Studies, *How We Approach the Bible*, p. 2.

21. *Bulletin of Wheaton College 1999-2000*, p. 4.

by faculty who believe them. Perhaps a case can be made that students need this sort of "incubation" in the evangelical faith — there will be plenty of time to face the world of different faiths later — but it might be enriching for both faculty and students to think and live with those who take different views within the faith, such as those held by Catholics, who still cannot be hired at Wheaton.

Beyond these pedagogical questions loom some theological ones. While Wheaton has adopted Calvin's worldview method of approaching the challenge of faith and learning, it does not have a theological tradition to bring to the task of integration. Calvin has a tradition of Reformed confessional theology, while Wheaton has a brief affirmation of evangelical faith on one hand and the Bible on the other. While it claims to integrate the Bible with other disciplines, it is hard to imagine the Bible as the sole, direct conversation partner. It would seem that biblical knowledge and injunctions have to be modulated through theological reflection in order to supply the kind of comprehensive and systematic account needed for real engagement of faith and learning, let alone integration. For example, in the dialogue between religion and science, one would have to have more available than simply the Bible to get at serious issues such as evolution. Theological reflection on the biblical themes must be added in order for a fruitful encounter to occur. Up until this point it does not seem that Wheaton has a theological tradition to draw upon. That lack may soon be addressed by the outpouring of systematic theology now coming from evangelical theologians. But for the moment there seems to be a missing link for doing the most persuasive kind of faith and learning engagement.

Finally, the overall vision of Wheaton is narrowed by its inclusion of several fundamentalist/literalist clauses about the Bible in its Statement of Faith. In addition to the "verbal inspiration" and "inerrancy" clauses, another insists that God "directly created Adam and Eve, the historical parents of the entire human race."[22] Likewise, its vision is narrowed by the prohibition in its Statement of Responsibilities of any use of alcoholic or tobacco products. Such constrictions set up obstacles for recruiting precisely the kind of moderate evangelical faculty that Wheaton currently possesses and wants to attract. The "faith requirements" of the college already make for a fairly small pool of applicants; those further constrictions

22. See Article 4 of the Statement of Faith of Wheaton College, www.wheaton .edu.

make the pool smaller still. Wheaton runs the risk of not having the quality faculty it needs to teach an ever-brighter pool of students in years to come.

Baylor University

It is fitting that Baylor follow Wheaton in our discussion because Baylor stands midway between our orthodox and critical-mass categories. Being Baptist, it shares Wheaton's evangelical connection. For many years Baylor has had the requirement that all faculty applicants attest that they are practicing Christians or Jews. Like Wheaton, Baylor proceeded for generations with an "add-on" approach to being a Christian university, with the enormous number of Baptists on the faculty and in the student body assuring that Baptist piety would flourish in the non-curricular activities of the university. Moreover, Baylor is surrounded by a pervasive evangelical and specifically Baptist ethos created by over three million Baptists in the state of Texas alone. Again, like Wheaton, Baylor is coming to understand that the comprehensive claims of the Christian account mean that there must be an engagement of faith and learning right in the middle of the educational processes of the school. Baylor, however, came later to that realization than Wheaton did.

Baylor is a much larger institution than Wheaton and has aspirations to become a Protestant version of Notre Dame — a significant graduate research institution. Besides twenty-one Ph.D. programs and a host of master's degree offerings, it also has five undergraduate schools in addition to its College of Arts and Sciences and Interdisciplinary Programs. It is simply a much larger and more complex institution than either Calvin or Wheaton, a fact that makes the challenge of maintaining Christian identity and mission all the more daunting.

There are other important elements in that challenge besides size and complexity. First among them perhaps is the problem of vision. There is no doubt that from its beginning Baylor intended to be a Baptist university. Its motto, *Pro Ecclesia, Pro Texana,* reflects that intent. But because of the challenge of the Enlightenment project in combination with a religious tradition that was pietist in character, Baylor had more or less adopted the aforementioned "add-on" model of Christian identity and mission, as had many other Christian schools. The content of education at Baylor was relatively untouched by Christian claims even though the ethos of the school was discernibly Baptist.

Enter a small group of academics that had come to the idea of the engagement of faith and learning through a number of different sources. Some had been introduced to the idea by encountering Arthur Holmes's *The Idea of a Christian College* and by interaction with the Calvin cohort of Christian scholars — Wolterstorff, Marsden, and Mouw, among others. Others were inspired by Catholic approaches to faith and learning. Others came to it on their own. About a decade ago, Baylor began to shape an academic vision that takes the Christian account seriously not only in its non-curricular aspects, but in its intellectual tasks as well. Leading this effort were two philosophers — one who is now provost and one who heads Baylor's Institute of Faith and Learning — as well as a theologian who is now president, and a sociologist who is now dean of the graduate school.

Traces of that fresh element in Baylor's vision can be found in many places, starting with its mission statement. It leads off with this: "The mission of Baylor University is to educate men and women for worldwide leadership and service by integrating academic excellence and Christian commitment within a caring community." Because "the university derives its understanding of God, humanity, and nature from many sources," it cherishes "the value of intellectually informed faith and religiously informed education." Further, "Baylor encourages all of its students to assess information from a Christian perspective" and intends to advance "the frontiers of knowledge while cultivating a Christian world-view." The mission statement also strongly endorses moral and religious formation of its students along with intellectual growth.[23]

Keying off the mission statement and their own strong convictions, Baylor's leaders have initiated hiring policies that aim to ensure that the faculty will not only be religiously observant themselves, but will be sympathetic to the notion of engaging faith and learning. To nourish historical ties with their parent denomination, they encourage a goal of hiring 50 percent Baptists. Realizing that many new faculty members will not immediately understand the task of integrating faith and learning, the provost probes their willingness to explore a faith and learning approach of their own. In addition to their conference with their department chair and pro-

---

23. "Baylor University Mission Statement," *Baylor University Undergraduate Catalog 1999-2000*, p. 4.

vost, prospective faculty members also face interviews with the dean and the president. The process seems to have real bearing on appointments, since a number of finalists have been turned down after such interviews. A real effort is being made to recruit faculty to fit the new vision of the university, and so far that effort appears to be successful.

Another major strategy to "integrate academic excellence and Christian commitment" is the establishment of twenty new distinguished professorships spread around the university. Baylor is recruiting especially those whose excellence includes religious reflection on their subject area. Thus far four such Christian and Jewish intellectuals have been recruited.

In addition, new Baylor faculty are now invited to attend a weeklong conference on "Scholarship and the Christian University" at which the interrelations of faith and learning are explored. The school offers an attractive stipend as an incentive to attend the conference. This is followed by an ongoing three-year faculty mentoring process in which new faculty are further exposed to the idea of engaging faith and learning, as well as many other subjects that pertain to gaining tenure.

Aiding these new initiatives is the Institute of Faith and Learning, directed by a philosopher, Michael Beaty, who has become a primary articulator of the faith and learning ideal. Besides being a resource for ideas and strategies, Beaty also engages in research on the attitudes and beliefs of faculty about the religious identity of Baylor. Other institutes and centers — the Institute of Church-State Studies, The Institute of Biblical and Related Languages, the Center for Ministry Effectiveness — add to the university's ongoing reflection on its religious heritage.

Baylor exemplifies its commitment to transmit the biblical vision to students in its two-course requirement in Bible within the general education curriculum, which itself constitutes about half the hours needed for graduation with a B.A. The other bachelor's programs require all students to take a course called "Biblical Heritage and Contemporary Issues." Still, it is likely that attempts at integrating faith and learning are considerably less frequent than the school's leadership would wish.

The religion department that is responsible for teaching those required courses is quite large — about two dozen members. The philosophy department is about half that size. In contrast to the "worldview analysis" emphasis of both the Calvin and Wheaton philosophy departments, the Baylor philosophy offerings are much more in line with standard offerings in secular colleges. The religion department itself is not unanimous in its

commitment to faith and learning integration, though it obviously supports the continuing requirements in Bible.

As the leadership of Baylor aims at being both a highly-ranked research university and a Christian institution, it has proposed new graduate
programs in several key areas.[24] Interestingly enough, new graduate programs will be introduced partly on the basis of their "relevance to the
Christian character of the university, especially through the character of
the faculty, and sometimes through [their] subject matter and ethical applications."[25] The powers that be seem to favor two new Ph.D. programs,
one in economics and one in philosophy.

Even with this impressive listing of the ways that Baylor is trying to
incarnate a fuller vision of the engagement of faith and learning, it is useful to add some critical reflections. First, we might begin with the content
of the integration process itself. The engagement of faith and learning is a
two-way conversation, in which a Christian intellectual tradition is
brought into dialogue with secular learning. As a university in the Baptist
tradition, however, Baylor has been inclined simply to offer biblical knowledge and wisdom to the conversation. But as we mentioned above in our
discussion of Wheaton, the Bible alone doesn't provide the kind of systematic and nuanced framework needed for a dialogue, with, say, economics.
The Bible may supply some general themes for a conversation, but in order
for them to be really useful, they would have to be elaborated and modulated through a theological/philosophical perspective. In other words, the
Bible must be supplemented with a theological tradition. Baptists simply
do not have much of a theological heritage, although they certainly carry
certain Baptist themes — religious liberty, soul competency, church-state
separation — that accompany their classical evangelical beliefs. What will
supply that theological tradition to make the integration of faith and
learning fruitful? Without a credible, shared theological tradition, faculty
tend to think that such integration consists primarily of biblical ideas simply trumping worldly knowledge, as often happens at Bible schools. For
the moment, it seems that Baylor is encouraging many theological flowers
to bloom. The new distinguished professors come from various religious

24. 1994-96 Self Study Steering Committee, Baylor University, *Exploring Three
Visions for Baylor, 1995-2005.*

25. "Position Paper for Baylor Graduate School" (internal document produced
by the Academic Task Force of the University Planning Council, April 1997), p. 3.

and theological traditions and approach faith and learning in a variety of ways. It is possible that as Baylor searches for that more systematic theological tradition, it will gravitate to the generally Reformed systematic accounts of the younger generation of evangelical scholars. Or perhaps other classical Christian accounts will be adopted. But for the moment, Baylor has no consistent theological framework to draw on in its approach to faith and learning.

If the content of the conversation between faith and learning is problematic, so also has been the manner in which the faith and learning ideal has been introduced. The current leadership has implemented its vision swiftly and very boldly, in a rather top-down fashion. For some on the receiving end the process seemed like steamrolling, which does not go well in a Baptist institution that has had strongly democratic governance in the past. Even the former president has reservations about the pace and manner of the change.[26] And other constituencies who have been ruffled by the bold and vigorous approach are putting up resistance.

The second problem is that the vision of faith and learning integration simply has not yet been understood or appropriated by a large majority of the faculty. A rather small number of visionaries have implemented this vision, but it is not yet deeply embedded or broadly shared. Besides the speed of introduction, why is this the case? First, as I argued in Chapter Two, most faculty members — even practicing Baptists — have been formed in their graduate education to trust only certain kinds of scientifically- or rationally-based knowledge. Such scholars are unlikely to grant intellectual status to the Christian account of life and reality and, lacking any sense of a credible Christian intellectual tradition, are disposed to see integration of faith and learning as the kind of thing done by Bible colleges, lacking intellectual respectability. Further, such faculty — 74 percent of those at Baylor — resist even the notion that the university should give special consideration to Christian perspectives.[27] While a large majority

26. Chancellor Herbert Reynolds, former president of Baylor University, conversation with the author, November 16, 1999.

27. Michael Beaty, Todd Buras, and Larry Lyon, "Christian Higher Education: An Historical and Philosophical Perspective," *Perspectives in Religious Studies* 24 (Summer 1997): 163. Perhaps Baylor is in a more vulnerable position in regard to these issues because so much has been done to survey the Baylor faculty. The Institute of Faith and Learning has done a thorough job of plumbing the opinion of Baylor faculty, students, and board members.

(90 percent) of the Baylor faculty support the traditional "add-on" or "two-spheres" approach to Christian higher education, a much smaller portion (67 percent) support integration of faith and learning, and even that still-substantial percentage supporting such integration can probably be attributed more than anything else to "good-team-player" support for the leadership's vision.[28] That two-thirds of the faculty supports the leadership's vision becomes less impressive in light of the fact that only 46 percent of the Baylor faculty think they are able to "create a syllabus for a course they currently teach that includes a clear, academically-legitimate, Christian perspective on the subject."[29]

There is a genuine difference of opinion about whether the new vision of Christian higher education — integration of faith and learning — will prevail in the long run at Baylor. Key leadership certainly has pressed it vigorously for almost a decade. But will it last? Larry Lyon, dean of the graduate school, and Michael Beaty, Director of the Institute of Faith and Learning, whose surveys have given such an accurate picture of the status of Baylor's new vision at the university, conclude that "the surveys suggest little reason to expect Baylor then will move away — in either direction [secularization or integration of faith and learning] — from the two-spheres view of a Christian university."[30] On the other hand, Provost Donald Schmeltekopf believes that Baylor will win the battle for a richer intellectual connection between faith and learning.[31] Time will tell who is right. At least the requirement that all faculty members hired be observant Christians and Jews should ensure that the battle takes place on relatively friendly terms.

The University of Notre Dame

Over 90 percent of the faculty of the University of Notre Dame believe that their institution can both remain Catholic and achieve excellence.[32] Nev-

---

28. Beaty *et al.*, "Christian Higher Education," p. 163.

29. Beaty *et al.*, "Christian Higher Education," p. 163.

30. Larry Lyon and Michael Beaty, "Integration, Secularization, and the Two-Spheres View at Religious Colleges," *Christian Scholar's Review* 29 (Fall 1999): 100.

31. Provost Donald Schmeltekopf, conversation with the author, November 16, 1999.

32. Lyon and Beaty, "Integration, Secularization," p. 93.

ertheless, 55 percent of them agree or strongly agree that their school should hire faculty without regard for religious commitments.[33] The tension between these two opinions within the faculty provides an illustration of the challenge Notre Dame faces. The vast majority of all its constituencies — board, alumni, faculty, students, administration, and supporters — desire Notre Dame to remain Catholic. Indeed, each of those constituencies except the faculty is overwhelmingly Catholic. Yet, as we observed in Chapter Four, Notre Dame is intensely motivated to break into the top circle of elite research institutions. Not only would such success bring further fame and fortune to an already famous and rich university, but it would also bring to Catholics everywhere the satisfaction of competing successfully with the most respected secular (formerly Protestant) universities. What Notre Dame did in football in the 1940s and 1950s would then be duplicated in academe in the new millennium.

Whether Notre Dame can achieve both great tasks — remain Catholic and achieve the status of a premier graduate institution — depends a good deal on the strength and clarity of vision the university has. Indeed, the very meaning of the phrase "remain Catholic" depends on that vision. In contrast to the relatively weak theological resources of the evangelical and Baptist traditions at Wheaton and Baylor, Notre Dame has the capacity to draw upon a rich store of Catholic theological and moral wisdom. Catholicism has a capacious and sophisticated intellectual tradition, so one would expect that tradition to be prominent in the university's vision. Indeed, the pope's apostolic constitution *Ex Corde Ecclesiae* presents an extremely rich mine of wisdom about Catholic higher education. Sadly, the ongoing debate over its call for juridical accountability to the church by Catholic colleges and universities obscures many of its more constructive offerings.

In a kind of theological prologue to its mission statement, Notre Dame lays out a trinitarian view of its mission. "A sacramental vision encounters God in the whole creation. In and through the visible world in which we live, we come to know and experience the invisible God. In mediation the Catholic vision perceives God not only present in but working through persons, events and material things. There is an intelligibility and a coherence to all reality, discoverable through spirit, mind and imagina-

33. Michael Beaty, "Review of *Dying of the Light*," *Journal of College and University Law* 26 (Summer 1999): 188-91.

tion." This affirmation of the intelligibility of the Creator's creation legitimates the Catholic support for all genuine learning, which finally is continuous with divine revelation. Other sentences in the prologue touch on the Second Person: "God's grace prompts human activity to assist the world in creating justice grounded in love." "A Catholic university draws its basic inspiration from Jesus Christ as the source of wisdom and from the conviction that in him all things can be brought to their completion." An implicit invocation of the Third Person, the Holy Spirit, insists that "God's way to us comes as communion, through the communities in which men and women live. . . . The emphasis on community in Catholicism explains why Notre Dame historically has fostered familial bonds in its institutional life."[34]

With this context in mind, the actual mission statement declares that the University of Notre Dame is "dedicated to the pursuit and sharing of truth for its own sake." The statement acknowledges the university's "responsibility to advance knowledge in a search for truth through original inquiry and publication," insisting that "No genuine search for the truth in the human or cosmic order is alien to the life of faith." We can call this a "convergence" approach, because it confidently assumes that empirical knowledge will converge with Catholic teaching. Yet the products of the free pursuit of truth, though grounded ultimately in God, are not viewed as completely autonomous: "The University welcomes all areas of scholarly activity as consonant with its mission, subject to critical refinement." Or, again, "As a Catholic university one of its distinctive goals is to provide a forum where through free inquiry and open discussion the various lines of Catholic thought may intersect with all the forms of knowledge found in the arts, sciences, professions, and every other area of human scholarship and creativity." Because all learning must be subject to "critical refinement" and must be examined where it "intersects" with "various lines of Catholic thought," there must be serious attention to the sources of Catholic thought itself. So the university commits itself to "pursue the religious dimensions of all human learning" so that "Catholic intellectual life in all disciplines [might] be animated and fostered and a proper community of scholarly discourse be established."

Notre Dame then makes clear that it does not belong in our "ortho-

---

34. *University of Notre Dame Bulletin of Information 1997-98,* p. 8. Quotations taken from the "Context" section preceding the university's mission statement.

dox" category with Calvin and Wheaton. It declares that its desired intellectual interchange "requires, and is enriched by, the presence and voices of diverse scholars and students." "What the university asks of all its scholars and students, however, is not a particular creedal affiliation, but a respect for the objectives of Notre Dame and a willingness to enter into the conversation that gives it life and character. Therefore, the University insists upon academic freedom which makes open discussion and inquiry possible." Yet, if there is to be the kind of conversation the university prizes, its Catholic perspective must be nurtured by the continuing presence of "a predominant number of Catholic intellectuals. This ideal has been consistently maintained by the University leadership throughout its history."

The statement goes on to affirm the university's commitment to nurture a blend of intellectual and moral virtues in its students, including a "disciplined sensibility to the poverty, injustice and oppression that burden the lives of so many." It strikes further Catholic themes by aiming to "create a sense of human solidarity and concern for the common good that will bear fruit as learning becomes service to justice." This formation takes place in "a way of living consonant with a Christian community manifest in prayer, liturgy and service" whose ultimate end is "building a society that is at once more human and more divine."[35]

It is clear that Notre Dame proposes a distinctive Catholic version of the dialogue between faith and learning, which is indeed embodied in the life of the university, as we will see. Still, other visions are competing with that Catholic version for dominance at Notre Dame. One is the temptation to capitulate to the cultural norms of success and glitz that have already made Notre Dame so wealthy and famous. More exalted, perhaps, but no less dangerous, is the "obsessive drive for prestige," as one commentator put it, which makes Notre Dame beholden to the academic models of the great secular universities it is trying to match or surpass. The Enlightenment model of autonomous reason and the postmodern model of epistemological perspectivalism, both vying for dominance in the elite secular universities, present seductive alternatives to its Catholic vision. What

35. *University of Notre Dame Bulletin of Information 1997-98.* These sentences and phrases are gathered from Notre Dame's mission statement; they are re-organized here to show their coherence with the trinitarian themes developed in the "Context" section preceding the mission statement.

makes the choice between Notre Dame's vision of Catholic humanism and the competing secular models so difficult is that the university has the resources to pursue both. Because of that, the struggle at Notre Dame is magnified more than at any other church-related college or university.

In this encounter Notre Dame is both aided and hampered by *Ex Corde*. Certainly the Catholic vision of higher education embodied in the pope's letter is consistent with Notre Dame's own intentions. The letter has been used to facilitate and strengthen what the university has already proposed in its commitment to remain Catholic; indeed, it has stimulated and intensified a discussion already underway. Perhaps it has even lifted the horizon of the university's aspirations. But *Ex Corde* is also a handicap, at least in the eyes of the vast majority of Notre Dame faculty, because its insistence on juridical accountability in the form of mandates for Catholic theologians and demands for a Catholic majority in the faculty seems to them an intrusion into the university's autonomy, if not into academic freedom itself.[36] This threat, they claim, damages the reputation of the Catholic university among those who already suspect that the church will not allow free inquiry in its schools. It makes them more resistant to the efforts to keep Notre Dame Catholic.

Though there is little sympathy with the juridical demands of *Ex Corde* among the administrative and faculty leadership, its positive vision of what a Catholic university ought to be is quite consonant with what Notre Dame is already trying to do. Because the university has enormous resources, it is able to foster its vision in ways that add real muscle to the Catholic motifs it cherishes. First and foremost, perhaps, Notre Dame continues to require two courses in theology and two in philosophy for all its students. The first theology course — "Foundations of Theology: Biblical/ Historical" — aims at a basic biblical literacy along with knowledge of the apostolic tradition in the first centuries of Christian history. If its instructors indeed do what the course intends, it communicates the classical deposit of faith common to all Christians. A second course must be chosen from among a wide variety of biblical, theological, and ethical topics. The

36. See the response to *Ex Corde* by the National Conference of Catholic Bishops in their "An Application to the United States," available at www.nccbuscc.org/education. The bishops have accepted the papal challenge to have Catholic professors of theology at Catholic colleges and universities seek a mandatum and to achieve a majority of Catholic professors at such schools; see pp. 8-9.

first philosophy course is an introduction that focuses more on the classical problems of the existence of God, human freedom, and moral obligation than most introductory courses would in secular schools. A second philosophy course is chosen from offerings grouped under the areas of images of humanity, morals and politics, and philosophy of religion.[37]

As one might guess, such ample requirements necessitate large departments of theology and philosophy. Notre Dame has to be one of the few large universities where those departments are larger than those of English and history. Each department runs at about three dozen professors, and both departments are crucial in bearing the Catholic vision on behalf of the whole university.

The theology department, which for some time had the reputation of taking a hypercritical stance toward the Catholic magisterium, now is under the chairmanship of a young Catholic intellectual who seems faithful to the magisterium and fully committed to transmitting the Catholic faith and its intellectual tradition to the students. It is definitely not a detached "religious studies" department, though its scholarly prowess is much respected. The faculty has published over three hundred books since 1965, an output which would be hard to match by any university department.[38] The department has been very active in cross-disciplinary conversations as an effort to stimulate a vibrant Catholic intellectual culture. Interestingly, the department offers no required course in Catholic theology or social teaching in addition to the introductory biblical/historical course, mainly because staffing such a course would deplete the department's resources. Nevertheless, that lack is a bit glaring in view of Notre Dame's commitment to the Catholic vision.

The philosophy department is a highly distinguished one. While the older neo-Thomist philosophy is still represented, a stronger voice is now projected by Reformed philosophers such as Alvin Plantinga and Peter Van Inwagen who are, among other things, powerful representatives of the Calvin College school of "worldview analysis." The department has concentrated strength in philosophy of religion and offers a classical Christian philosophical alternative to the many secularist departments in the elite American universities. While the philosophy department cannot offer the

37. *University of Notre Dame Bulletin of Information 1997-98*, pp. 164-68, 137-39.

38. Notre Dame Web site, www.nd.edu/aboutnd.

coherent framework for organizing all the knowledge in the university, as the classical Thomist department once did, it is able unabashedly to make philosophical arguments for Christian truth claims.

Another important strategy employed by Notre Dame to enhance its Catholic character is its creation of a remarkable number of centers, institutes, journals, and programs that engage Catholic interests and themes. These "strategic hamlets" within the university are not agencies located in the third drawer of some professor's desk; they are well-funded programs with their own offices, staffs, programs, and facilities. Again, Notre Dame's resources are crucial here, for few church-related colleges or universities could afford to sustain them adequately. Among the many centers are the Cushwa Center for the Study of American Catholicism, the Center for Social Concern, the Center for Ethics and Religious Values in Business, the Reilly Center for Science, Technology and Values, and the Center for Philosophy of Religion. Among the many institutes are the Erasmus Institute, the Medieval Institute, the Keough Institute for Irish Studies, and the Kroc Institute for International Peace. Most departments have programs of study that key off Catholic themes and concerns, such as the Department of Government and International Studies' Program for Research on Religion, Church, and Society. A number of quality journals such as the *Review of Politics* carry classic Catholic concerns that often are ignored in secular journals. As centers and institutes have been created, the university has successfully filled their directorships with important Christian, often Catholic, intellectuals, whose presence has been important in shaping the university's intellectual climate.

Moreover, Catholic religious themes are not limited to the theology and philosophy departments or to institutes, centers, and programs. Catholic thought influences the foci of many departments. The economics department, for instance, has traditionally focused on social justice issues; the government department has specialized in political philosophy; the sociology department has emphasized the study of family and religion; and the music department has concentrated much of its efforts on sacred music.

Faculty hiring has been an important factor in keeping all these important emphases and embodying the Notre Dame vision in general. The dean of the School of Arts and Letters watches carefully over the hiring process. Besides a commitment to the traditional criteria of teaching, research, and citizenship, identification with and potential contribution to the unique mission of Notre Dame is also very important for new faculty.

This includes "the infusion of the liberal arts ideal with a spiritual dimension; the goal of educating the whole person; the development of interconnections among the disciplines; the interrelation of learning and morality and of reason and faith; and the ideal of service to the world. Certain concerns and principles have traditionally been associated with the Catholic intellectual tradition, to which candidates might contribute: for example, the dignity of the human person and a sacramental vision that finds divine presence in the world; the unity of knowledge and an openness to the mystery of transcendence; universal human rights and international social justice; and respect for intellectual community and for the wisdom of the ages."[39] Though non-Catholics and even non-religious candidates could measure up to many of these criteria, the dean also has an affirmative action plan for Catholics. All other things being roughly equal, Catholics are hired over non-Catholics because, in the dean's words, "the identity and unity of a Catholic institution depends on our having a strong representation of Catholics on our faculty."[40]

In addition to this general policy, the provost and the deans make "target of opportunity" grants available to departments that identify and recruit Catholic candidates who particularly enhance the Catholic character of the university. These grants provide temporary budget support as a strong incentive. Indeed, as far back as 1993, President Malloy's *Final Report — Colloquy for the Year 2000* made the following its first recommendation: "In recruiting new faculty, each department must make energetic efforts to hire faculty of the highest caliber who seek to participate in the intellectual life of a dynamic Catholic university. All who participate in hiring faculty must be cognizant of and responsive to the need for dedicated and committed Catholics to predominate in number among the faculty."[41] There is some disagreement as to how vigorously the policy has been prosecuted.

These "affirmative action" efforts may be attributed to the fact that the percentage of Catholics in the faculty has been declining. Currently, the figure most often quoted estimates that 55 percent of the faculty mem-

---

39. Mark W. Roche, "Profile of the Ideal Candidate for Notre Dame" (unpublished manuscript of speech to department chairs in Arts and Letters), p. 1.

40. Roche, "Profile of the Ideal Candidate," p. 6.

41. Edward A. Malloy, C.S.C., *Final Report — Colloquy for the Year 2000*, University of Notre Dame, 1993, p. 5.

bers are Catholics, but many of these are nominal or even ex-Catholics. More realistically, a number of professors have suggested that only about 25 percent of the faculty are "serious" Catholics. Thus the efforts to bolster Catholic faculty presence. Oddly enough, it seems that Notre Dame makes little effort after faculty are hired to educate them into its Catholic tradition. Part of this lack is no doubt due to the size and complexity of the institution; nevertheless, it remains a weakness. In contrast, the Catholic presence among other constituencies is far more secure: the trustees are 90 percent Catholic, the student body is 85 percent Catholic, and the administration is overwhelmingly so. The faculty seems to be the main point of concern.

Certainly one cannot examine the mission statements and the public rhetoric of Notre Dame without seeing a powerful Christian vision of higher education at work. It is not the Calvin model of integrating faith and learning that is so influential at the other institutions we have examined; it is a uniquely Catholic approach that assumes that empirical knowledge will converge with Catholic teaching. Reason and empirical research are given high autonomy. And because there is such a large body of Catholic religious and social thought, the university can assert confidently that it is important and weighty enough to be taken up by many members of the faculty and the student body. Many of its institutes and centers exist to provide full support for those pursuits. So, from many points of view, the Catholic identity and mission of the university seem secure far into the future. Several influential faculty members believe this to be the case and scoff at those who worry about secularization.[42]

However, as I mentioned earlier, other visions are at work in the Notre Dame faculty. Some fit nicely with Notre Dame's mission, but others do not. Faculty members who hold to contrasting visions are often uninterested in or hostile toward the attempts to preserve the Catholic character of Notre Dame. Furthermore — and this may be the most seductive challenge — the university has so much desire to make it to the very top of research universities it is too often willing to hire the most prestigious applicant regardless of whether or not that person fits the Notre Dame mission. The rhetoric and actions of the administrators do not always affect hiring,

---

42. See, for example, Richard P. McBrien, "What Is a Catholic University?" in *The Challenge and Promise of a Catholic University*, ed. Theodore Hesburgh, C.S.C. (Notre Dame, IN: University of Notre Dame Press, 1994), pp. 153-64.

tenure, and promotion at the grass-roots level of each department. And at that level, the picture is not so promising. In one typical department, only about 20 percent of the members are strongly committed to the Catholic character of Notre Dame; another 20 percent are hostile toward religious considerations in hiring, wanting only the best person in a narrowly technical sense; the rest are in the middle, perhaps capable of being swayed either way. In many cases, the direction of the department depends heavily on the chair. And up to this point even the persuasive powers and incentives of the dean and provost do not seem to make that much difference. Indeed, some committed Catholics think that the administration is so aimed at prestige that it will not resist the secularizing tendencies in the departments. It is at this ground level that the future of Notre Dame is most uncertain.

St. Olaf College

Though not ordinarily given to praising the Christian character of any college, James Burtchaell nevertheless congratulates St. Olaf College on an attractive "lamination of scholarship with piety and theology," "a Lutheran identity . . . purposefully claimed," and "an institutional integrity with responsiveness to the church."[43] Certainly one of St. Olaf's advantages in earning Burtchaell's praise is its symbiotic relation to a strong ethno-religious culture that has remarkable density and resilience in Minnesota and its environs. Norwegian immigrants were attracted to that region, and those who came tended to be serious about their pietist Lutheran heritage. They supplied the college an abundance of faculty and students, if not great monetary support. For many years that ethno-religious subculture permeated the college and made it unmistakably Lutheran and Norwegian. Among its original aims was a strong religious and liberal arts education to prepare laity for their callings in the world. This aim followed naturally from its sponsoring tradition and continues to the present day.

St. Olaf has transcended its pietist tradition, however, by assembling a number of remarkable Christian intellectuals throughout its history. When its ethno-religious unanimity began to diminish after World War II,

43. James Burtchaell, *The Dying of the Light: The Disengagement of Colleges and Universities from Their Christian Churches* (Grand Rapids: Eerdmans, 1998), p. 518.

this emergent intellectual tradition became fertile ground for extensive theologizing on the identity and mission of the college.[44] The level of sophistication and continuity of that reflection nearly match that of Calvin College. Indeed, one of the marks of St. Olaf's seriousness about its Lutheran Christian heritage is the interminable character of its discussions. Its mission statement is now undergoing revision.

The current mission statement is unabashed about its religious commitments. In the first line the college identifies itself as a "four year college of the Evangelical Lutheran Church in America," a not insignificant first step. It provides an education "rooted in the Christian Gospel." Moreover, since "life is more than a livelihood, it focuses on what is ultimately worthwhile and fosters the development of the whole person in mind, body and spirit." Further, it "offers a distinctive environment that integrates teaching, scholarship, creative activity, and opportunities for encounter with the Christian Gospel and God's call to faith." The college intends that its graduates "combine academic excellence and theological literacy with a commitment to life-long learning." "It encourages [students] to be seekers of truth, leading lives of unselfish service to others."[45]

Behind that mission statement and the profuse reflection on identity and mission is a long tradition of Lutheran theology. Like Notre Dame and Calvin, St. Olaf brings to its discussions an identifiable theological tradition. Luther and the numerous Lutheran thinkers who followed him are living voices at St. Olaf. Of the many Lutheran themes that enter into the fray at St. Olaf, the most important one is vocation. Lutheranism has taught that all Christians are given callings by God to use their gifts in service to their neighbor in the places of responsibility — family life, citizen, worker, church member — they have been given. Historically, faculty have modeled and taught this doctrine so pervasively that it has become a central, if not the central, theme of St. Olaf's life. The intertwined themes of

---

44. See, for example, *Integration in the Christian Liberal Arts College*, ed. Howard Hong (Northfield, MN: St. Olaf College Press, 1956), in which it was argued that systematic theology must be the organizing center for the re-integration of the liberal arts curriculum. At its centennial, St. Olaf brought out *Identity and Mission in a Changing Context* (Northfield, MN: St. Olaf College Press, 1974), in which Harold Ditmanson, an influential theologian for a large segment of the life of the college, argued for a particular kind of context for Christian education.

45. From St. Olaf College Mission Statement, available on St. Olaf's Web site, www.stolaf.edu/publications/viewbook/section2f.html.

calling and service have been so central that the volume published on the occasion of the college's 125th anniversary is entitled *Called to Serve: St. Olaf and the Vocation of a Church College.*[46] This theme of vocation or calling is articulated in the mission statement as "God's call to faith" and to "unselfish service to others" as well as to become "responsible and knowledgeable citizens of the world."

The statement also proposes that students "encounter the Christian Gospel and God's call to faith" and develop "theological literacy." Certainly the first phrase's intent is realized in the ethos of the college — especially its chapel program — as well as in the academic curriculum. But both phrases apply to the curriculum. St. Olaf requires two courses in religion and one capstone course in ethics. The first course is called "The Bible in Community and Culture" and includes a number of variations that the students can choose. They range from "The Bible: Its Ancient Meaning and Its Continuing Impact" to "The Bible for Pagans." The courses seem to aim at leading the students through a current issue back to biblical texts. Unfortunately, there seems to be little effort to teach the whole biblical narrative or a coherent biblical theology.

A second course requirement in theology allows a wide variety of choices running from the straightforward "Essentials in Christian Theology" and "Lutheran Heritage" to "Introduction to Feminist Theology." The courses by and large do get into disciplined theological teaching and learning; they definitely increase theological literacy among students in a significant way.

The third required course, which used to be another religion course, is now a senior integrative course, "Ethical Issues and Normative Perspectives." Offered by many departments, the course aims "to analyze ethical issues from a variety of perspectives that provide norms of justice and well-being and guide moral reasoning," including "[o]ne or more perspectives from the Christian theological tradition."[47] In order to prepare faculty from widely dispersed departments to teach the course, the college offers intensive summer courses for faculty to learn philosophical and theological ethical perspectives. This is a major effort to engage the Christian moral tradition with ethical issues arising in fields of study across the curriculum.

46. Pamela Schwandt, ed., *Called to Serve: St. Olaf and the Vocation of a Church College* (Northfield, MN: St. Olaf College Press, 1999).

47. *A World of Possibilities: St. Olaf College Academic Catalog 1997-98*, p. 36.

As with the other schools surveyed, St. Olaf operates with a large theology department. It carries fifteen tenured faculty and five or six more on terminal appointments, totaling about twenty full-time professors. Once completely Lutheran, its Lutheran representation now runs at less than half. Other Christian traditions are represented as well as other world religions. St. Olaf has a long record of concern for world cultures and religions that dates from its close relationship to the missionary movement of the American Norwegian Lutheran church. That interest in worldwide missions has been translated into a wide-ranging emphasis on study abroad, which is included as one of the three main pillars of St. Olaf's mission statement — the college intends an education "incorporating a global perspective." Fully 50 percent of each graduating class has studied abroad while matriculating at St. Olaf.

The trajectory of the theology department is interesting indeed. Once confessionally Lutheran, pastoral, and closely related to the chapel, the department went through a period of serious conflict between those who wanted to adapt a "religious studies" approach and those who believed it should produce and represent normative Christian theology, between those who wanted to speak "about" the tradition and those who wanted to speak "for" it. After considerable fireworks, the department has now settled into what its chairman thinks is a fruitful compromise in which it "combines both approaches to the benefit of both." That compromise or ambivalence is picked up across the campus by those who lament the loss of the school's former role as the steward of the Lutheran heritage. Nevertheless, there is no doubt that the broader Christian heritage is "privileged" in the department's work, which is considerable. The department is very influential in the interdisciplinary efforts of the college and continues to produce significant scholarly contributions.

Over a decade ago the college recruited Robert Jenson, then of the Lutheran seminary at Gettysburg, to its theology department. Jenson is a distinguished Lutheran systematic theologian who was brought to St. Olaf to add Lutheran luster to the department and to renew its role as the bearer of the Lutheran vision on campus. This worthy attempt did in fact polish the Lutheran reputation of St. Olaf and provided the occasion for Jenson to continue to produce fine theological work. But the college's intention to instill new leadership in the department did not work out for various reasons, and the department has remained as stalemated as before, losing an important chance to regain direction.

St. Olaf could not be described adequately without mentioning its renowned programs in the performing arts, particularly its choral music. While these programs contribute immensely to the St. Olaf ethos, which we will discuss in the next chapter, it is important to note that they are also academic programs. As such they are powerful instruments of the college's identity and mission as a Lutheran Christian college. Instructors who see their teaching as a calling infuse the arts with Christian meaning.

Following the Lutheran theological distinction between law and gospel, the college aims at cultivating the minds of the students with Christian learning, not converting their hearts, which would be the proper work of the gospel in the church. While the college talks easily of the growth and development of students, it would be reluctant to talk of transformation, the language of Calvinists and evangelicals.

As for cultivating new and continuing faculty into the tradition of the school, St. Olaf employs several instruments. During the celebration of its 125th year, the college is encouraging wide discussion of the volume *Called to Serve*. Each new faculty member is brought into a mentoring program initially funded by the Lilly Fellows Program but now sustained by St. Olaf. The St. Olaf Forum stimulates a continuing discussion for all faculty on the relation of faith and learning at St. Olaf. The Boldt Professorship is an in-house, revolving position that allows a worthy faculty member to teach an ongoing seminar on the liberal arts mission of the college and to invite outside speakers on that issue. A revolving new chair in honor of Martin Marty, the chairman of the college regents, will be dedicated to the intersection of religion and the particular discipline of the holder of the chair. The summer programs in theological ethics for faculty teaching the "Ethical Issues in Normative Perspectives" course reaches many members of departments beyond philosophy and theology.

Since the college has recently had a painful retrenchment program because of overstaffing, there have been few new tenure-track faculty recruited lately. But the academic dean has carefully screened those who have come aboard in the last five years for their willingness to identify with and contribute to St. Olaf's mission. There is also an active effort on the part of the administration to increase the percentage of Lutheran faculty, in view of the fact that no more than 30-35 percent of the faculty is estimated to be Lutheran. (Though I consider St. Olaf a "critical-mass" school, the college keeps no statistics of the faculty's denominational ties, if any.) However, it is instructive that the college does not include in its anti-discrimination policies the clause on religious membership; it still has the legal capacity to seek out Christians in general and Lutherans in particular.

The board of regents is made up of roughly thirty persons, about 60 percent of whom are Lutherans, including two bishops and a pastor. Its chairman, Martin Marty, the distinguished Lutheran historian of American religion, is highly sophisticated in his understanding of the history and nature of Christian higher education. Such leadership certainly augurs well for the future of St. Olaf.

The engagement of faith and learning on the part of faculty in the non-theological and non-philosophical fields is mixed. It certainly goes on in the capstone course on ethical issues and among a minority of faculty. But many are uninterested. Part of their reticence is that they fear doing it badly. As one faculty member put it, "At St. Olaf, to do the faith/learning thing badly is worse than not doing it at all; at Calvin one must do it, even if badly." However, some of the reticence is due to apathy and even hostility toward the task. In the quest to become a nationally recognized liberal arts college, St. Olaf has been tempted by the same siren as Notre Dame. The drive for sheer excellence resulted in the theologically careless hiring of a significant cohort of faculty.

This disturbing factor leads Burtchaell to offer his gloomy and somewhat cryptic prediction for St. Olaf's future after so glowingly depicting its past and present as a Christian college, declaring that the school "is entering into a divestiture of its Lutheran identity that, so much longer in coming, could be swifter in its eventual accomplishment."[48] What could Burtchaell mean by such a summary judgment? In my estimation, there are at least two pertinent factors: the failure to hire the faculty to carry forward the religious DNA of the institution and a theology that, even if maintained scrupulously, might well undermine efforts at a vigorous engagement of faith and learning.

During the 1980s and the early 1990s, St. Olaf did not, for whatever reason, hire many faculty members who fit the strong religious dimension of the college's mission. Those faculty, now moving into long-term tenured positions, seem to present a major challenge to the Christian and specifically Lutheran identity of the school, particularly in light of the retirement of the last great cohort of Norwegian Lutheran faculty that carried St. Olaf's heritage for so long. There are certainly younger partisans of the Lutheran cause on campus, but they are fewer in number. In general, the

---

48. Burtchaell, *Dying of the Light,* p. 518.

current faculty does not relate as closely to the chapel program as that earlier generation. They are less inclined to relate faith to learning, because their grounding in the faith is less prominent than before. They are less likely to have the life-long commitment to St. Olaf. Yet, in many ways, St. Olaf is a better college — more scholarly, more professional, and more cosmopolitan. But will the soul depart as the secular accolades increase?

The school faces another serious problem, particularly in the realm of faith and learning. Oddly enough, this problem has been complicated by St. Olaf's recently retired president, Mark U. Edwards, Jr., whose interpretation of Lutheran theology leads to a split between faith and learning. The former president's reading of the Lutheran tradition leads him to argue that secular learning through the instruments of reason and experience should be completely autonomous, unchallenged by the wisdom of the Christian intellectual tradition. For him education is purely in the realm of the law, the earthly kingdom which God rules with his "left hand," to use Lutheran parlance: "Situated within this realm (the earthly kingdom of God's law), we in higher education are called to pursue truth with all the intellectual rigor at our command. In this respect a college of the church should differ in no significant respect from a secular college or university."[49] According to Edwards, a Lutheran college is true to its identity when it abides by "the secular standards of what a fine college should be."[50] Certainly one would expect a Christian college to measure up to some secular standards of excellence, but does that mean a complete acceptance of Enlightenment philosophical naturalism or postmodern relativism as those orientations shape the learning of the modern secular academy? Apparently so, for in a later article in *The Christian Century,* Edwards chastises the Calvinists who want to integrate faith and learning. Rather, he opines, the scholarship and learning of Lutheran colleges should show no substantive difference from secular efforts. In his version of the Lutheran approach, "the Christian substance appears in the Christian calling of the faculty, staff and students and in the Christian context surrounding the academic enterprise — only rarely in the results of scholarly inquiry itself."[51]

49. Mark U. Edwards, Jr., "Lutheran Heritage at Lutheran Colleges" (unpublished manuscript, October 8, 1995), p. 6.

50. Edwards, "Lutheran Heritage," p. 7.

51. Mark U. Edwards, Jr., "Christian Colleges: A Dying Light or a New Refraction?" *Christian Century,* April 21-28, 1999, p. 463.

Were this version of Lutheran theology taken to its logical conclusion it would deprive the gospel of any intellectual content and the law of any moral content. The biblical narrative and theological reflection on it would not be given any epistemological status to engage secular learning. It would champion a form of Lutheran quietism in the realm of education. Much as German Lutherans in the 1930s separated the two kingdoms (government under law separated from Christianity under the gospel) and allowed the Nazi movement to go unchecked by appeal to the intellectual and moral content of the Christian vision, so this approach would allow modern secular learning to go unchallenged by that vision. It would constitute a nearly certain formula for the separation of faith and learning, not their engagement. It would leave the Lutheran college with only an add-on approach to Christian presence. While it is certainly true that the canons of secular reason have to be taken seriously and cannot simply be trumped by an appeal to the Christian vision, it is just as surely true that those canons should not go unchallenged in a critically responsible way. The educational process at a Christian college should be different in substance, not only in context.

However, it would be unfair to suggest that Edwards has taken his approach to its logical conclusion. On the contrary, he seems to have nuanced and expanded his views more recently.[52] He also has demonstrated a very strong commitment to the Lutheran and Christian character of St. Olaf beyond the intellectual realm. He has vigorously affirmed the sense of calling that has defined St. Olaf from its beginning and supported the ongoing discussion of what it means to be a Lutheran college even though he disagrees with the positions on faith and learning taken by a number of Lutheran colleagues on that issue. He has worked carefully with the dean to insure that new hires fit the mission of St. Olaf.

Even with these disagreements and tensions over the nature of St. Olaf's approach to faith and learning, the rapid slide into secularization that Burtchaell predicts seems remote indeed. During the recent celebration of the 125th anniversary of its founding, the college once again probed its identity and mission as a college of the church. A spring 2000 conference entitled "Called to Serve — Faith, Understanding, Action" again struck the college's traditional Lutheran themes. With many

52. Mark U. Edwards's opening address to the "Called to Serve" Conference, St. Olaf College, April 7, 2000.

strengths at its disposal (including its considerable Christian ethos, which we will discuss in the next chapter), St. Olaf seems likely to hold onto its heritage of faith well into the future, despite the challenges involved.

Valparaiso University

It is impossible to speak of Valparaiso's vision of Christian higher education without referring to its forceful and energetic former president O. P. Kretzmann, who served the university from 1940 to 1968. A charismatic rhetorician and visionary, Kretzmann stamped the university with the indelible mark of his imagination. That imagination lives on in the several generations who knew and admired him, as well as in the programs he instigated and the buildings he built, paramount among them the soaring Chapel of the Resurrection, completed in 1959. Installed in 1940, toward the end of the Great Depression and near the beginning of World War II, Kretzmann articulated a grand vision for a university that had struggled for existence throughout the 1930s. He envisioned a university that stood at the crossroads of Athens and Jerusalem. While neither shrinking from nor negating the challenges of the secular knowledge of Athens, he confidently proclaimed that the universal truth of the Christian faith was just what the world and university needed at that time. He saw a Christian university that was different from those that "have not been integrated by a unified and permanent philosophy of life and history."[53] Kretzmann's vision of Christian humanism was one in which there were no insurmountable problems in the university's pursuit of its two-fold task: "the search for Truth and the transmission of Truth."[54]

Kretzmann exemplified the creative possibilities that could arise in the combination of a strong but intensely parochial religious tradition (the heavily German and unswervingly conservative Lutheran Church–Missouri Synod) with a liberating cosmopolitan flair. Coming from a traditional Lutheran clergy family — five brothers became Lutheran pastors — Kretzmann grew up in polyglot New York City and imbibed the

---

53. O. P. Kretzmann, "The Destiny of a Christian University in the Modern World," in *The Lutheran Reader*, ed. Paul J. Contino and David Morgan (Valparaiso, IN: Valparaiso University Press, 1999), p. 111.

54. Kretzmann, "Destiny of a Christian University," p. 110.

worldly wisdom and sophistication of the great metropolis. He embodied that combination of disciplined conservative religion and worldly sophistication, and tried to impose it on his great project — Valparaiso University.[55]

His and Valparaiso's vision was informed by a Christian humanism more akin to the Catholic approach than to dialectical Lutheranism. Confident in the Christian account of life and reality — after all, the strong tradition of confessional Lutheranism permeated both faculty and students — the university aimed at a synthesis of Christ and culture. There was little doubt that the full Christian vision was the norm, and whatever was best in culture could be the vehicle of Christian meaning. Valparaiso could be a luxuriant expression of Christian culture. Based upon a firm and disciplined, if not narrow and parochial, religious tradition, Valparaiso could allow a thousand flowers to bloom in an atmosphere of freedom and creativity. Instead of the "over-againstness" to high culture one might expect from a "sectarian" religious tradition, the university promoted a confident synthesis of Christ and culture. Its motto, "In Thy Light We See Light," expresses the conviction that the normative light of God's revelation allows everyone within the university to see real light in human culture. The soaring Chapel of the Resurrection, constructed on the highest ground of the campus, symbolized that God's revelation stood above and integrated the life of the mind that took place around it. The chapel's architecture and art remain a witness to that grand integration. Its exuberant and powerful Christ rising from the cross communicates a triumphant and hopeful strain.

Kretzmann founded, edited, and wrote for *The Cresset — A Review of Literature, Arts, and Public Affairs,* which continues to the present day as a vehicle of Lutheran reflection on culture. He also founded Christ College, one of the oldest honors colleges in the country and an ongoing effort at forging a uniquely Christian liberal arts curriculum. For some time the content of the required theology courses was coordinated with the texts and worship life of the daily chapel services. The university was able to draw upon a significant number of Missouri Lutherans who were theolog-

55. These historical facts and insights can be garnered in *The Lutheran Reader* as well as in an as-yet-unpublished history of the university entitled *Flame of Faith, Lamp of Learning* by Richard Baepler, former Dean of Christ College and Vice President for Academic Affairs, now retired.

ically educated but then went on for advanced education in other disciplines — economics, philosophy, law, business, and literature, to name a few. Gifted Missouri Synod faculty and students gravitated toward Valparaiso as a place where their talents could be freely developed and expressed, in contrast to the more controlled and limited atmosphere in the Missouri-owned teachers' colleges. These ingredients led to a rather natural and spontaneous engagement of faith and learning.

A good deal of this original vision continues today in a younger generation that is still connected to many that worked directly with Kretzmann. The retired stalwarts still come to chapel and offer wisdom to those who desire it. Elements of that vision persist in the university's mission statement (tellingly elaborated on Valparaiso's Web site under the rubric of Faith and Learning): "The University aims to develop in its members these values (respect for learning and truth, for human dignity, for freedom from ignorance and prejudice, for a critically inquiring spirit), together with a sense of vocation and social responsibility. It holds that these values receive their deepest meaning and strength within the context of the Christian faith."[56]

Right after its mission statement, the university addresses directly the issue of faith and learning:

> The University's concern for the personal and intellectual development of each student is rooted in its Lutheran heritage. This Christian philosophy of education guides both the design of its curriculum and the approach to learning that it fosters. Beyond the courses in theology which the curriculum provides, the University emphasizes a Christian freedom which liberates the scholar to explore any idea and theory, a vocation freely uniting faith and intellectual honesty. . . . Standing together at the center of campus, the Chapel of the Resurrection and Moellering Memorial Library express the University's belief in the creative relationship between faith and learning.[57]

Perhaps the jewel in Valparaiso's crown is Christ College, its honors college. It is "dedicated to the cultivation of intellectual, moral and spiritual virtues," an emphasis that grows out of the vision of its current dean, Mark Schwehn, one of America's leading authorities on Christian higher

---

56. *1999-2000 General Catalog of Valparaiso University*, p. 5.
57. *1999-2000 General Catalog of Valparaiso University*, p. 6.

education.[58] Besides affirming that these needed virtues are religiously generated, the honors college points to its very name as a symbol of the fruitful combination of the humanities and the Christian intellectual tradition. It has successfully drawn bright Lutheran students, who constitute 70-80 percent of its approximately three hundred students. After working through the major traditions of human thought in its rigorous first year core, it requires a course in the Christian tradition and several courses that probe the methodologies of the natural and social sciences as well as the humanities. The college has its own faculty, almost all of whom are trained in theology in addition to their own special discipline.

The two extensive core courses in the first year of the standard, non-honors curriculum contain a number of Christian readings. Further, two courses in theology are required, one at the foundational level, which can be an introductory course in Bible, Christian thought, Christian ethics, or world religions. A second course requirement in the non-honors curriculum involves a wide variety of choices in Bible, theology, church history, ethics, or world religions. These courses are required not only in the College of Arts and Sciences but also in the undergraduate schools of engineering, business, and nursing.

Given such an array of required religion courses, Valparaiso, like the other schools surveyed, maintains a large theology department of around a dozen professors. Along with its heavy service commitments, the department is educating around forty majors. Until the late 1980s it was entirely Lutheran. The 1990s brought a great transition, however, the result of eight or nine of its Missouri Synod stalwarts retiring. However, a number of them had already left the Missouri Synod after the great church turbulence of the mid-1970s, as did a number of currently serving Lutherans. (Neither Valparaiso nor its theology department can be understood without attending to the fallout of that great conflict.) As the traditional source of theologians was cut off or shunned, the department recruited in new fields with very mixed results. A portion of the department has turned toward a religious studies approach, while a minority has embraced a strongly revisionist theological posture. Neither cohort is interested in the old role of the department as the bearer of the Lutheran vision in the university. Realizing

58. For Schwehn's full elaboration of the role of religiously generated virtues in academic life, see his *Exiles from Eden: Religion and the Academic Vocation in America* (New York: Oxford University Press, 1993).

this disunity in the department, the university has established three endowed chairs for distinguished Lutheran scholars in ethics, theology and literature, and the healing arts. But that has not brought complete peace or cohesiveness to the department, even though it has brought acclaim for the widely respected accomplishments of those scholars.

Valparaiso has bolstered its Lutheran and Christian identity by organizing a remarkable number of programs, projects, and initiatives, many of them funded by the Lilly Endowment. The Lilly Fellows Program in the Humanities and the Arts was established in 1991 precisely to stimulate a nationwide conversation on church-related education. Along with a large array of conferences and workshops, it includes a training program for six postdoctoral fellows who teach at the university and construct ways of relating faith and learning. Valparaiso is planning a Program in the Theological Exploration of Vocation, supported by Lilly, which is intended to work this doctrine into the larger offerings of the university. It is home to the Valparaiso Project on Education and Formation of People in Faith and to the Project on Visual Culture of American Religions, both of which are also funded by Lilly. Each of these programs and projects is administered by a Christian intellectual who makes significant contributions to the larger educational world as well as to Valparaiso.

In the day-to-day life of university departments, the integration of faith and learning is a rather mixed bag. The natural sciences have a number of evangelicals who integrate faith and learning along Reformed lines. There continue to be outstanding Lutheran intellectuals and those from other theological traditions who make significant scholarly contributions and who in their classrooms engage the Christian intellectual framework. But there are whole departments that have little interest in such engagement. There are even small pockets of secularist resistance.

Valparaiso is taking more care these days in its hiring policies. The department chairs are encouraged by the dean of Arts and Sciences to recruit only candidates who are committed to the mission of a Christian university in the Lutheran tradition. The provost interviews all finalists with the same criterion in mind. In recent years the president has insisted on strong Lutheran appointments in the theology department and the chapel. The board of directors, which is 92 percent Lutheran, presses the administration to increase Lutheran numbers.

Unfortunately, new hires are given little disciplined introduction to the tradition of the university. Their orientation only touches upon

Valparaiso's vision of faith and learning, and they meet only a few times during the year to discuss it. There are, of course, many resources for new and continuing faculty to learn about Valparaiso's tradition on their own. In celebration of its seventy-fifth anniversary as a Lutheran school, the university published an excellent book on its history and vision, *The Lutheran Reader,* which includes many helpful essays as well as the massive study Valparaiso did in 1992 on its Lutheran character. *The Cresset* produces an annual issue on the nature of the Christian university. The anniversary is also the occasion for an anticipated new history of the university by Richard Baepler entitled *Flame of Faith, Lamp of Learning.* Further, many conferences and concerts will be held to commemorate the school's founding as a Lutheran university. Like St. Olaf, Valparaiso seems in constant reflection about its identity and mission.

The Christian faith finds its way into the life of the university in ways as diverse as Valparaiso's academic offerings themselves. A new museum of art has sacred art as one of its emphases. The law school accentuates pro bono work and focuses academically on matters of church-state relations and church law. The theater department has a liturgical drama group called "Soul Purpose" that performs widely. The university hosts a deaconess-training institute that prepares women for church vocations. Its academic programs in choral and instrumental music are excellent vehicles for the expression of Christian faith.

With all these good things, what, then, presents any sort of danger for the future of Valparaiso as a Christian university in the Lutheran tradition? The threat resides precisely in this: Valparaiso's relation to its sponsoring tradition is increasingly tenuous. While there are still many Missouri Synod administrators and faculty at the school, that number is declining. There are many reasons for this. One is that official Missouri Synod has increasingly been captured by a reactionary faction that looks with suspicion upon Valparaiso's brand of free Christian humanism. The denomination gives no financial support to the university, and many of its congregations refuse to send students to it. Some congregations still support the school with money and students and these are eagerly cultivated by the university. Further, because of the turmoil of the past and the doctrinal repression in the present, the Missouri Synod educational system is not producing nearly the number of solidly formed intellectuals it once did. Missouri Synod parishes are not offering the number of students to the university they once did. Thus, Valparaiso has a much smaller natural supply of prospective faculty and students from its own sponsoring tradition. Because of these developments, it looks to the Evangelical Lutheran Church in America for an additional supply of both faculty and students. To some extent that strategy is working, as is its effort to recruit more Catholics and evangelicals. But the university's relation to these other communions is fluid and informal. Can they be counted on in the future? Can the university persist as a Lutheran university without its deep though indirect connection to Missouri Synod Lutheranism?

The tortured recent history of Valparaiso's Missouri Synod connection presents a unique challenge. The painful effects of the great Missouri Synod conflict of the mid-1970s linger within the university. Those wounded in that division have highly ambivalent attitudes toward Valparaiso's sponsoring tradition, and some go beyond ambivalence to downright contempt. Those attitudes don't help the university's continuing relationship with Missouri Synod parishes and persons. Moreover, a number of faculty members feel homeless with regard to religious life. Their beloved tradition died . . . or was killed. Since the attack came from the right, they distrust all classical or conservative Christians — including evangelicals — and lean toward a liberal revisionism that moves too easily in the direction of secularization. It will be at least another decade before these attitudes wane with the retirement of the affected generation. So, in this confusing situation, from whence will the resolve come to recruit faculty who are committed to the classic Lutheran character of the university?

Given this potential for theological upheaval, it is clear that the original Kretzmann vision needs to be renewed or reinterpreted along more Lutheran, dialectical lines. The generation that articulated the originating vision is passing from the scene. A replenished theological vision for the university needs to be forcefully and clearly articulated by those in key leadership positions. Then the university has to have the resolve to hire according to that vision and educate its new faculty into it. Without more clarity and resolve, the critical mass of Lutheran intellectuals so long enjoyed by Valparaiso may be diluted and even dissolved.

Concluding Reflections

It seems clear that the vision of each of the six schools is connected to the strong religious traditions that have sponsored those schools. Those traditions — Reformed, evangelical, Catholic, and Lutheran — have provided the resources for a compelling vision on the part of each college or university, which has become the organizing paradigm for the life and mission of each school. That religious vision constitutes a comprehensive, unsurpassable, and central Christian account of life and reality. Confidence in that account has enabled each school to make the religious vision paradigmatic.

Each religious vision takes on articulated form in the mission statement of each college or university. In most cases that articulated form is only implicitly theological. Its full theological elaboration is found elsewhere in the school's intellectual resources. In some few cases, such as Calvin and Notre Dame, the mission statement itself is explicitly theological, but even those are fairly sketchy and await elaboration elsewhere in the school's reflective apparatus. Nevertheless, judgments can be made about the theological adequacy of the schools' articulated vision. Chapter Two argued that the slide by so many other schools into secularization was precipitated at least in part by inadequate theologies, and the vision articulated in the mission statements examined here has been crucial in helping to avoid (at least for now) a similar slide.

The six schools in this study have either possessed or striven for adequate theological articulations. While both Wheaton and Baylor inherited weak theological articulation because of their pietist background, both have sought more adequate explications in systematic theology, which is increasingly providing disciplined reflection on the biblical narratives that both schools have rightly taken as normative. Those systematic reflections offer more organized and methodical accounts of, for example, a Christian view of human nature, which than can be employed in the efforts to integrate faith into broader fields of learning.

All six of the schools were confident enough in the efficacy of the Christian vision to prevent a lapse into the kind of liberalizing theology that played such an important role in the secularization of the elite mainstream Protestant colleges and universities. The classic faith, articulated in creedal affirmations (Wheaton) or in coherent theologies (Notre Dame, Calvin, St. Olaf, Valparaiso), or evidenced in faithful religious participation (Baylor), was not thinned to near transparency by adaptation to the philosophical or educational trends of the day. Such adaptations, often attempted with the laudable intent of rescuing the faith from "irrelevancy," have been way stations to the complete extirpation or marginalization of the classic religious vision in all too many schools.

Though half of the six schools (Wheaton, Baylor, and St. Olaf) have struggled with the limitations of the "two-spheres" or "add-on" approach, all of them seem to be trying to move beyond it. In all six, the Christian theological account has the necessary epistemological status to provide a real partner in the dialogue with various fields of learning. Without such status for the Christian intellectual tradition the life of a college, its faculty, and its students is bifurcated into two unconnected realms of faith and learning. And it is clear which realm wins out in the educational world if such a bifurcation is fostered at even church-related colleges and universities. Religious ethos will in time be overcome by secular learning without the necessary Christian curricular vision to reinforce it.

None of the schools currently struggles with the kind of reactionary responses to secular learning in which a rigid biblicism or repristinating confessionalism holds sway. Wheaton is protected from militant fundamentalism by its board's commitment to the moderate evangelicalism of Billy Graham, though it could face real tensions with several of its constituencies as it slowly purges fundamentalist vestiges from its Statement of Belief. Baylor has insulated its governance — and thereby its vision — from the direct control of the Baptist General Convention of Texas, even though that convention is currently in the hands of "moderates." Valparaiso has always been an independent Lutheran university, which status has protected it from the depredations of a marauding Missouri Synod right wing. Notre Dame worries about losing its autonomy to a conservative hierarchy, but that seems far-fetched even if there are juridical requirements or mandates for its theologians and for Catholic faculty majorities. Such requirements will more likely be irritants that can be managed than tragedies that cannot. Calvin, being so directly connected to the Christian Reformed Church, may be susceptible to ongoing theological skirmishes, but it is difficult to envision the kind of warfare that would do it great damage. St. Olaf has little to worry about from its sponsoring tradition, since it rarely monitors theological expression. So in spite of the dangers of reactionary impulses that may harass the schools here and there, secularization is by far the more dangerous opponent.

The Catholic, Reformed, and Lutheran religious traditions have provided these schools with adequate theologies, if they are indeed given proper epistemological status in the educational processes of the various schools. No more need be said about the substance of those theologies. But it seems important to end this discussion of the "vision" dimension of these schools with two provisos — one philosophical and one pedagogical.

In the pre–Vatican II Catholic university, philosophy played an integrating role among the disciplines. Moreover, it was the handmaiden of theology, providing the framework for the theological penetration of the university as well as important warrants for theological claims. That role of philosophy has seemingly departed forever. However, the Reformed approach exemplified by Calvin College employs philosophy as a means of analyzing the worldview assumptions present in the many disciplines. By exposing them as worldviews based on faith commitments, that approach has opened the door for serious dialogue with those disciplines on the part of Christian worldview claims. This has been an extremely important development that has relativized and "cut down to size" the sometimes arrogant claims of secular fields. This Kuyperian approach has provided a way for Christian theology to return to the quest for truth on at least equal terms with secular approaches. Indeed, in Calvin's faith and learning integration model, Christian theology has the upper hand.

The specific Kuyperian philosophical approach need not be required for philosophy's new role in the Christian college or university. Catholic and Lutheran philosophers have long had their own means of doing this in-depth analysis of presuppositions.[59] The role of philosophy in the future of all these schools will be indispensable on several fronts beyond worldview analysis. First, it should focus on epistemology, probing the methodological claims of all the fields. Every Christian school should have courses on the philosophy of science, social science, history, literature, religion, and the arts. The claims of reason, experience, and imagination have to be critically scrutinized along with those of revelation. Such philosophizing can set the rules of engagement between faith (revelation) and learning (reason, experience, imagination), so that extremely fruitful conversations can go on.

Each theological tradition will relate the claims of revelation and secular learning in different ways. Catholics will see more convergences because of the high view of reason they hold. But they also will hold those claims up to "critical review," as the Notre Dame mission statement puts it.

---

59. For example, see the brilliant analysis of the social sciences as anti-theologies in John Milbank, *Theology and Social Theory: Beyond Secular Reason* (Oxford: Blackwell, 1990).

The Reformed will tend to give reason lesser status, not only because it is fallen but because it is finitely related to and employed by specific traditions. Thus, secular learning will more often have to retreat before Christian worldview claims. Lutherans will see revelation and reason in a paradoxical relation, one that will sometimes lead to irresolvable divergences along with significant overlapping convergences, all having come about after a long and tense conversation. The most important thing for these schools is not that they carry on the conversation the same way, but that the conversation goes on in a serious and authentic way — something that cannot happen if the theological account is not given epistemological status.

Pedagogical implications follow from these epistemological and theological stances. The Reformed, in both their classical and evangelical guises, will be more likely to aim at the transformation of their students. Their epistemological confidence accompanies more sanctificationist theological commitments. They will address both mind and heart. Catholics and Lutherans will be less insistent, it seems to me, because their epistemologies are not so confident, though Catholics may well join the Reformed in their sanctificationist hopefulness. But none of the parties will retreat to a "detached" posture so characteristic of the religious studies approach regnant in so many colleges and universities. This is partly because they know that there is no such thing as a "detached" perspective, but mostly because they think their religious account of the truth is so precious that they must pass it on.

6 | *Ethos*

The focus of the following chapter will be on the "way of life" elements in the schools before us. If the preceding chapter centered on the intellectual, especially theological, dimension of the religious account that shapes the life of each school, this chapter will give attention to the non-curricular practices, traditions, patterns of life, and values that add as much religious character to each school as the intellectual dimension of its religious life. When these two elements, vision and ethos, are borne by persons from the sponsoring tradition and combined richly in the life of a college or university, a genuine Christian educational community emerges from the religious account of that tradition.

Calvin College

It is again altogether fitting to begin with Calvin College, which has had such an admirable history of defining its vision clearly. Does it have as rich an ethos? We can begin with campus worship, one of the Christian practices indispensable in maintaining and transmitting an ethos.

Though the college has always had worship services, the chapel building itself was a latecomer to the profile of buildings at the college. Calvin has been determined to focus its efforts on bringing a religious perspective to bear in the classroom, and it long considered a separate building for chapel to be unnecessary or even detrimental to that cause. It symbolically chose to hold its chapel services in an auditorium used for several different educational endeavors instead. But since the decision was made to build a chapel and develop a vibrant worship life around it, there has been no turning back. It is instructive to note that along with its chaplaincy, Calvin has created the position of dean of the chapel, which is occupied by a distinguished preacher and writer. Cornelius Plantinga, formerly a professor at Calvin Seminary and one of the Christian Reformed Church's leading theologians, was recently appointed to that post. That was a strong symbolic move to indicate the importance of worship and preaching at the college.

The protected chapel time is a daily twenty-minute period between 10:00 and 10:20 A.M. Attendance is voluntary. The worship schedule is varied, ranging from faculty/staff interpretations of scripture to simple services of song and prayer to the popular Friday hymn sing. Three to six hundred community members attend on the first three days of the week. Attendance falls to 50-200 on Thursday but rebounds strongly to a capacity 800-900 for the hymn sing on Friday. The chapel is also packed on Sunday night for LOFT, "Living Our Faith Together," which is a blend of traditional structure and contemporary music planned by a group of students and a minister.

Worship is not confined to the chapel, however. The seven dorms of roughly 250 students apiece host twenty to thirty minutes of devotional time on three evenings per week. Three of the dorms have "praise bands" that lead hymn sings in the context of the devotions.[1] An apartment complex for older students has devotions on Wednesday evenings. The character of these devotional sessions and of LOFT has been shaped by the significant number of non-Christian Reformed evangelical students who have arrived at Calvin in recent years. The evangelical emphasis on expressiveness, spontaneity, and "born again" enthusiasm coexists with the more restrained Dutch Calvinist piety of the students from the Christian Reformed Church, which itself has felt the influence of evangelical worship styles in recent years. It will be interesting to see how Calvin's future ethos will be affected by this evangelicalism.

There are approximately seventy Bible study groups in the dorms, each made up of about half a dozen students. Each dorm has a spiritual activities coordinator, and the dorm staffs meet weekly with prayer and de-

1. Information about student worship and devotional life comes from Sue Rozeboom, Assistant to the Dean of the Chapel.

votions. Other religious activities are sponsored by the Cross Bearers, a campus-wide organization of fifty leaders devoted to the stimulation of spiritual growth on campus. The campus chaplain has organized a mentoring program wherein a student is matched with a member of the faculty or staff. Approximately a hundred students and a like number of faculty and staff participate in this program, which focuses on, among other things, the spiritual life of the students. Several academic and administrative departments quietly set aside a specific time for weekly or monthly prayer.

Piety seems to be alive and well among Calvin's faculty, staff, and students. Often, however, "orthodox" schools like Calvin get saddled with the stereotype of focusing only on personal, perhaps even other-worldly, religious piety with little attention to the ills of the world. Nothing could be further from the truth at Calvin. Indeed, Calvin got into voluntary community service long before most state schools ever thought of it. Already in 1964 a group of students organized the Student Volunteer Service program. It grew steadily; by the late 1970s, 50 percent of the graduating Calvin women and 35 percent of the men were involved in community service.[2] As the college began to see that service was also the occasion for learning, it established the Service Learning Center in 1993 and integrated service into a selected number of courses. It now has a high degree of involvement in its surrounding community, and it offers spring break service journeys to a number of destinations. All told, about 1800 Calvin students and a third of the faculty are involved in service activities in any given year. Tellingly, the college justifies its involvement in service by appealing to its Christian mission. Students learn that "the least of these" are God's children, and that they can learn much from those they serve, just as the Bible contends that the last shall be first and that servers are served. Further, as students become fully present in the many places in which they serve, they are transformed and then become agents of transformation in the surrounding community.

Calvin is willing to insist that its faculty and students live a moral and well-ordered life, a Christian life according to Reformed ideals. Rather than a laissez-faire approach to student life with a predominant rhetoric of freedom, the college proposes a Christian vision of life on

---

2. See Calvin's "History of Student Service" on its Web site, www.calvin.edu/admin/slc.

campus. Positively stated, this vision aims at a loving, caring, and just community in which "the tasks of our daily life are guided by faithfulness to the Word."[3] However, it is further recognized that all persons will not live up to that "law of love," so the college is willing to elaborate a code of proscribed conduct. The code is a detailed catalogue of actions that are essentially violations of the Ten Commandments. Students are not required to pledge avoidance of such bugaboos as dancing and drinking (though drinking is prohibited on campus), but are nevertheless expected to comport themselves in a responsible Christian manner. The guidelines for life together are not shaped by the utilitarian nostrums of a "public health ethic"; rather, the college appeals to specifically Christian morality in both its positive and negative imperatives. And it seems ready to stand behind them.

These standards for community life are obviously not left up to definition by a professionalized and secular student affairs division, as is the case with many colleges. The faculty is much involved in shaping them. Indeed, the new curriculum to be unveiled in 2001 will deal more intentionally with character formation and with the virtues necessary for Christians to cope with everyday life in the world. Such an ambitious goal, in addition to the requirements of integrating faith and learning on the intellectual level, entails a lot of faculty cohesion and commitment. Though inhabiting a fairly large liberal arts college, the faculty and staff at Calvin seem to exhibit a goodly number of covenantal commitments, befitting a Reformed view of life together. The faculty and staff see a lot of each other, and they take responsibility for each other. They care enough about the college's identity and mission to have principled disagreements. Commitments to the school go far beyond the contractual attitudes of many who teach at schools that do not share so many basic convictions. The faculty, staff, and students share a common narrative and history that gives solidarity to the life of the college.

Calvin has a history of being strong in several sports, especially basketball and cross country. Its success — Calvin won the NCAA Division III Men's Basketball Championship in 2000 — adds a good deal to its school spirit, as do its fine choral programs. It sponsors many events that illustrate its commitment to the integration of faith and learning. Its January Series is well known in the region and increasingly around the country; fif-

3. *Calvin College Student Handbook 1998-99*, p. 1.

teen consecutive weekdays are used during its interim term to showcase speakers of note on a variety of subjects. Its summer seminars in Christian scholarship have already been mentioned. Calvin also hosts major conferences on faith and writing. A typical year will find several dozen writers, including some very well known names, invited to connect their faith commitments with their writing. These faith and writing events draw up to two thousand participants every other year. The college's special events are an extension of its firm commitment that Christianity deals with the life of the mind as well as the heart.

An unusual quality of Calvin is its egalitarian character, which follows perhaps from its Reformed distaste for pomp and display. Almost all students who apply are accepted; then the winnowing begins. Standards of behavior apply to all. There is no such thing as "merit pay." Faculty salaries are publicly known, since they depend only upon longevity and rank.

Built on all these different pillars — public worship, rich devotional life, vigorous commendation of the Christian way of life, community solidarity, sports, and special events of a highly intellectual nature, the community ethos at Calvin has a "thick" quality. The college not only possesses a sharp theological vision of its identity and mission, its community is shored up by a rich variety of practices that give that vision living texture. Much of this is dependent, of course, on the unanimity with which Calvin begins — all faculty and staff must be participants in a particular religious tradition — and students come from that tradition or from other traditions that admire what Calvin has to offer. But the college combines all these ingredients into a vibrant and effective Christian community of learning, not one that is repressive or dour. No doubt there are more than a few students for whom this is all too much, leading them to rebellion or apathy. No doubt Calvin's basic unanimity becomes a bit safe and bland. Certainly Calvin could afford to represent other Christian traditions on its faculty. But, all in all, the college has combined educational quality with commitment to Christianity in an impressive way, which, for all intents and purposes, seems to be assured for the foreseeable future.

Wheaton College

It would be a safe prediction that a school whose Christian character was historically of the add-on variety would have a strong Christian ethos about it, even after it had adopted an integrationist approach to faith and learning from its Reformed sister school. And the prediction would certainly be accurate. As far as a public, pervasive religious piety goes, it would be hard to surpass Wheaton College. Not only does the institution foster and encourage such piety, but the large numbers of enthusiastic evangelical students also bring it to the school from their home congregations. Besides the eerie absence of smoking students, a remarkable feature of Wheaton's daily life is its natural display of evangelical piety. Students pray together with faculty over a cup of coffee in the student lounge before they launch into a discussion of a literary text. Faculty members pray before class. Students witness to each other. In addition to their many opportunities for worship on campus during the week, over half the students attend local churches on a Sunday morning.[4]

With this kind of momentum, even required chapel three times a week comes as a boon, not as a burden, for at least the great majority of students. Wheaton is the only school in our study that requires chapel of all undergraduate students throughout their time there (Baylor has a modified requirement system). At Wheaton chapel attendance is part of the students' "spiritual life commitment" included in its "Statement of Responsibilities," which all students must sign upon admission. (They are, however, allowed 9 absences per semester.) All 2400 students fit in Edman Chapel three times a week, from 10:35 to 11:15 A.M., where they participate in a distinctly evangelical style of worship.

Under the direction of a chaplain who is an ordained Presbyterian minister, the chapel services generally include sacred music, extemporaneous prayer, Bible reading, and an address or sermon by someone of spiritual stature. Since the chaplain has involved students in the planning of chapel there have been few complaints about its required nature. While only 25-50 faculty come on any given day, a much larger number tune in to the service on campus TV or radio. The president speaks at chapel once a month, while faculty, chaplain, and staff take their turns. Outside guest speakers are often nationally known figures in the evangelical world as well as a surprising number of mainstream Christian intellectuals. There is also provision for a special chapel for faculty and staff on Thursdays and one for graduate students on Wednesdays in the Graham Center.

4. The data in this section was gathered in interviews by the author with various Wheaton College personnel during a visit to the college in November 1999.

Religious life in the dorms is just as impressive as the worship in chapel. A dozen student leaders with the help of 125 sub-leaders sustain Discipleship Small Groups that reach 500-600 students. These groups are dedicated to the spiritual formation of students through Bible study, prayer, and mutual support. Flowing from Wheaton's historic commitment to foreign missions, its World Christian Fellowship meets in small groups during the week but in one large group of 500-800 for Sunday revivals to challenge students to explore their role in fulfilling the Great Commission. A striking feature of Wheaton is its wall of names in the administration building that honors the hundreds of Wheaton students who have gone into foreign missions. Instead of athletes or donors, the school honors missionaries. The chaplain's office also oversees three full-time and three part-time counselors, who help students through the standard crises but do it in a Christian way. Since Wheaton has a graduate program in clinical psychology with a strong Christian orientation, the chaplain's office has ready access to counselors with a Christian perspective.

Perhaps even more powerful than these formal, organized programs sustained by the college are the ways students challenge other students. Students are continually confronted with the clarion call to live "For Christ and His Kingdom." Heroic standards of Christian perfection become the marks by which students judge themselves. Through these standards they are spurred on to stronger efforts to live up to Christian ideals.

Much student energy is directed into ministry and service projects. As one might guess, Wheaton's emphasis on evangelism makes it difficult to distinguish between evangelism and service. Both are generally and genuinely mixed. To put it in biblical terms, the Word accompanies the cup of cold water, and vice versa. Over six hundred students participate in the Office of Christian Outreach programs, forty-four ministries ranging from tutoring to jail visitation. There are also extensive summer "holistic" ministries at home and abroad. Though evangelicals are often stigmatized as caring only for souls and not bodies, Wheaton has had for twenty-five years a strong program called Human Needs and Global Resources (HNGR). This program consists of sixteen to eighteen hours of rigorous preparatory academic work and then a six-month internship in a developing country with a Christian organization involved in holistic responses to poverty.[5]

5. *Catalog of Wheaton College 1999-2000*, p. 87.

Enthusiastic participation in these many programs is assured by the kind of students Wheaton draws from all over the country and abroad. Since evangelical communities are growing in the United States and increasing in both economic and educational status, a large contingent of bright evangelical students want to come to Wheaton. But on top of that is an additional screening device, "The Statement of Responsibilities," which all students and faculty are required to sign.[6] The statement lifts up five biblical principles that are then elaborated into very specific behavioral components of a Christian lifestyle. Perhaps the most controversial are those that prohibit the use of tobacco and alcohol, not only on campus but also in private life off campus. The statement includes many positive injunctions and virtues but does not hesitate to proscribe behavior that the Bible "condemns as morally wrong," including pre-marital sex and homosexual behavior. Through the statement — and the enforcement of it in both informal biblical and formal juridical ways — the college cultivates "a campus atmosphere in which moral and spiritual growth can thrive," one in which students are encouraged to make conscious choices for a Christian lifestyle rather than "mere acceptance of prevailing practices in society at large."[7]

All of this is not foisted upon the students by a distant faculty beholden to a different set of standards. On the contrary, faculty themselves are not only willing signers of "The Statement of Faith" (discussed in Chapter Five) but also the "Statement of Responsibilities." While a few "interpret" their way around its proscriptions, the vast majority consider it a gesture of Christian integrity to abide by those proscriptions even if they don't agree with them. One of the criteria for hiring both faculty and staff at Wheaton is their willingness and ability to act as spiritual mentors for each other and for the students. It is not unusual to see faculty and students in serious discussion and prayer over important spiritual issues. The college as a whole has enough confidence and clarity in the Christian account of religion and morality that it is willing to embody that account in a concrete way of life.

While sports are done well at Wheaton, they do not play a dominant role. Wheaton also has an excellent Conservatory of Music that is visible

6. *Catalog of Wheaton College 1999-2000*, pp. 16-17. See also the on-line catalog at www.wheaton.edu.

7. *Catalog of Wheaton College 1999-2000*, p. 16.

and audible in the life of the college. Its Billy Graham Center provides a strong endorsement of evangelism and world missions with its many institutes and its fine museum on the history of evangelism. Wheaton's commitment to spread the Gospel in these many ways is certainly a distinctive quality of the school. It makes its appellation "evangelical" seem very accurate indeed.

Through these various instruments, Wheaton unabashedly aims "to develop exceptional Christian students into whole and effective servants of Jesus Christ."[8] This means that both the classroom and the dorm provide exercises in Christian formation. However, it is in "Christian community" that Wheaton makes its most potent claim on student lives.

Student response to this strong evangelical claim on their minds and hearts seems varied. The large majority wholeheartedly endorses the evangelical ethos that envelops and challenges them. They use the occasion to deepen and enrich their commitments. Already highly motivated and intelligent, they enthusiastically engage the institutional purposes that Wheaton sets out so clearly. This large cohort of students strives for Christian maturity. Another group seems to cooperate with a lesser degree of sincerity and maturity. Since they are rewarded to act in a Christian way, they do so out of peer reinforcement. They may leave many tensions in their lives unresolved but on the surface seem cooperative and enthused. A third and much smaller group reacts against the pervasive ethos but yet are unwilling to give up their faith. They augment their struggles and doubts with a genuine search for a faith that may look very different from the norm at Wheaton. A fourth group — very small indeed — completely rejects Wheaton's evangelical mission and ethos. They often label themselves agnostics and, depending on the time remaining until graduation, typically withdraw from the institution.[9]

As to the institutional ethos tended by the board, administration, staff, and faculty, some interesting things may be afoot as the college continues to move toward the more open world of moderate evangelicalism. Will the remaining remnants of fundamentalism and moral perfectionism

8. *Catalog of Wheaton College 1999-2000,* p. 17.

9. Interview by the author with Kevin Cumings, Dean of Student Life at Grand View College in Des Moines, Iowa. See Cumings, "Student Culture at Wheaton College: Understanding Student Life on an Evangelical College Campus" (Ph.D. dissertation, Loyola University of Chicago, 1997).

(the prohibitions against drinking, smoking, and dancing) be shed without damaging conflict with some of the more sectarian traditions that have historically supported Wheaton? Or, if they are not shed, will Wheaton be able to recruit enough quality faculty to teach its bright students? Will the movement into sophisticated mainstream culture facilitated by Wheaton's increasing intellectual excellence dampen its enthusiasm for missions and for a disciplined Christian lifestyle? Does Wheaton have the capacity to shed some of the vestiges of a "harder" evangelicalism without blending into the Protestant mainstream? For the moment, the evangelical ethos seems intense and distinct, but the American culture of success can be seductive indeed.

◆   ◆   ◆

It is appropriate at this point to move to the discussion of ethos at the two Lutheran schools, St. Olaf and Valparaiso. They are similar in size to Calvin and Wheaton and thus have more in common with them with respect to ethos than with their larger compatriots, Baylor and Notre Dame. Further, all four have until recently shared a kind of "outsider" flavor — Wheaton as an evangelical school only newly escaped from its disrepute as a fundamentalist bastion; Valparaiso, St. Olaf, and Calvin as ethnic enclaves sponsored by relatively anonymous minority religious traditions. These qualities gave each school a special kind of "over-againstness" that enabled them to maintain a distinctive ethos. Each, however, has found that those qualities have been diminished by the social changes of recent years. The Lutheran schools especially have experienced this loss of distinctiveness that once came with their ethnic and religious isolation. Thus, they have had important challenges before them to maintain a Lutheran Christian ethos without the props supplied by ethnic and religious homogeneity.

Part of this loss of unanimity is intentional, however, for St. Olaf and Valparaiso do not fit our orthodox category like Calvin and Wheaton. Theological and pedagogical reasons if not economic imperatives have led them to become critical-mass schools. They invite pluralism among faculty, staff, and students. Indeed, they are sometimes so bedazzled by current cultural trends — "inclusivity" or "diversity," for example — that they have not always thought hard enough about what kind of diversity they really want and need and what kind they should avoid. Be that as it may, these schools have embraced a kind of diversity that Calvin and Wheaton have rejected; that fact presents them with a more daunting task in cultivating Christian ethos.

One of the most important features of the ethos of a critical-mass school is that its ethos is more lightly and subtly offered. These schools commend a way of life to students and faculty; they do not challenge them to live up to the clear, public, religiously grounded standards of a very specific and detailed Christian way of life. They do not conceive of themselves as bearers of a Christian counterculture that is committed to the transformation of persons and society. Further, the Lutheran schools have theological reasons for their reluctance to codify and enforce a detailed blueprint of the Christian life; they are grounded in a theology more focused on justification than on sanctification. Therefore, there is more room for faculty and students alike to exercise their freedom to opt out of the ethos without feeling out of place or unwelcome. Because there is less solidarity around a particular way of life, there is also less capacity to transmit it to the next generation. Many other lifestyle choices are available on campus. The normative one has to be "caught" and freely accepted. There is freedom to fall by the wayside, and many do. In many ways life at these schools is very much like life in the "outside world," which they consider a strength of their approach.

St. Olaf College

St. Olaf is the only school among the six with an organized student congregation, one dating back to 1952, long before the fad of organizing student congregations waxed and then waned. Its pastor, who is also the college pastor, has the aid of a full-time associate pastor as well as a cantor. The college pastor is a visible and influential person at the college, where he is on the president's strategic planning team, and in the community. The congregation has a full-fledged council with four commissions: Extra-Campus, which focuses on both international justice issues and charitable activities abroad; Life and Growth, which aims to enrich student life with fellowship experiences, Bible study groups, and discussions; Stewardship, which connects its members to service opportunities and collects money for noteworthy projects, especially in Tanzania; and Worship, which helps to plan the many services that go on in the chapel during the year. These services are held in the large (capacity 1600), centrally located, neo-gothic Boe Memorial Chapel, which also hosts many concerts, lectures, and festivals. It is connected with and architecturally complemented by the fine, newly built student center. St. Olaf's architecture itself seems pedagogical. The solid gothic building style suggests, as one professor put it long ago, "the permanence and power of the religious and intellectual ideas which it is to shelter."[10] The campus is also adorned with religious art and sculpture. There is no doubt this is a college connected to the church.

In addition to the main Sunday service, chapel is held daily through the week with an additional Wednesday evening communion service. The daily services are held during set-aside times of twenty minutes each morning. Even the bookstore closes down for chapel. About 100-200 St. Olaf students and faculty attend on any given day, though special holy days such as Ash Wednesday will find the chapel filled to near capacity. These services are dramatically enhanced by the artistic resources made available by the college's extensive programs in instrumental and choral music as well as other performing arts. On Sundays, for example, six of the college choirs take turns providing music for worship. But ensembles running from trombone sextets to faculty soloists enrich ordinary mid-week services as well. These services are shared with the campus community by St. Olaf's radio station, WCAL, the nation's first listener-supported radio service, which also is beamed to many thousands more through its outlets in the Twin Cities and Rochester. Several of the religious and musical programs produced on campus are broadcast nationwide. Christian worship enriched by fine music is a strong part of the public ethos at St. Olaf.

In many Lutheran colleges, music — especially choral music — plays an important part in expressing and transmitting the religious aspirations of those colleges' ethos.[11] In St. Olaf's instance, this tradition is not one among many; it is the pioneer and premier among them all. F. Melius Christiansen, one of the great heroes of St. Olaf history, was not only the founder of choral music at St. Olaf at the beginning of the twentieth century, he was also the "inventor" of the sacred choral concert in the country

10. Carl Mellby, as quoted by DeAne Lagerquist, "Campus Culture" (unpublished manuscript), p. 4.

11. One distinguished but crusty retired eminence remarked to me with sharp but humorous precision: "Too much can be made of this music stuff. Don't you know that music is the opiate of the Lutheran masses?"

as a whole. St. Olaf has maintained and built on this powerful tradition to the point where the college is synonymous with fine choral music. The choir has been so important that it now has a book written about it by the college historian. In fact, the college has eight choirs, three bands, and two full orchestras. Most of these ensembles — a total of five hundred student musicians — work together in its annual Christmas Festival. Sixteen thousand people attend the concert in person while millions hear and see it through public radio and television. All told, the numerous music programs at St. Olaf are estimated to involve from 30-40 percent of the student body. Music at St. Olaf is not a spectator sport.

Moreover, the directors of the music programs self-consciously imbue their teaching and conducting with Christian content. Faculty and students alike savor the transparency of sacred music to spiritual aspiration. Students conduct devotions before concerts and in some cases even before practice. St. Olaf's current head conductor, Anton Armstrong (who graduated from St. Olaf and also spent many years directing choirs at Calvin), affirms that "the St. Olaf choir exists to praise God in sacred song."[12] It is certainly not a stretch to claim that many students find their spiritual lives deepened significantly by participating in the extensive music life of the college.

It seems that students are surrounded by conductors, instructors, staff, and fellow students to whom the Lutheran doctrine of the calling is essential. The already mentioned book, *Called to Serve: St. Olaf and the Vocation of a Church College,* contains essays from "Oles" both past and present, both famous and obscure, who have had their occupations transformed by the beckon of God into genuine callings. This "sense of the calling of all Christians" is one of the leitmotifs of the college that is effectively communicated to many students. Moreover, St. Olaf is fortunate to be in an area of the country where there are many college-bound Lutheran students to recruit. It has been able to keep its Lutheran student enrollment at about half and add a significant portion of Catholics as well (16 percent). Students with these religious backgrounds prove receptive to what St. Olaf has to offer.

In addition to the extensive work of the student congregation's Life and Growth Commission, there are many other groups and agencies at

---

12. Anton Armstrong, chief conductor of the St. Olaf choir, interview with the author, October 1999.

work in the dorms to nurture young Christians. The Christian Activities Network, the Fellowship of Christian Athletes, Young Life, InterVarsity Christian Fellowship, Thursday Night Bible Study, the Catholic Student Organization, and the Forum for Inter-Religious Dialogue are examples. Because very few students live off campus and because the college has a restrictive car policy, students tend to stay on campus or in Northfield, quite a small town. This makes St. Olaf a tightly knit community in which these various forms of Christian outreach can work effectively. Christian outreach must be effective in generating or confirming the faith of many students because St. Olaf supplies more seminarians to divinity schools and seminaries than any other Lutheran college or university.[13]

Adding to this cohesion and to the formation of the Christian virtues of love and justice are the many possibilities for service. The Student Volunteer Network coordinates opportunities in Northfield and the surrounding area. Many of the standard outlets are available — Habitat for Humanity, Project Friendship, Bread for the World, Amnesty International, and local church and hospital service. Obviously St. Olaf students take these activities seriously, because St. Olaf has been for the last seventeen years the number one source of volunteers for the Lutheran Volunteer Corps (a Lutheran version of a domestic Peace Corps) and the leading point of origin among liberal arts colleges for candidates for the Peace Corps itself. Indeed, St. Olaf as an institution tithes its students. While 70 percent of its graduates are employed immediately after graduation and 20 percent attend graduate or professional school, fully 10 percent of its students commit themselves to service organizations.[14]

St. Olaf takes a far less aggressive *in loco parentis* role than either Calvin or Wheaton. The many opportunities listed above are just that, opportunities, and students are not required to respond to them. Moreover, they tend to focus on service and social ethics. There is little public rhetoric about the kind of personal Christian moral ideals so evident at Calvin and Wheaton, though the notions of service and vocation are strongly grounded in religion. Beyond the obvious prohibitions of drugs and weapons, St. Olaf also maintains a no alcoholic beverage policy for everyone on its grounds or for any of its programs if they include students. The college has no Greek organizations. The aims of the residential life program are

13. Quoted by Lagerquist in "Campus Culture," p. 22.
14. *St. Olaf Academic Catalog 1997-1998*, pp. 9-10.

couched in fairly secular language — "the development of sensitive and responsible individuals" — and allow generous visitation hours in co-ed dorms. The counseling center looks essentially like one at a secular school, though counseling is also available through the college pastor's office.[15]

The institutional ethos of St. Olaf encourages students to encounter Gospel claims in a whole range of ways. It would be nearly impossible for a student to evade some sort of serious encounter with the Christian account in either its intellectual or lifestyle dimensions. But St. Olaf, unlike the colleges in our orthodox category, would not use the language of transformation or conversion with regard to student lives. Growth and nurture would be better words. Furthermore, as befitting a critical-mass college, it is understood that not everyone is Lutheran or even Christian. Church claims and opportunities can be ignored or rejected without anyone feeling like an outsider. Among those not part of the critical mass are persons of conflicting visions and ways of life, among them the sort supplied by the culture of the great graduate schools. As their presence is made known on campus, the classical Lutheran and Christian vision is certainly challenged. The drift toward liberalizing theologies is one response to those challenges, so the liberal causes that accompany liberal theology are visible. For example, already in 1989 the student congregation at St. Olaf voted to become a "Reconciled in Christ" congregation, which means that it "publicly welcomes and affirms gay and lesbian people as children of God and participating members of our congregation."[16] This announcement, though years old, occupies a prominent place in the congregation's brochure. But the position it announces stands in an ambiguous relationship to the "classic Lutheran teachings" the brochure mentions earlier.

Since Northfield is quite small, the majority of faculty members live near the college, but growth in the number of commuters to and from the Twin Cities — currently estimated at about 20 percent — is a worrisome development. Many faculty continue to involve themselves in the lives of the students, but not so much as spiritual mentors and pastors, as do the faculty of Wheaton or Calvin. Nor are they as a whole as closely bound to the college's identity and mission as the earlier generation of Norwegian Lutherans was. While there is still a kernel of that group present at the college, the next generation of faculty and staff will have to bear the ethos of the college with-

---

15. *St. Olaf Academic Catalog*, pp. 237-38.
16. St. Olaf College student congregation brochure, p. 2.

out the natural influx of faculty and students from the once dominant ethno-religious tradition. How much "mass" is enough to be "critical"? Nevertheless, there is little doubt that St. Olaf has significant momentum as a Lutheran college going into the future. With the right choices, its ethos — full of music, worship, and calling to service — will endure.[17]

Valparaiso University

Valparaiso shares many of the same gifts and challenges as St. Olaf, but there are significant differences between the two schools. One is simply that their sponsoring traditions are quite different, though those traditions have less effect than they once had. Furthermore, as mentioned in Chapter Five, Valparaiso has a complex relationship to its sponsoring tradition, the Lutheran Church–Missouri Synod. Another significant factor is that St. Olaf has opted to remain a liberal arts college while Valparaiso decided to become a small, comprehensive university replete with business school, engineering school, nursing school, and law school. This fracturing of the student body into various schools makes the "ethos challenge" for Valparaiso more daunting than that faced by St. Olaf.

The religious ethos of Valparaiso University is carried to a large extent by the worship services and programs of the Chapel of the Resurrection, which has a full-time dean and pastor to the university (one pastor with two titles), an associate with dual titles, and an organist. The chapel was completed in 1959 with a capacity of three thousand, with additional space for assembled choirs and orchestra in the loft. An enormous Schlicker organ covers the whole western wall of the loft. The nave alone is two hundred feet long, with walls sixty feet high. Its chancel is housed in a tower one hundred feet high that is shaped like a nine-pointed star and surrounded by stained-glass panels that symbolize the work of the Holy Trinity. A huge marble altar fronts a cross from which a gold-figured risen Christ seems to be springing. The chapel, baptistery, and accompanying 140-foot-high campanile are adorned with the "highest art for the Glory of God."

---

17. An interesting assessment of St. Olaf's overall performance with regard to its heritage was made by a distinguished member of the college: "In comparison with its past, St. Olaf gets a C+; in comparison with what most other schools are doing now, St. Olaf gets an A."

It is within this magnificent space that daily chapel is held from 11:15–11:35 each morning. One hundred fifty to two hundred persons gather for worship in a variety of styles as the week progresses. As many retired as current faculty appear for these services. There are two main services on Sunday morning, an early one in the small Gloria Christi Chapel below the main chancel, and a later one in the nave. Sunday attendance generally runs less than a third of capacity for both chapels, but on special occasions will swell to capacity. While the chapel is not officially a congregation, it functions like one in many ways. There are marriages and baptisms and memorial services in the chapel. In addition to serving as a church away from home for many students, it serves as a primary church for a number of university people alienated from the school's sponsoring tradition or from denominational life in general.

There are smaller services on Sunday and weekday evenings, with the Wednesday evening praise service drawing over three hundred evangelically oriented students. While the preponderance of services are distinctly Lutheran — Valparaiso is known for its "high" liturgical practices — students from many denominations participate. Indeed, there are enough Catholic students at Valparaiso to warrant a nearby St. Teresa of Avila Catholic Student Center staffed by a full-time priest, who also leads one of the regular weekday services in the Chapel of the Resurrection. The Lutheran (37 percent of the total undergraduate enrollment), Catholic (23 percent), and evangelical (20 percent) students seem to share much of the worship yet have their own special times to get together for worship and study. It is estimated that one-third of the students participate regularly in Valparaiso's voluntary chapel life.[18]

Like St. Olaf, Valparaiso has a strong tradition of choral and orchestral music both in its formal curriculum and among its extra-curricular activities. The chapel consistently draws upon the talents of students and faculty alike to enrich the daily worship. Worship can be a marvelous religious and aesthetic experience when such talent is expressed in dignified worship in a magnificent chapel. Further, many students are enlisted into the planning and leading of worship. Such experiences have left their mark on generations of Valparaiso students and faculty.

As is the case at St. Olaf, Valparaiso's programs in music and the arts

18. Dean of the Chapel Joseph Cunningham, interview with the author, February 2000.

become vehicles for the formation of students into a Christian orientation toward the world. (The university has 140 music majors.) The conductors of its choral and orchestral programs are strong Christians who encourage student-led devotions before concerts and who themselves point out the Christian resonance in the great works of art that are performed. Valparaiso's theater program includes a troupe of actors called "Soul Purpose," which performs dramas at the university and churches throughout the country. The tours of these ensembles become spiritual journeys for many of the students. True to its ethnic heritage, Valparaiso's repertoire is more German than English or Scandinavian. The climactic concert for the university's 75th anniversary in 2000 will be a gala performance of Bach's St. Matthew's Passion.

The chapel also sends out tentacles to all the dorms and Greek houses. (National fraternities and sororities have existed at Valparaiso since World War II in spite of the Missouri Synod's suspicion of secret societies; Valparaiso and Baylor are the only schools among our six that allow Greek organizations.) These residential ministries are led by student chaplains, who conduct worship and Bible study for a student population that tends not to come to chapel. These formal programs of the chapel are supplemented by the activities of a number of religious groups — among them Valparaiso University Christian Activities Board, Fellowship of Christian Athletes, the St. Teresa of Avila Center, and Inter-Varsity Christian Fellowship. InterVarsity draws over a hundred people to its Friday night meetings, and the Fellowship of Christian Athletes reaches the preponderance of student-athletes. These combined activities are estimated to reach over three-fourths of the students at Valparaiso.[19]

In this connection it is important to note the impact of Valparaiso's basketball program on the life of the university. Faced at the beginning of the decade with consistently losing teams, Valparaiso decided to beef up its athletic programs. The star among them has been its basketball team, which has appeared in five straight NCAA Division I men's basketball tournaments. This would not be remarkable in any religious sense were it not for the team's coach, Homer Drew, who is an unmistakable Christian presence at the university and in the larger world of athletics. His strong public witness to his players and to the university in general concerning

19. Cunningham, interview.

the importance of Christian faith, as well as his exemplary demeanor, have contributed markedly to the religious atmosphere of the university.

Like all colleges and universities these days, Valparaiso emphasizes service. Again working through the chapel, the university encourages students to participate in Crop Walk, Adopt a Family, World Relief, Shelter Ministry, and a number of service jaunts on spring break. While the university has no official relation to it, the Hilltop Neighborhood Association provides an outlet for service for many students right in the backyard of the university. A number of courses involve service and learning components. Yet, all told, the university seems less vigorously involved in service than the majority of schools surveyed.

In student life, the university publicly "holds to the ideal of a community of Christian scholars living together in freedom and civility, in an environment conducive to Christian faith and supportive of the Christian ethic." Its honor system "is in every way consistent with the highest principles of Christian ethics and morality."[20] Though presented openly as the ideal way of life, these principles are more commended than sanctioned. There are some domains of university life, especially the fraternities, where Christian principles seem to have little relevance. Valparaiso has had a painful history of tension with its fraternities. The student services offices, though no doubt run by Christians, have little in their programs to distinguish them from those of a secular school. The faculty as a whole is more distant from the religious and moral formation of the students than they were when it was more heavily Lutheran.

These generalizations are less accurate when applied to Christ College, the university's fine honors college. In that community there is much more direct involvement of the faculty in the lives of the students. It is also heavily Lutheran (about 70 percent), and the strong intellectual challenge given to the students is generously supplemented by attention to the calling of each student. Many of its students successfully move into professional and educational work guided by self-conscious Christian motivation.

Like most critical-mass schools, Valparaiso gives a lot of room for students and faculty to ignore or reject its public religious ethos, and of course many do. A significant portion of students, more than at Calvin, Wheaton, or St. Olaf, are commuters who do not participate in that public ethos. The very roominess of the Valparaiso campus, as well as its division into differ-

20. *Valparaiso University General Catalog 1999-2000*, pp. 30-31.

ent professional schools, seems to work against a common way of life. The
lifestyle of many students in their day-to-day lives is distinctly secular.

Valparaiso senses that it must work hard to recruit a continuing supply of Lutheran students and faculty if its ethos is to remain Lutheran. And
it does. Since its ties to the official Missouri Synod are either weak or non-
existent, it tries hard to connect with that cohort of Missouri Synod parishes that will support it. It runs conferences for Lutheran elementary and
secondary teachers. It solicits confirmation rolls from those parishes that
will give them to the university. It organizes and hosts Lutheran youth conferences. It continues to house a Lutheran Deaconess Association. It cultivates the many Missouri Synod alumni that are likely to encourage their
children to come to Valparaiso. It also intentionally recruits Lutheran
young people from the Evangelical Lutheran Church in America. And to
some extent these steps pay off, especially in the honors college. The roster
of student and faculty names at Valparaiso still contains many recogniz-
ably German surnames of Missouri Synod provenance. These students and
faculty continue to provide definitive leadership in shaping the ethos of
the school.

Valparaiso, like St. Olaf, celebrated the anniversary of its founding
during the year 2000, though Valparaiso has only 75 years of existence as a
Lutheran school while St. Olaf has 125. If its intent to remain a Christian
university in the Lutheran tradition could be measured by the importance
of Lutheran themes in its celebrations, there would be little fear for the future. Every celebratory conference, lecture series, festival, concert, publication, and worship service is deeply shaped by concern for its Lutheran
identity and mission. Its official rhetoric and commitment are solid; what
is less solid is its ethos at the grass-roots level.

Nevertheless, that observation must be accompanied by the recognition that Lutheran schools such as St. Olaf and Valparaiso do indeed make
a difference in students' lives. There is empirical evidence to vouch for that.
The Lutheran Educational Conference of North America, disturbed that
only 5 percent of Lutheran high school graduates were going to Lutheran
colleges and universities, commissioned a study by the consulting firm
Hardwick-Day to find out the differences between students graduating
from Lutheran schools and those graduating from "flagship" public universities. Evidence of such differences, if flattering to the Lutheran schools,
would be used to help convince more Lutheran families to encourage their
young to attend Lutheran schools.

The evidence turned up by Hardwick-Day was fairly impressive. Compared to students at flagship public universities, students at Lutheran colleges like St. Olaf and Valparaiso find a more pervasive emphasis on faith and values (84 percent to 35 percent), find more occasions to interact creatively with students with similar values (79 percent to 59 percent), discover more possibilities to develop spiritually (79 percent to 24 percent), experience a much better integration of values and ethics in classroom discussions (65 percent to 25 percent), learn more about their faith and values during their college years (60 percent to 10 percent), know faculty on campus who serve as models of spiritual life (38 percent to 8 percent), integrate faith into other aspects of life better (60 percent to 14 percent), and are more likely later in life to engage in religious and church activities (64 percent to 28 percent).[21] Such findings certainly bear witness to these schools' capacity to shape students through both the intellectual and ethos dimensions of their tradition.

Baylor University

It would be difficult to escape elements of Baptist ethos in Baylor University's life even if it were a secular school. The presence of six thousand Baptist students would dictate that such elements were tangible. Over three million Southern Baptists supplemented by hundreds of thousands of independent Baptists in the state of Texas would reinforce that tangibility. No doubt even the University of Texas has a Baptist "feel" about it. Baptists constitute virtually an "established" religion in Texas. However, Baylor, unlike the University of Texas, is not a secular school. It has in fact for many years cultivated its Baptist ethos as the main ingredient of its identity and mission. Now, as elaborated in the previous chapter, there are strong efforts to integrate faith and learning. Hand in hand with that effort, a prominent Baptist ethos endures, one that is now even more consciously tended than earlier.

Baylor, though much larger than any of the schools discussed thus far in this chapter, requires chapel attendance of its undergraduate students. This is no easy logistical maneuver for a body of about 11,500 stu-

21. Hardwick-Day Study, summarized in DeAne Lagerquist, "The Religion Thing" (unpublished paper on St. Olaf's religious life, 1998), p. 24.

dents. The challenge is somewhat mitigated by the fact that Baylor requires chapel attendance for only two years of the four that most undergraduates take to get their degree. Further, students may skip seven of the twenty-seven sessions of any given semester. But if they miss more than seven, they must repeat the requirement. Most students complete this requirement in their first two years.

The chapel period is actually called Chapel-Forum. Until recently the "forum" meant that many of the speakers lectured on broadly secular matters. But the newly appointed dean of the chapel has insisted that the speakers address religious themes. Each term has a religious theme to which activists, musicians, authors, actors, and nationally-known speakers respond. For example, the focus for a recent term was on those "who excel in their callings as an expression of their commitment to Christ."[22] A variety of well-known speakers were featured, running from serious academics through pop music artists to Nobel Prize winners. The point being made was that lay Christians have great opportunities to witness to their Christian commitments in their work in the world.

Chapel-Forum must handle 4,000 students in the fall and about 2,200 in the spring. There are two sessions in Waco Hall each Monday and Wednesday; half of the term's students meet at 10:00 A.M., and half meet at 11:00 A.M. Though there is no worship per se, there are prayers offered by the dean of the chapel or other leaders. Since there are many non-religious students, Christians of other traditions than Baptist, and adherents of other world religions, attendees at the Chapel-Forum are not required to participate in hymns, liturgies, or common prayer, but must tolerate prayer that is offered by the leader. They also must hear the Christian witness offered by the speakers, though no particular response is required. In this instance, Baylor has an unusual blend of coercion and freedom for such a large school.

There are other major efforts to nurture student Christian discipleship on campus. Baptist Student Ministries (BSM), which occupies a building on campus and is funded by the Baptist General Convention of Texas and the university, has historically carried on various ministries at Baylor. One of its main approaches is Spring Revival Week, which typically includes a series of preaching events accompanied by a Christian music group. Evening and luncheon meetings are coordinated with the preaching

22. Baylor University Spring 2000 Chapel-Forum brochure, p. 1.

ministry. BSM also organizes a modest number of Bible study groups (CORE) that reach several hundred students. In order to increase the reach of these groups and to expand and coordinate its ministries, the BSM now reports to the dean of the chapel. Hopes are afoot to expand the Bible study groups fourfold.

Two other ministries are notable. Campus Crusade for Christ has a staff of seven and carries on a full range of programs both on campus and off. Touchstone, a program of Face To Face Ministries, generates an attendance of a thousand for its Monday evening sessions at First Baptist Church. It is estimated that, all told, half of Baylor's students are reached by these various ministries.[23]

It has been noted that Baylor has few overtly religious symbols or buildings, a condition perhaps appropriate to its mildly iconoclastic Baptist heritage. But it does have a carillon that wafts familiar Christian hymns across the campus after each class period. Many students seem to appreciate this element of Christian atmosphere.

Like almost all contemporary universities, and especially like church-related universities, Baylor has a strong emphasis on service, though it seems not to have gone heavily into service/learning ventures. During each semester one Saturday is devoted to Stepping Out, a program in which roughly 2,500 students spend a day in Waco tutoring, painting, cleaning, and other service activities. The university has an organization entitled Baylor CAN (Community Action Network) that entails each member devoting thirty hours of time per semester to community service in order to maintain membership. It also sponsors Students Tutoring for Literacy, Adopt-a-School, and Santa's Workshop, a pre-Christmas event to which 700 preschool Waco children come to be entertained and given gifts. Baylor also hosts the usual array of national organizations such as Habitat for Humanity and Circle K International.

The university confronts a serious challenge in imparting its religious ethos: only about 4,000 of its 13,500 students are housed in its residence halls. The majority live around the university in privately owned dwellings. Twenty-five percent of its students, almost as many as inhabit its dorms, live in off-campus fraternity and sorority houses. Since the university has little influence over these many students, the ambience of the nearby neighborhood seems like that of any large university — definitely

23. Todd Lake, Dean of the Chapel, interview with the author, March 24, 2000.

not pious. While there are no doubt many serious Christians among the off-campus student population, there are also a fair number of rebels against the dominant Baptist ethos of Baylor and Waco.

Nevertheless, the university takes it commitment to nurture the Christian life seriously. Its catalog states: "It is expected that every employee and every student will conduct himself or herself in accordance with Christian principles both on and off the campus. Personal misconduct either on or off the campus by anyone connected with Baylor detracts from the Christian mission of the university."[24] The student handbook then elaborates in some detail what is proscribed. While these injunctions are supported by a network of resident assistants in the dorms, the large majority of off-campus students are not held accountable in any direct way for them. *In loco parentis* applies only to those living on campus. Fraternities are particularly ready to act according to their own lights, while sororities are friendlier to the Christian ideals that the handbook elaborates. However, when gross violations lead to individual student distress, interventions by college authorities are not uncommon.

Faculty, though a bit uncertain about the integration of faith and learning in the classroom, are eager to encourage the Christian ethos of the school. They are willing to create a caring and supportive environment for students in their classrooms and beyond. The strong impression given by both faculty and students is one of friendly hospitality. For its size Baylor is definitely "user-friendly," and this most certainly is related to its Baptist ethos.

The university has created many institutes and centers to connect with and serve its Baptist constituency. The Center for Ministry Effectiveness, Center for Family and Community Ministries, Youth Camp, and Youth Ministry Teams provide strong links with a large and living Baptist tradition in Texas that will continue to supply Baylor with bright and committed Baptist students. Baylor's Texas Baptist constituency is a resource whose importance and influence is hard to overestimate.

Baylor has a number of special events. Its major one is primarily social. The Diadeloso (Day of the Bear) is a sixty-six-year-old tradition of a spring daylong festival of odd sports, movies, and fun shared by eight to ten thousand university people. The more serious of Baylor's special events are now being oriented to the faith and learning activity mentioned in

24. *Baylor University Undergraduate Catalog 1999-2000*, p. 25.

Chapter Five. For instance, a major conference in the spring of 2000 entitled "Religious Faith and Literary Art" brought fifteen noteworthy figures
to the campus, including the novelist John Grisham.

There is little doubt that many forces legitimate and encourage a
Baptist Christian ethos at Baylor. And because of their number among students, staff, and faculty, Baptists likely will continue to exert significant
cultural and religious influence on the life of the university. As a large institution, however, with a majority of students living outside its purview,
Baylor will continue to harbor not only the Baptist way of life, but also a
quite worldly one often at odds with the Baptist ideal.

University of Notre Dame

Though there may be an intense academic struggle going on at Notre
Dame between those who want to reach the highest pinnacle of excellence
without regard to Catholic identity and those who would give priority to
Catholic identity in the university's intellectual life, there is no such struggle going on in the area of ethos. In this realm, Notre Dame is intensely
and unequivocally Catholic, with or without the support of its more ambivalent faculty. Furthermore, because of its affluence the university can
devote tremendous resources to the cultivation of its Catholic ethos. It
would be safe to say that none of the other schools surveyed could match
the massive resources that Notre Dame contributes to nurturing the religious identity of its students. This is not to say that all this effort succeeds
with all its students. Like all our critical-mass schools, Notre Dame offers
and encourages but does not require its students to participate in its many
programs. But at Notre Dame it would be hard to escape completely the
claims of the Catholic way of worship and life.

The central worship facility of the university is the Basilica of the
Sacred Heart, a beautiful and impressive Gothic building built in the late
nineteenth century but fully restored in the mid-1980s. Staffed by the
priests of the Congregation of the Holy Cross, the basilica offers at least
two masses daily on ordinary weekdays, Sunday evening vespers after a
full morning of masses, and special campus-wide liturgies at certain
times during Holy Week. Students, faculty, and staff attend in numbers
running from a hundred to full capacity. Like an ordinary Catholic parish, it follows the rhythm of the church year and offers such staples as

confession and Pre-Cana marriage preparation, particularly since so many current and former students desire to be married in it. Unlike ordinary parishes, it has a number of student musical ensembles to call upon to enrich its liturgies and to offer concerts. It offers daily rosary at the Grotto, a cave-like devotional site modeled on Lourdes near the basilica, at which hundreds of students daily light candles and say prayers. The staff of the basilica also makes available on the university's Web site reflections on the assigned scripture for the week. The basilica's staff of priests also offers its services in many other facets of the extra-curricular life of Notre Dame, so the basilica has effects far beyond its own worship and programs.

While the basilica is the symbolic hub of religious life at Notre Dame, it is not the place where most students worship. Rather, the twenty-seven single-sex dorms provide the worship "homes" of the 6,500 Notre Dame students who live in them. (The 80 percent of the Notre Dame undergraduate population that lives in university dorms furnishes a sharp contrast to the 30 percent of Baylor undergraduates living on campus.) It is significant that the university keeps its dorms at a human scale of 100-300 residents. In fact, in recent years it converted two large student high-rise buildings to classrooms and offices and built several smaller dorms in their place.

These relatively small dorms provide the space for an extraordinary approach to college life: the rector system. Each of the twenty-seven dorms has an adult rector (over thirty years of age) who is most often a priest or nun, though the number of lay rectors is slowly increasing. It is worth noting that the president of the university, Edward Malloy, C.S.C., has been such a rector for his whole time at Notre Dame. A recent advertisement soliciting applications for the position states:

> Within its undergraduate residence halls, the University strives to create communities of faith and learning that serve as catalysts for the integration of students' intellectual, spiritual and social development. The Rector is the principal person in charge of an undergraduate residence hall. The position is held by priests, male and female religious, and committed lay people.
>
> Together with a graduate student Assistant Rector and undergraduate seniors serving as Resident Assistants, the Rector educates, counsels, and accompanies students in the life of faith, and calls students to ac-

countability in accordance with University behavioral expectations. The Rector also acts as liaison to other University departments responsible for student welfare and the physical condition of the residence hall.[25]

The men's halls have two graduate assistant rectors to the women's one to help the rector coordinate the many facets of dorm life. The rector chooses his or her own assistants from a list of applicants. The rector functions as the parent in the university's policy of *in loco parentis*. This means that the life in the dorm is conducted under the umbrella of the rector's authority, which even extends to allowing underage students to drink, much as a family might allow a youngster to have a glass of wine at its table. On the other hand, the rector also enforces the university's behavioral policies, which are taken seriously. The "parietals" limit visitation hours between men and women, while other regulations inveigh against drunkenness and other social nuisances. The rectors and the assistant rectors perform security rounds — sometimes all through the night — to insure compliance and a civilized dorm life.

But the central thrust of dorm life is not constituted by these restrictions, real though they may be. The central thrust is positive, especially in the provision of worship services as well as spiritual support and guidance. Each of the dorms has a chapel; the rector and his or her assistants plan and preside over worship life there. The men's dorms have mass daily while the women's dorms have mass twice a week. (Since the women religious cannot say mass, it is a challenge to find a male to say mass daily in the women's dorms. Besides, it seems to be a fact that women students are more likely to attend mass in the men's dorms than vice versa.) While mass is offered in each of the dorms, students may gravitate to the location and style of worship they prefer.

While attendance at the daily masses is expected to gather only a small portion of the student dorm population on any given day, a higher expectation is placed on attendance at the weekly Sunday mass, usually at 10:00 P.M. This mass is intended to begin the new week with worship, and something like 80 percent of the dorm population attends on a given Sunday, though it may not always be in their own dorm. Over the course of a term, virtually everyone attends one or more Sunday masses. Musical ensembles organized in the dorms support the masses, and the style of wor-

25. Advertisement in *Commonweal*, March 10, 2000, p. 42.

ship runs mostly to contemporary music and informal demeanor. Even the Protestant students tend to come to the masses.

In addition, the rector, assistant rectors, and senior resident assistants are expected to provide support, counseling, and spiritual guidance to the students in their dorm. Many students attest to the important influence both rectors and assistant rectors have had on their lives. And this influence reaches through generations, since many Notre Dame students have parents who also attended the university.

Dorm life also includes recreational, fund-raising, and service activities. These functions have "commissioners" appointed to organize them; service activities have two commissioners, to indicate their importance. At least half the students in the dorms are estimated to work in service projects generated and coordinated by the service commissioners.[26] Add to this the dances sponsored twice a term by each dorm and the fund-raising done at football games and one gets the picture of a very busy dorm life.

The university's intense effort to forge community life at the dorm level results in an amazing 96 percent retention rate from the first to the second year. Those returning students typically spend the next three years in the same dorm under the same rector. This continuity in community life adds to the power of Notre Dame formation. The adult presence — particularly the presence of about forty Holy Cross religious — adds immeasurably to the capacities for civilized living and student spiritual formation.

As if these dorm activities were not enough, the university has a well-staffed and highly active campus ministry. It trains those who wish to become catechists, runs Emmaus small groups that engage in spiritual reflection, sponsors Keeping the Faith lectures, prepares adults for confirmation and initiation into the Catholic church, holds marriage preparation courses, organizes seven ensembles for liturgical music, and, above all, offers a wide array of retreats. A twenty-six-hour freshman retreat is offered six times a year dealing with community, faith, and the hopes that students have for their years at the university. A retreat called the Notre Dame Encounter is offered five times a year. It is a three-day event attended by fifty-

26. These impressions and estimates were given to the author by Kathleen Sprows Cummings, Lilly Fellow in the Lilly Program in Humanities and the Arts based at Valparaiso University. Cummings was an assistant rector at Notre Dame during her years in its graduate program.

five students each time it is held and led by a staff of eighteen, among whom are eight adult spiritual directors. These retreats usually run at capacity and are held at several retreat centers on or near the campus. Campus Ministry even holds a Wednesday evening interdenominational prayer service for non-Catholics.

Campus Ministry also focuses on special groups and their spiritual needs. Since the university has seven hundred international students from seventy-five countries, worship and spiritual sustenance are oriented toward particular cultural groups. In addition, it provides special programs for graduate and married students. It has a ministry to gay and lesbian students, which entails some delicate maneuvering. This ministry emphasizes the Catholic teaching that homosexual orientation is not a sin in itself and assures such students of their acceptance in the community of faith and at the university. The ministry is largely silent about homosexual activity itself. Rather, the ministry indicates that it "wants to help you live in such a way that your life can be a strong statement of what you believe," which seems to be more an affirmation of modern expressive individualism rather than Catholic moral teaching. Nevertheless, the ministry is as important as it is ambiguous in its relationship to Catholic tradition.

Besides the service activities generated out of the dorms, there is also a Center for Social Concerns, which operates under the larger umbrella of the Institute for Church Life. This location of the center attests to Notre Dame's forthright justification of service as a Christian, not merely a civic, duty. The center coordinates the service activities of roughly two thousand student volunteers in over fifty student and community organizations. It also refers students to courses in the university that include a service component. Some of the opportunities are under the "peace and justice" rubric, which presses forward the Catholic commitment to social action. This strong commitment to service by the whole university leaves a mark on the students. Like St. Olaf, Notre Dame sends about 10 percent of its graduating seniors to at least a year of voluntary service.

The university tends its relation to the Catholic Church by maintaining a number of practical institutes and centers that go along with its many academic institutes and centers dealing with intellectual matters. Besides the Center for Social Concern, the Institute for Church Life also includes the Center for Pastoral Liturgy, which serves schools and parishes by helping to enrich their worship life. It also includes Retreats International, which makes use of the international Catholic network of retreat centers to organize retreat trips for students and other Catholics. Notre Dame hosts the Alliance for Catholic Education, which recruits and helps to train teachers for Catholic schools in underprivileged areas. The Alliance has 140 graduates. The university also hosts a Congregation of the Holy Cross seminary in addition to a service organization called the Holy Cross Associates, which entails at least one year of living in communities devoted to service.[27]

The buildings, statuary, and artwork around the campus definitely symbolize Notre Dame's religious commitments. There are crucifixes in many if not most of the rooms in the university. The huge mural on the side of the library depicting Christ and the history of the church (the so-called "Touchdown Jesus") is there for all to see. The cross-topped spire of the basilica towers above all other buildings and complements the golden dome of the administration building. Many statues of key figures in the history of Notre Dame abound on campus as if to solidify communal memory.

Certainly sports have played a very important role in the ethos of Notre Dame, and one would be hard pressed to argue that that role is without a religious dimension. The quip about "Touchdown Jesus" blessing the football stadium at the opposite end of the quad from the library is not altogether facetious. Sports play an important role in the assertion of Catholic pride. The day of a home football game resembles an enormous picnic — replete with all sorts of entertainment — of a gigantic extended family. On such occasions one can easily get the impression from the assembled crowd that God prefers a victory for Notre Dame.

There is indeed a powerful religious ethos at Notre Dame. Its communal solidarity is enhanced by generations of Catholics that have attended it and care deeply about it. No doubt some students opt out of that ethos; certainly some even rebel against its pervasiveness. Perhaps Notre Dame's very success tempts its participants to idolize the symbols of that success overmuch. But there is little doubt that the richness and momentum of its genuine Catholic ethos will carry far into the future.

◆　　◆　　◆

27. These many programs of the university may be examined at the university's Web site, www.nd.edu.

The six schools of this study have many important things in common. Certainly all of them have a distinct and public religious quality about their communal lives. Though there are varying degrees of "thickness" to their communal identity, there is no doubt what they stand for. There are many factors going into an ethos that is discernibly connected to a sponsoring religious heritage, and all six of these schools make serious efforts to maintain that connection. Coupled with educational programs that take seriously the Christian intellectual heritage, these schools' extra-curricular ways of life provide an educational experience wherein the Christian account of life and reality is publicly relevant to all the major aspects of their lives. In other words, they offer their students educational quality with a real religious soul.

Such schools exhibit the kind of character that adds rich diversity to American higher education. They contribute variety to a homogenizing educational world in which matters of substantive meaning and morality are kept at arm's length. They certainly seem to contribute to a civil society with a serious need for responsible citizens. Indeed, there are many secular reasons for rejoicing that such schools continue to thrive. But for Christians, the main reason for rejoicing lies elsewhere. For them it lies in the fact that these schools take seriously the Christian faith's relevance to the entirety of their lives, including the intellectual dimension. They proceed with the conviction that the Christian account of life and reality is comprehensive, unsurpassable, and central, and combine that conviction with high-quality education in a truly inspiring way.

PART THREE

Strategies for Maintenance
and Renewal

Now that I have surveyed the current plight of most church-related colleges and universities and speculated about the underlying causes of their
secularization in Part One, and spent Part Two in a description and analysis of six colleges and universities that have not succumbed to the secularization process but instead have maintained a robust connection with the
vision, ethos, and persons of their sponsoring heritages, it is time to discuss the necessary strategies and tactics for maintaining a meaningful relation to those heritages. Though many of those strategies and tactics have
been implied in Chapter Six, it may be helpful to make them explicit in a
systematic way.

Chapter Seven will be devoted to those strategies and tactics necessary to maintain and perhaps even strengthen the connection to heritage
that is already present in orthodox and critical-mass schools. Certainly the
six schools examined in this text are not the only relevant ones; there may
well be even better examples that are less well known. This chapter may
provide something of a map for schools that are currently intentionally
pluralist but have the necessary leadership and resources for moving to the
critical-mass stage. While it is indeed difficult for such schools to move toward a closer relationship with their historically related church, it is not
impossible. Chapter Seven may help.

Chapter Eight will deal with a most important topic: it will suggest
strategies for moving from an accidental kind of pluralism to a more intentional sort. A great many, perhaps the majority, of schools related to
churches are so loosely related that the vision, ethos, and persons of the

sponsoring church are only minimally present in the life of the school. Some have gone so far on the secularization route that there is no turning back; there are simply not enough people who care enough about the religious connection to make an effort to renew it. But there is a large contingent of moderately secularized colleges in which there are yet people who care, where the flame has not gone out completely. These persons can become the leadership cadre for reviving a meaningful connection to the school's sponsoring heritage in particular and through it to the Christian tradition in general. Working in concert, such persons can effect significant change. They can enact strategies that will give Christian perspectives and practices more presence in the school's life. Through such actions the college can more honestly and meaningfully claim a relation to its historic parent. While it may never reach the critical-mass stage, the college can yet strengthen its Christian ties so that the designation "church-related college" actually carries some meaning.

7 | *Keeping the Faith*

What has been learned in the foregoing analysis of these six schools? How and why have they been able to preserve educational quality with religious soul? What are the essentials in maintaining a strong connection with each school's sponsoring religious heritage, one in which the vision and ethos of that heritage are publicly relevant to all aspects of the school's life?[1] In the following chapter I will outline those essentials for those schools — like the six I have examined — that already are orthodox or critical-mass schools. The focus will be on the ways that they keep the faith. Those strategies are also relevant for those intentionally pluralist institutions interested in recruiting a critical mass of persons from a particular religious tradition.

Sponsoring Religious Traditions

At the outset it is important to note a necessary precondition for these sorts of schools to flourish. The sponsoring traditions have to produce enough persons who intensely believe that the Christian account is pervasively relevant to the life of a college or university. This precondition is essential for these schools to keep the faith. Religious colleges and universi-

---

1. An excellent article that explicates these essentials is Mark R. Schwehn, "The Christian University: Defining the Difference," *First Things*, May 1999, pp. 25-31. This chapter could well be viewed as an elaboration of Schwehn's main points.

179

ties are part of larger ecological wholes and are dependent on them for sustenance.

It seems that some traditions — including many mainline Protestant denominations — simply are not providing sufficient numbers of the persons described above to constitute the critical mass necessary to establish and maintain identifiably Christian colleges and universities.[2] Of course, these traditions certainly are bringing forth persons of faith; in fact, many of their faithful members populate their own schools as well as other church-related schools. But too often there are not enough of them acting in concert to maintain schools in which the Christian account is the organizing paradigm for the collective identity and mission.

On the other side of the ledger, it is obvious that the evangelical tradition and the Roman Catholic Church are nurturing enough members who believe in the intellectual and lifestyle relevance of the faith to carry out concerted efforts in Christian higher education. Evangelicals have large numbers, intensity, and increasing wealth. The many churches that make up the evangelical tradition nurture ample numbers of young people who want to attend evangelical schools that connect faith and learning. As mentioned earlier, many such people are now moving through the graduate schools of America and are joining an evangelical intellectual renaissance that is already underway. Evangelical students make up majorities at Wheaton and Baylor and now a significant portion of the student body at Calvin. There are many smaller churches — the Christian Reformed Church, for example — that continue to supply persons who intensely support the kind of Christian higher education described in this book.

The huge and sprawling Catholic community spawns many "cultural Catholics," a characteristic that fits what Ernst Troeltsch called the "church type."[3] Indeed, these "cultural Catholics" frequently constitute the largest denominational group on many campuses, including the secularized Protestant ones. But such a large and varied community also produces many intense Catholics who want to join educational ventures of a dis-

---

2. This is a generalization that may not apply in all instances. Oklahoma City University, for example, attempts to take its Methodist heritage seriously. But even the exceptions are unlikely to fulfill the criteria of the critical-mass category. There may indeed be schools from mainline traditions that are intentionally pluralist schools, but the preponderance does not rise even to that level.

3. Ernst Troeltsch, *The Social Teaching of the Christian Churches* (London: George Allen & Unwin, Ltd., 1931), pp. 993ff.

tinctly Catholic kind, such as Notre Dame. Happily, many such Catholics also want to join serious Christian ventures under Lutheran or other Protestant auspices. Whether such Catholics wish to join less glamorous or more secularized Catholic enterprises is another question. But certainly there are enough committed Catholics to sustain the flagship Catholic colleges and universities.

The generous supply of intense evangelicals and Catholics will also insure strong financial support for the orthodox and critical-mass schools. While direct support — that which moves from the churches or orders themselves to the general budgets of the schools — will no doubt continue to diminish in terms of percentage of many schools' overall budgets, the indirect support — that given by individuals to specific causes within the schools — will continue to be enormously important. In fact, indirect aid will probably increase in importance. Buildings, programs, professorships, chaplaincies, centers, and institutes — especially those having to do with specifically religious purposes — will likely be the beneficiaries of this important largess.

Vibrant religious traditions that believe in the public relevance of their heritage for higher education often organize offices in their judicatories that watch over and stimulate their denominational schools' efforts. The pope and his *Ex Corde* letter is a powerful case in point. Lutherans and Southern Baptists have their own church offices that monitor and encourage Christian higher education in their tradition. Such offices are very helpful in keeping important conversations about religion alive among all their institutions.

The old Protestant mainstream denominations bring forth many intense Christians, but perhaps not enough to supply the necessary critical masses for sustaining their own colleges as Christian colleges. Those more intense mainstream Protestants then often join evangelical, Catholic, and Lutheran educational ventures, where they become supportive allies. Wheaton, for example, has many such mainstream Protestants on its faculty.

Lutherans have always put themselves in a special category, neither mainstream nor sectarian (in the sense of Troeltsch's "separatist" religious communities), with some considering themselves "evangelical Catholics." But the Evangelical Lutheran Church in America, the largest Lutheran church, has taken on many characteristics of the Protestant mainstream. Something noteworthy about both the church and its schools is revealed in the fact that only 5 percent of its graduating high school students find their way to Lutheran colleges and universities. Perhaps that percentage can be increased by serious efforts by both church and college.[4] If successful efforts are not forthcoming, it is likely that only a few ELCA schools will survive as critical-mass schools; most will be at best intentionally pluralist.

The Missouri Synod, on the other hand, has taken a sectarian turn in which those concerned with a stringent doctrinal orthodoxy hold the sword of Damocles over its churches and its schools, creating a significant challenge to the development of both theology and liberal arts. Such narrowness leads many conservative Missouri Synod churches to distrust the more open Lutheranism that shapes Valparaiso University. That distrust seriously affects Valparaiso, diminishing its traditional national supply of good students. The sectarianism of the Missouri Synod also has diminished its production of the kind of intellectuals who in earlier days filled the faculty slots at Valparaiso.

Thus, the challenges facing the Lutheran schools to achieve or maintain a robust connection are daunting. The few that will be able to sustain a critical mass will have to be very intentional and inventive. They cannot rely on the strength and momentum of their sponsoring heritages to do their jobs for them. Most, it seems, will at best have to be content to be or become intentionally pluralist.

In all cases, however, orthodox and critical-mass schools have to cultivate strong relations with their sponsoring religious traditions — churches, judicatories, clergy, lay people, and youth. These various constituencies have to continue to know and care about their schools, and the schools have to care about their constituencies. One decisive mark of secularized schools is the lack of mutual recognition and care by both school and church, when neither sees the other as crucial to their mission. Conversely, the schools surveyed here take much care to tend their connection

4. One of the interesting things about the Lutheran schools is the network of communication they enjoy. Both the Lutheran Educational Conference of North America and the Evangelical Lutheran Church of America's Division for Higher Education and Schools stimulate reflection on and conversation among Lutheran colleges and universities. Thus, the intensity of Lutheran interaction about the nature and mission of their schools is unique among Protestants. Those umbrella organizations also serve as important links between church and college. They keep church concerns on the agenda of the colleges, some of which are forgetful of such concerns.

with those constituencies. They recognize their mutual interdependence. By so doing, these schools are likely to continue to receive the necessary supply of students, administrators, board members, donors, and faculty.

Governance Issues

While James Burtchaell suggests that the formal severance of colleges from their sponsoring churches was a fateful occurrence, he finally opines that "these stories of legal estrangement are important sidebars to the main story of alienation, but they are not the main plot."[5] The analysis presented in these pages confirms Burtchaell's assessment. True enough, the orthodox schools will continue to be formally accountable to their sponsoring traditions, bringing both bane and blessing but insuring that the religious traditions continue to be publicly relevant in the lives of those schools.

Critical-mass schools have generally diminished their legal accountability to their sponsoring churches or orders, for the many reasons recounted in earlier chapters. However, all the schools in our survey continue to preserve some formal links with their sponsoring body, such as assured slots on the board or provisions for their trustees and some policies to be confirmed by the sponsoring church or order. These links are important symbolic reminders of institutional accountability and need to be preserved. Still, a school's key continuing components — its internally selected board, administration, and faculty — are the main players in its governance. Their voluntary accountability to the sponsoring tradition is the most crucial feature in their connection to it.[6] This accountability takes on a kind of "chicken and egg" character. Without a critical mass of intense adherents to the tradition in the board, administration, and faculty, that voluntary accountability will not hold. But without that voluntary accountability there will be no critical mass of such communicants in

5. James Burtchaell, *The Dying of the Light: The Disengagement of Colleges and Universities from Their Christian Churches* (Grand Rapids: Eerdmans, 1998), p. 828.

6. Even the *Ex Corde* requirements — mandates for Catholic theological faculty and insistence that a majority of faculty be Catholic — will do little to change the reality that it is voluntary accountability that is pivotal. While withdrawal of recognition as a Catholic school by the bishops would be very damaging indeed, it still remains the case that coercive power is far less important than voluntary accountability in keeping a strong connection between the Catholic tradition and its schools.

the composition of these bodies. Therefore, accountability of critical-mass schools to religious traditions will be sustained indirectly through their continuing voluntary commitments. Such an arrangement resonates with American notions of academic freedom and institutional autonomy while, if tended properly, also maintaining a powerful link of pledged accountability to their sponsoring traditions.

It is of course important to ask whether a college or university needs to be related to a specific tradition rather than to a broader context of the Christian faith. Cannot a school be a "generic" Christian college or university? There seem to be many reasons to answer that question affirmatively. After all, church-related schools have shunned "sectarian" identities from their very beginning. No one has wanted to be "narrowly sectarian." Furthermore, schools with lax approaches to Christianity have often used that label in order to discredit those with other perspectives. For example, Lutheran schools have sometimes comforted themselves in their trajectory toward secularization by smugly claiming that they are at least not like Calvin College, which allegedly doesn't respect secular learning. Isn't it better to eschew participation in the "narcissism of small differences" and simply be a Christian college? Finally, it is certainly true that serious Christian colleges of most traditions share more with each other than with their secular counterparts. Shouldn't we aim at being Christian colleges and dampen our denominational peculiarities? Then we could give up these sometimes-futile efforts to staff our schools with communicants of a particular tradition that in fact is not producing enough persons to fill the bill.

There is definitely something persuasive about these arguments, particularly the one that we ought first of all be Christian in a broad sense. I think that point is correct, yet it seems very likely that one can only be a Christian school in that broad sense if one is anchored in a specific tradition. There are at least two reasons for this observation. First, we always come to Christianity through a particular tradition and we continue in the faith as practitioners of a particular tradition even though we may be capaciously ecumenical in our attitudes. It is the same with churches and church-related institutions. Generic churches or church-related institutions are rarer than truffles in the desert. If one scratches the surface of any church, a particular tradition always becomes visible. C. S. Lewis made this point well. He coined the phrase "mere Christianity" to refer to that great common core of Christian faith and practice. It is, he said, like a great central hall in which we meet Christ and witness the spectacular work of God. Around the side of this grand hall are smaller rooms in which meals are served, wounds healed, skills taught, and friends made. Don't stay long in the great hall, he said; find a smaller one where there is nourishment for the mind and soul. Without that smaller hall, the great hall lacks Christian texture and specificity. So it is, it seems, with colleges.[7] They need grounding in a specific tradition before they can become genuinely ecumenical.

A second reason for connection to a specific tradition has to do with accountability. It is difficult to be accountable to a general, perhaps even universal, group or reality. Such a connection lacks the "bite" of specific claims. Too often in the history of higher education, claims of adherence to a "broad" Christianity have turned out to be mere way stations on the path from denominational affiliation to complete secularization. To be really accountable, a school needs to have a set of specific referents — persons, practices, traditions of thought, and common memories. Only when it is accountable to them can it then branch out into a larger set of purposes. Such logic applies even more stringently to schools that are *voluntarily* accountable to a tradition. They need something specific to which to be accountable.

Critical Mass

After all this use of the phrase "critical mass," how should we characterize what it describes? Exactly what proportion constitutes a critical mass? I propose that we look at it in terms of three concentric circles, each containing roughly one-third of whatever constituency in the school we are talking about. The first circle, the inner one, is the most important for the purposes of this particular discussion. It is constituted by a group of intense communicants who not only identify strongly with the religious dimension of the school's mission, but have a solid understanding of the sponsoring tradition — both its vision and ethos, and of how these elements should relate to the various dimensions of the school's life.[8] Further,

---

7. I am indebted for this use of C. S. Lewis's thought to Dwight Moody, Dean of the Chapel, Georgetown College, who preached an unpublished sermon on why his college had to be Baptist, not simply Christian.

8. As a rule of thumb, I would measure "intensity of commitment" by whether

they have the strength of commitment to defend and promote the tradition's relevance to the life of the college or university. It is definitely possible that some non-communicants inhabit this core, but in their cases the non-communicants are so "inside" the tradition and its influence in the school that they could just as well be communicants. Often they become just that. Even if they don't, however, they are true colleagues in the cause.

The next circle outward — again, roughly one-third of the total — is constituted by communicants and non-communicants alike who warmly support the religious dimension of the school's life and participate in it. But neither their intensity toward nor their understanding of the tradition and how it should work out in the school's life are as great as that of the inner core. They are not likely to take leadership roles in furthering the cause of Christian higher education, yet they are willing followers. They support what the inner core proposes, not uncritically but with generous benefit of the doubt. These first two circles contain roughly two-thirds of the population of each relevant group and thereby create a critical mass. This mass shares "first principles" but certainly not unanimity in how those principles should work out in concrete cases. There is room for many lively debates within that shared consensus.

It is with regard to this necessary consensus that so much talk of "diversity" and "inclusiveness" is unhelpful. It would be silly not to affirm diversity in the categories of race, ethnicity, political persuasion, class, geographical region, and gender. But at the level of fundamental notions about what Christian higher education should be about, diversity within a school can lead to a watered-down approach that affirms nothing in particular. Proponents of strategies used by orthodox schools have a point when they argue that diversity at such a fundamental level leads to education at the lowest common denominator. These schools, understandably, refuse to take such risks.

Critical-mass schools, however, do take such risks, especially with the third concentric circle from the center, the group that may well provide meaningful and helpful diversity. Ideally, even this group will give tacit approval to or at least tolerate the cause of Christian higher education in a par-

---

or not a person would lead an organized movement to reclaim the school's religious connection if he or she were part of only a small remnant of "true believers." By "knowledge of the tradition" I mean a grasp of the basic theological themes of the Christian account as they are construed by the particular tradition.

ticular denominational tradition. Some might even appreciate the tradition as a solid foil for their perspective. Such persons make up a loyal opposition. But, by and large, this group is, at best, not interested in making a place for Christianity in higher education and, at worst, hostile to it. Often persons in this camp are hired for their other strengths — research capacities, for example — and waltz by "institutional fit" requirements. Others are there because those who hired them lacked sufficient clarity about those requirements or the courage to follow through on them. Yet others are in this group because, for various reasons, they have changed their beliefs and attitudes about the cause of Christian higher education in its more robust form. But most of those in this category just want to be left alone, absolutely free to pursue their own teaching and research interests. If the partisans of the Christian cause do not bother them, they are content. A goodly number of this group may well be good for a college or university on other grounds. On the one under discussion, however, I believe they need to be outnumbered two to one in any college determined to keep its religious connection vibrant.

Thus, I see the composition of critical-mass schools in thirds. It is not true that two-thirds or more must be communicants of the sponsoring tradition, though it is true that at least a third (coming from the first two concentric circles) should be. The most important third can be made up of communicants and non-communicants alike who believe intensely in the public relevance of the Christian account as it is refracted through the lenses of the sponsoring tradition.

Selection Processes

Board

Boards of orthodox schools are selected primarily on the basis of their religious convictions. Other considerations — wealth and leadership abilities, for example — are no doubt important, but first things come first. Board members are usually formal representatives of specific church traditions by constitutional directive, so there is little concern about selecting persons who may stray from fundamental assumptions. But there may be much contention over the working out of the fundamental principles. Orthodox believers care much about theological distinctions and are sometimes prone to argue endlessly over precision.

In a critical-mass school, the ruling board should have two-thirds of its members represent the sponsoring tradition, for two reasons. First, boards are the real insurers that a tradition is borne forward by the school, for it selects both its own members and the president, and it has much influence on administrative policy and on the selection of other constituent groups. It carries the tradition through time. Second, it is more likely that at least one-third of the board will have the necessary intensity and understanding if two-thirds of the board is drawn from that particular tradition. The rest of the communicants may provide needed support even if they do not exhibit vigorous leadership. The final third should appreciate and support the overall identity and mission of the college even if they are not communicants. Critical-mass colleges often have such supporters who are "unmusical" about their religious purposes but contribute essential gifts on other fronts.

Administration and Staff

At the outset of our discussion of selection practices, it is important to note that both the orthodox and critical-mass schools in our survey do not include "religion" in their list of categories upon which they do not discriminate. This legal caveat is very significant because it signals to all prospective participants in the enterprise that religious identity and conviction are crucial to the school's mission. Conversely, if religion is included in the list of non-discriminatory categories, the school admits that religious identity and conviction are not central to its mission and therefore cannot select its members according to such criteria. Moreover, the courts have made it clear that if religious factors are central to the identity and mission of a school, and this predisposition is clearly stated in its hiring policies, it is perfectly proper to select members of the community on the basis of religious criteria.

The whole administration in orthodox schools is composed of communicants of the sponsoring tradition, but the critical-mass schools offer a more complex case. In such schools the president and cabinet should all qualify for our "inner circle," though every cabinet member does not have to be a communicant of the sponsoring tradition. Presidents of both types of schools are crucial for maintaining Christian identity and mission, although in many ways orthodox schools are less dependent on charismatic leaders than critical-mass schools are. Christian identity and mission are more firmly embedded in orthodox schools and therefore can be carried by the whole enterprise even if the president is not such a leader. However, all of the six schools surveyed had at one time or another real "giants" who by force of personality and vision provided charismatic leadership. Most of those giants lived and worked in an era in which the president had much more comprehensive influence over all the activities of the college or university, while the contemporary president has much of his or her energy given over to fund-raising and has much less direct control over internal policies, particularly academic ones. With the professionalization and specialization of academic life, the contemporary president simply cannot be the benevolent dictator of times past.

Nevertheless, the president is crucial in setting the overall direction of the school. He or she must believe that the Christian account of life and reality is publicly relevant to all facets of the school's life and understand and embody the sponsoring tradition. It is most helpful if he or she can articulate a compelling vision of the school's identity and mission to key constituencies, particularly the board and faculty. However, if the president is not an accomplished rhetorician, someone else high in the administration must be such a spokesperson. Without a compelling vision from those entrusted with leadership, schools quickly lose their cohesion and momentum. Further, the president or another cabinet-level official must be something of an educational philosopher, sophisticated enough to spell out a Christian vision of higher education that can help to organize and integrate the curricular and non-curricular offerings of the college and to differentiate that vision from the secular models that now dominate the educational world. If such skills are not available at the administrative level, they must be found among the faculty and utilized by the administration.

The provost or dean of academic affairs is indispensable in making sure that academic policies and practices — particularly faculty hiring — favor the Christian purposes of the school. In five of six of the surveyed schools the provost (or dean of academic affairs) personally interviews all finalists for faculty positions. In the sixth the provost makes sure that the deans of the various divisions of the school engage in careful hiring according to mission. In many of these six schools, the provost or dean of academic affairs is the primary articulator of vision and educational philosopher.

Orthodox colleges insist that the dean of students, who is responsible for the guidance of much of student life, operate programs from a Christian perspective, but the dean of students of a critical-mass school is less likely to operate from such a point of view. Secular models are much more likely to hold sway at such a school. That laxity is a problem, however, because other concepts of human flourishing can quickly supplant Christian ones as models for guiding student life. At their best, critical-mass schools also insist on a common vision on the part of directors of development, business managers, and admissions managers, to ensure that the various activities they oversee function as part of a unified whole.

In all our schools, the chaplain or dean of the chapel operates on the cabinet level, if not *de jure*, then *de facto*. These colleges and universities realize that the formal spiritual life of the campus is at the center of college identity and mission. Further, the leadership in these schools values the insight of the dean of the chapel on many aspects of institutional life and dignifies the role of chaplain by seeking such insight out.

An often overlooked but exceedingly important position in the chain of command is the department chair. In orthodox schools department chairs are deeply embedded in and committed to the religious ethos and vision of the college. No chances are taken here. The situation is often different in critical-mass colleges and universities, however. In fact, in several of our schools the department chair is the weak link between the public vision of the school and ground-level activities that sustain it, particularly faculty hiring. Sometimes the problem is that the department itself elects the department chair, and if the department is conflicted or contrary, the elected chair may hire faculty who do not fit the public identity and mission of the school. In other cases the chair is appointed on a rotating basis and therefore has no lasting effect on the hiring process. It seems important that department chairs be appointed by the provost or dean so that they are "on board" in hiring for mission. In the long run such an arrangement will help to ensure that the faculty who are hired will be supporters and participants in that mission.

Finally, it is important to select staff — from the upper-echelon salaried workers to those who earn hourly wages — who are sympathetic with the purposes of the school. Colleges and universities with a strong ethos find that these staff members are often important bearers of ethos. St. Olaf College, for example, includes several essays about key staff members in its commemorative volume.[9] These devoted employees are important figures for many students, who find them models of Christian care and wisdom. Some are amazingly committed to their schools and thereby help to create solidarity in the whole community. Certainly staff need not be communicants, but they should be carefully selected and then inducted and instructed into the tradition of the school. Often these faithful staff members persist much longer in the life of the school than administrators and faculty.

Faculty

Faculty selection for orthodox colleges seems easy enough on the religious side of the equation; schools like Calvin or Wheaton require explicit confessions of faith. Faculty who apply to such schools should be under no illusions about the sort of school to which they are applying. However, such policies certainly diminish the pool of applicants. The challenge for orthodox schools is to keep faculty standards high in the traditional areas of teaching, scholarship, and service. But even more of a challenge might be to acquire the kind of talent needed to integrate faith and learning well. Integrating faith and learning poorly may be worse than not trying it at all. Doing it well requires both talent and thorough preparation.

Faculty selection for critical-mass schools is both the most important and the most difficult of tasks. It is most important because faculty members are the ground troops, the ones who directly encounter the students. If the Christian account is to be publicly relevant to the central task of the school — its education — then the right kind of faculty is indispensable. Faculty members will not only have to be adept at teaching, scholarship, and service, but also at a fourth category: institutional fit. Ability to contribute to the identity and mission of the Christian college is as important a criterion as the traditional three.

However, the selection process is difficult because contemporary academic culture is biased against precisely the kinds of questions that need to be asked of prospective faculty. Christian colleges and universities need

9. Pamela Schwandt, ed., *Called to Serve: St. Olaf and the Vocation of a Church College* (Northfield, MN: St. Olaf College Press, 1999); see the essays on a groundskeeper, pp. 111-17, and a coach, pp. 125-33.

to find out what the religious convictions of the prospective professor are; yet the current academic culture prohibits such personal questions. Colleges need to make assessments of prospective faculty members as whole persons if they are to teach whole students, as the rhetoric of church-related liberal arts colleges claims. Yet contemporary academic practices discourage probing into anything more than the prospect's narrow expertise. Department chairs, deans, and provosts in critical-mass schools find it hard to ask these necessary questions. Even when they do ask them, it is hard to turn candidates down on those grounds. Furthermore, it is often difficult to discern a genuine answer to these thorny questions from a strategic one. Hiring the right persons for critical-mass colleges requires tact, discernment, and courage; even for the committed persons who do it, such hiring is no easy task. One helpful tool in such situations is a requirement of written reflections by prospective faculty on their possible contributions to the school's religious identity and mission.

Students

Critical-mass universities and colleges seem to aim at a higher proportion of communicants than the guidelines I have suggested. Notre Dame runs at 85 percent Catholic, for example. Only Valparaiso has less than a third of its students coming from its Missouri Synod denomination, although if all Lutherans are included, the numbers improve. But what I have suggested is more complex than simple denominational designations. A school is fortunate indeed if one-third of its student body is passionately devoted to its particular faith and learning engagement, even after four years of study. It is also fortunate if another third is supportive of its vision though finally not all that intense or knowledgeable about it, even after four years.

Therefore, the critical-mass school ought to hold religious identity and involvement as a major criterion for entrance. It should aim at a critical mass — at least one-third of the student body, and preferably more — of its own communicants. But that third can be supplemented by recruitment of students from other traditions that are sympathetic with what the school intends as a Christian institution. For example, evangelical students are already drawn to Calvin, and in the future they will make up the slack when the Christian Reformed student population inevitably falls below 50 percent. Valparaiso, hard pressed to reach more than 20 percent from the Missouri Synod, can aim at Lutherans from other traditions as well as Roman Catholics. What is important is that one-third of the student body be intensely receptive to the religious purposes of the institution and another third be supportive of them.

Ethos

Chapel[10]

Leaders who believe in the paradigmatic character of the Christian account for their schools find public time and space for worship. The Christian practice of worship is essential for the identity and mission of all six examples of thriving Christian higher education. While only one requires chapel of all undergraduate students all the time (Wheaton) and another requires chapel of all undergraduate students some of the time (Baylor), the other four have opted for voluntary chapel. Notre Dame and Calvin have high attendance at their voluntary services, while the two Lutheran schools draw somewhat less. But in all cases there are public times and places for chapel. All in principle protect the times at which chapel is held, though the principle may be violated in fact. The times are made short enough so that there are not too many temptations for others to hold competing meetings. All have public spaces for chapel, though Baylor has its Chapel-Forum in a meeting hall. Further, only Baylor does not technically worship. It conducts religious services, but does not insist or expect that all present participate.

What lessons are there to be drawn about the place of chapel in these six schools? One is that they make it clear that chapel is publicly endorsed as an official activity of the institution. The endorsement not only involves a prominent place and time for the chapel, but also provision for strong staffs and support. Relatively lavish resources are given to these chapel programs, especially compared to more pluralist church-related schools.

10. I realize that the use of the terms "chapel" and "dean of the chapel" and "chaplain" is biased in favor of Protestant language. Catholics use other terms. However, it is simply too complex in the following sections to include both usages, for which I apologize.

The leaders of chapel in these schools are distinguished and influential players in the overall lives of the schools. Interestingly, they are also pastors to the community who have mature pastoral skills; they are not primarily intellectual provocateurs or social activists. Nevertheless, they have intellectual gifts that support the engagement of faith and learning in the schools' larger missions.

One disturbing problem for all these schools is the declining rate of faculty attendance at chapel. To some extent this reflects the hectic character of current academic life, but it does reveal some faculty apathy toward and even disapproval of the worship life of the institution.[11] It might be time for faculty involved in faith and learning at these various schools to pledge themselves to at least weekly attendance at chapel. The importance of faculty support for chapel might also be a major topic for the faculty "socialization" projects that are gaining momentum in most of these schools. Faculty presence is very important for the morale of the chapel staff and the students that attend.

Additional Student Religious Formation

Certainly chapel is one of the main instruments of student religious formation, but it cannot be the only one. Choral and instrumental music are potent instruments of religious formation, especially in the Lutheran schools. Further, all six schools in this study nurture additional programs, including devotional and study groups in residence halls. These programs evidently draw students who are unlikely to appear at chapel, yet they are normally organized or at least coordinated by the chapel office. While the chapel office monitors the activities of other religious groups on campus, it wisely encourages — within reasonable parameters — a wide variety of ministries, some of which may be sponsored by off-campus agencies.

Although all six schools have admirable ministries in student residences, some are particularly strong because they observe two important truths. First, the best attempts at formation take place when students re-

11. A worship leader of one of the schools mentioned that some faculty do not come to chapel because they feel uncomfortable with one worship tradition — the Christian one — being privileged. Such is the sensibility of some faculty among even these explicitly Christian schools!

side on campus. When large numbers of students commute or live close to campus in non-university housing, the chances of reaching them with serious religious programming diminish considerably. The existence of off-campus fraternities is particularly problematic for nurturing Christian ethos, as they tend to dilute the overall sense of campus community. Second, the highly successful approach employed by Notre Dame illustrates the importance of adult presence in student residential halls. The fact that adults (rectors and assistant rectors) live, worship, and serve with the students contributes much to the quality of life of each dorm. Moreover, since the rector is normally a priest, the sense of religious presence is also elevated. Though it is certainly expensive, colleges and universities wishing to deepen the religious life of their students should seriously consider a similar approach. Additional benefits of this approach include an enhanced civility and a more persuasive version of *in loco parentis*. Student life is not set completely free to generate its own norms but rather is shaped according to the moral ethos represented by an authoritative adult.

Student life offices should also be staffed by Christians that are willing and able to guide their policies and programs according to the Christian vision of human flourishing. Perhaps professional training in student services in secular graduate schools is necessary, but an understanding and commitment to an explicit Christian ethos is just as important. If that is not present, a blunt utilitarianism emerges that is aimed at simply doing no harm. The higher and larger aspirations of the Christian vision of life are then left unarticulated, and those students who aspire to such a vision are left high and dry. Moreover, those who do not aspire to such heights are generally not dissuaded from self-destructive actions by the display of even the direst effects of those actions. Without a guiding moral force undergirded by thoughtful religious belief, student life offices tend toward benign oversight of a lowering of the moral expectations of the whole community.[12]

12. A most bizarre example of this occurred some years ago at Roanoke College when it was at the nadir of its relation to its religious heritage. Two middle-aged Lutheran matrons who staffed the student health center thought the public health of the college would best be served by their handing out condoms in the student dining room a few days prior to spring break. The students found it a bit embarrassing to take such contraband from women who could well be their mothers; furthermore, the women themselves would never condone in their own behavior the kind of separation between sex and love that they were encouraging in students by their actions.

It is similar with the community service programs that now abound in our schools, including the six we have examined. The Christian rationale behind the schools' commitment to them needs to be rehearsed publicly and brought into reflective conversation with student experience of service. It is wonderful that so much service goes on in colleges and universities. It is fine that American civic ideals are being revived across the country in all sorts of schools, including Christian ones. But Christians have motivations and reasons for serving the neighbor that transcend civic responsibility. Without rehearsing the Christian rationale, that sense of civic responsibility can easily marginalize Christian motivations, and the service activity itself then does not figure into the spiritual maturation of Christian students. If integration of faith and learning is important in academic life, it is also important in service to and by students.

Living traditions — and these six schools are themselves living traditions — also carry many practices, habits, celebrations, and memories that make them unique and attractive communities. All six schools have colorful corporate lives that include significant religious dimensions; because they are also communities of belief nourished by their religious traditions, they exhibit characteristics that can only be called "covenantal." They are dense networks of both meaning and obligation that persist over time. When new students or faculty enter these communities, they know they are coming into something more descript than the ordinary run of colleges and universities. It is important that these schools have effective ways of introducing all new members of the community — including staff — into the living tradition that is theirs. It is also important that the treatment of all members of the community be consistent with the high ethical ideals that are publicly professed. Hypocrisy is perhaps an inevitable element of any community of high ideals, but a healthy community has effective means of narrowing the gap between ideals and reality.

Vision

The six schools employ religious visions to organize and direct their identities and missions. Their mission statements — as well as the rhetorical flourishes of their leaders — are rarely articulated in a careful and systematic theological manner. Such systematics would not make for stirring reading for any of the key constituencies of the school. However, the statements are always implicitly theological. One must look further for the careful and systematic theologizing, which is often found in the documents the school has prepared as background for its mission statement. Its theology of education may also be found in the study documents it uses to acquaint new faculty with its religious tradition. The Reformed, Catholic, and Lutheran schools have had long histories of theological reflection on their identities and missions. Because two of the schools — Wheaton and Baylor — have evangelical/pietist backgrounds, their theological articulations have been developed later than the other four. But they have made up lost ground quickly.

Each of them has avoided the theological deficiencies we outlined in Chapter Two. The formerly pietist schools, which once had a- or anti-theological attitudes, have adopted to a great extent the Reformed theological model of both articulating the faith and of integrating faith and learning. None of the colleges or universities has fallen into the trap of extremely liberal theology, wherein the Christian theological account is eroded over time in favor of contemporary philosophical or cultural currents. Each has maintained confidence in the Christian account as the guiding paradigm for the life of the college. Though St. Olaf has been tempted by a deficient Lutheran "First Article" theology, its dominant Lutheran vision has resisted the weaknesses of that approach. None of the schools is currently threatened by a reactionary or fundamentalist outlook that would prevent both lively theology and dynamic engagement of secular learning.

What then constitutes an adequate theological vision? In order to elaborate the marks of such a theology I wish to return to the categories with which I began — comprehensiveness, unsurpassability, and centrality. An adequate theological vision, one that can properly shape the identity and mission of a Christian college or university, is one that is comprehensive in scope, unsurpassable in its claim to be a vehicle of ultimate truth, and central in its relationship to the issues schools face.

Comprehensiveness

A comprehensive theology draws upon the whole Christian narrative as it is elaborated in the Bible and in trinitarian Christian theology. Only this largeness of scope will provide the kind of light needed in order to see the truth and falsity, possibilities and limits, in the many smaller secular sources of light that are a part of a modern college or university. Furthermore, a theology confident in the comprehensiveness of the Christian account will draw upon the vast stores of wisdom the Christian intellectual tradition has built up over the millennia. Christians have thought seriously and persuasively about the origin and destiny of the world, about human nature and its sinful predicament, about the meaning of nature and history, about the meaning of our own personal lives in that larger story, about human longing and fulfillment, about the Christian meaning and conduct of life in this world. Christians have thought about the public and visible dimensions of our whole lives, not just the mysterious and ineffable dimensions of our private existence. A Christian college has to employ a theology that is public and comprehensive, not merely private and pietist, because a public, comprehensive theology is the only sort that provides an adequate conversation partner for the many fields of inquiry in a modern university or college.

Several caveats are in order here. The engagement of the Christian theological account with the several disciplines does not go on all the time and by everyone in every classroom. A good deal of the time in any decent classroom is given over to transmitting knowledge of the field in question as understood by the world at large. But at the depths and boundaries of every field profound issues appear that can be brought into dialogue with the comprehensive Christian theological account.

Second, not everyone on a faculty can be expected to master the vast wisdom of the Christian intellectual tradition. Certainly a number of persons in the theology department should have this capacity and the willingness to use it on behalf of the college. A large contingent should have a solid lay knowledge of Christian theology, enough so that they can relate their own fields of inquiry to their Christian convictions in a meaningful way. Another segment may not have the expertise necessary to carry on such an engagement but should have the goodwill to support and appreciate it when others in the school do it.

Finally, I do not mean by comprehensiveness an arrogant overconfidence that the Christian account as interpreted by any number of different persons has all the answers to all the questions. Christian theology conveys wisdom and insight, but there is much to be filled in by secular knowledge. Some of that "filling in" will complement Christian wisdom, but some of it will create dissonance, if not indigestion, to mix metaphors. There will be much room for mutual critique and, sadly, for irresolvable differences in some cases. Nevertheless, this comprehensive Christian theological account must be given genuine intellectual status in a Christian college.

Unsurpassability

An adequate theology confidently flows from the classical core of Christianity, from its fundamental truth claims. The core of Christian religious and moral belief is articulated in the ecumenical creeds but elaborated in what is called the apostolic tradition, the Great Tradition, or "mere" Christianity. It is this that must be unsurpassable and finally non-negotiable. A Christian college or university must have a critical mass of participants who actually believe in its truth.

Among the six schools, Calvin and Wheaton most vigorously hold to the Christian vision's unsurpassability. Both are willing to override secular claims with Christian ones in their academic life, though that is not done as easily or crudely as the outside world suspects. Since the critical-mass schools invite people into their enterprises who believe that other views of life and reality do in fact surpass the Christian account, these schools run real risks. They risk the chance that those who hold those other views may in fact become the critical mass and depose the Christian account. That has happened in many church-related colleges and universities. They gamble that students may be persuaded that those other views surpass the Christian account and thereby lose their faith in it. That also has happened to many students who have lost their faith while in schools their parents thought would strengthen it.

The critical-mass schools, however, think their ventures are worth the risk. They contend that only in genuine dialogue with opposing views can the Christian account achieve a genuine unsurpassability in the minds and hearts of faculty and students alike. Further, they believe that only a theology that genuinely engages the world of learning, with all the risks that entails, can extend and apply the meanings from that core, draw out implications that have not been thought of before, find the flexibility and creativity to engage secular proposals that seem to have little obvious relation to that core, and garner the courage to submit the core itself to scrutiny. It is the last possibility that is frightening, but such is the exhilarating uncertainty of free academic life.

I suspect there is room for both philosophies of Christian higher education. There is good reason to believe that college-age persons need a protected shelter for the formation of — perhaps even indoctrination into — the Christian vision and ethos. The world has changed. Youth are no longer shaped by a coherent culture that gives them a firm identity as young people. There are so many competing philosophies of life battering the young that it seems to make sense to use a longer time to prepare them for the struggle ahead. Few of the Calvin or Wheaton graduates seem terribly wounded by their longer time in a Christian incubator. Indeed, there seems to be a good deal of evidence that that incubation has made them more resilient in the face of secular intellectual temptations. Their approach may lead to fewer casualties. Critical-mass schools risk those casualties for an education that they believe is truer to the world in which students are soon to live. They want the intellectual dialogue and conflict to take place under their auspices, not later, when there may be few intellectual allies around. In both of these approaches the possibility exists for fruitful engagement of the comprehensive Christian faith.

Centrality

An adequate theology of education has confidence that the Christian account is central, that it addresses the essential issues and values of life and reality. Perhaps an example will be helpful. Glenn Tinder, a distinguished political philosopher, has argued in *The Political Meaning of Christianity* that the Christian view of human nature is definitive for Western politics. In his parlance "the exalted individual" is a translation of the Christian teaching about each person being created in the image of God and each being redeemed by Christ. Humans are, as he puts it, "sacred but not good."[13] In addition to being exalted by God, they debase themselves. They are fallen; they have a propensity to idolize themselves and their works. This dual definition, he argues, is at the center of Western politics. On the one hand, it means that each life is irreplaceable, has rights, cannot be treated with impunity, and has a dignity far beyond utilitarian calcula-

13. Glenn Tinder, *The Political Meaning of Christianity* (Baton Rouge: Louisiana State University Press, 1989), pp. 76-78. His larger argument is distilled in his article "Can We Be Good without God?" *The Atlantic Monthly,* December 1989, pp. 69-85.

tions. On the other hand, it asserts that humans left to themselves will abuse their freedom by making a hell out of the world they have been given.

Without this background of Christian teaching and its ontological grounding in God, politics will become either cynical — judging humans by the quality and intensity of their lives, as is now happening in the West — or dangerously idealistic — looking to politics for messianic purposes, as happened in both fascism and communism. For Tinder, then, as for serious Christian schools, Christian theological and moral teachings address the central issues of human existence. Christian schools should not only be the guardians of such an intellectual heritage, they should also employ it as a normative perspective in many fields of inquiry. Christian anthropology, with its ontological moorings, is relevant not only to political science but also to psychology, sociology, and literature, to name but a few fields of inquiry.

Our six schools are likely to take the Christian theological account as central for their intellectual inquiry and for their life together, though there would be many cases where such a practice would be honored more in principle than fact. But the principle is important in a world in which Christian normative perspectives have often been removed from the deliberations about the most important issues of our time.

◆　　◆　　◆

Until this point I have talked about the Christian theological vision in general without much mention of denominational nuances. That is because it is important to emphasize that being a Christian college or university means adhering to the general core of the Christian account before we get to our Christian differences. We are first of all catholic — meaning universal — Christians. We share so much of a common inheritance of doctrine and practice that it is a mistake too eagerly to emphasize our differences, which do not amount to much when we compare them with secular approaches. These are, first of all, Christian schools; we should not overemphasize the differences involved.

After affirming this commonality, however, it must be admitted that there are real differences in religious outlook that affect both vision and ethos. The theologies of the Reformed, Lutheran, Catholic, and evangelical traditions are indeed different. Each theology has a different way of relating revelation and reason, Christ and culture, grace and nature. Those differences in theology take the schools along distinct paths. Notre Dame is simply different than Calvin. St. Olaf and Valparaiso are different than Wheaton. All are different than Baylor.

Richard Niebuhr's famous book *Christ and Culture,* for all its limitations after all these years, remains helpful to sort out those specific theological traditions in a basic way.[14] The three great central, magisterial traditions of the church are represented in our six schools: the Lutheran (Christ and Culture in Paradox); the Catholic (Christ Above Culture); and the Reformed (Christ Transforming Culture). As we have already observed, the evangelical traditions represented by Wheaton and Baylor seem now to be incorporating a Reformed perspective in their approach to higher education, yet maintaining room for other views.

The Reformed theological tradition views reason, culture, and nature as more pervasively fallen than does the Catholic tradition. This means that secular approaches to truth must have their implicit worldview assumptions analyzed and critiqued. The chastened secular product can then be integrated into a specific and detailed Christian worldview. This does not mean that all secular knowledge is faulty; it does mean that it must fit with the Christian worldview. Nor does it mean that all current formulations of Christian truth are infallible; theology itself must be in a constant state of reformation. This approach obviously has curricular, non-curricular, and pedagogical implications for all the schools that employ it.

The Catholic tradition assigns more autonomy to reason, culture, and nature. When all three work properly, they rise toward and converge with Christian revelation. However, even the Catholic tradition does not assign total autonomy to reason and culture. As the Notre Dame mission statement has it, secular reason must be subject to "critical refinement." The pope's interpretation of reason in his encyclicals differs markedly from that employed by secular philosophers of a modern or postmodern stripe. Reason is defined and interpreted differently in the ongoing traditions of thought. Nevertheless, Notre Dame's mission statement does not speak of "worldview analysis" or of the transformation of human knowl-

14. H. Richard Niebuhr, *Christ and Culture* (New York: Harper and Brothers, 1956); see especially Chapter One, where he introduces five ways that Christians have related Christ and culture historically.

edge in order to claim it for Christ. In the Catholic view, genuine human knowledge already belongs to Christ.

The Lutheran view is more dialectical than the preceding two. It has more confidence in reason than the Reformed but less than the Catholic. Since the incarnate Christ (the embodiment of goodness and wisdom) wound up on a cross, there seems to be a paradoxical relation between God's truth and goodness, on the one hand, and human reason and culture on the other.[15] Revelation both affirms and contradicts reason. Thus a Christian college must both appreciate and be wary of human claims to truth and goodness, including its own. A genuinely Lutheran approach would engage in a serious and extended conversation with all secular approaches. It would employ the full Christian theological account as the honored conversation partner in the dialogue with secular culture. But this dialectical approach, while persuasive in principle, has many flaws in practice. Lutherans have often separated Christ and culture, grace and nature, revelation and reason. The dialectical model at its best demands a critical mass of faculty willing to learn enough of the theological account to employ it effectively in dialogue with their own fields of inquiry. It also benefits from a critical mass willing to appreciate and support the conversation when it is done well by others. Thus far, few Lutheran schools have had the resolve to forge such a critical mass at that first, more challenging level.

Nevertheless, with all its limitations, I find the Lutheran approach compelling.[16] However, in attempting a theological account that aspires to be comprehensive, unsurpassable, and central, Lutherans, like Reformed and Catholic Christians, would be exceedingly foolish if they failed to draw upon the great stores of broader Christian truth and wisdom that are available to them. Lutheran thought is anemic in relation to the capacious stream of the great Christian intellectual tradition. Lutheran, Reformed, and Catholic believers can give their own distinct twists to the tradition they wish to pass along, but all benefit when they admit joyfully that the whole is far richer than its parts.

15. I have elaborated an interpretation of the Lutheran posture toward politics and culture in *The Paradoxical Vision: A Public Theology for the Twenty-First Century* (Minneapolis: Fortress Press, 1995).

16. My case for the Lutheran approach to Christian higher education can be found in "A Lutheran Vision/Version of Christian Higher Education," *Lutheran Forum*, Fall 1997, pp. 77-85.

Embedding the Vision

It is clear that each school's animating vision, in both its religious and more specifically theological versions, has to be articulated and embedded in the ongoing life of the college. It has to be articulated in the mission statement of the college and in the school's presentation of itself in admissions and development materials. But above all it has to be embedded in people.

First, it has to be inculcated in new members of the community, not only but especially faculty. A school's particular religious and theological account has to be communicated in an effective way to all entering parties. This takes time and resources, and probably involves required participation. Calvin and Wheaton are particularly strong in this regard, with Baylor gaining strength. St. Olaf comes next, with Valparaiso a bit deficient. Oddly, Notre Dame does very little along these lines with its faculty, though it is far more vigorous with its students.

Second, the animating vision has to be borne by a first-rate theology department willing to take up that burden. The theology department has to be the trustworthy guardian of the school's particular tradition of thought. It has to be unified in this sense of its mission. While all in the department certainly need not be experts in that tradition, a strong cadre of teachers and scholars ought to be. When the school needs the pure notes sounded, the department ought to be able to do it eagerly and clearly. Certainly other traditions of thought might well be included in the department, even non-Christian traditions of thought. It would add more to genuine religious education and dialogue for believers in those traditions to teach them. While Wheaton and Calvin have theology departments that are willing to represent the host tradition of thought, it seems that they make their departments unduly exclusive. Lately Notre Dame seems to strike a nice balance. Baylor seems a bit unsettled, while the two Lutheran schools enjoy only a modicum of common vision.

Third, Christian colleges ought to make opportunities available and attractive for faculty to take courses in Christian theology. If genuine engagement of faith and learning are to take place, non-theologians need to acquire at least a solid lay education in basic Christian theology. After all, Christian schools are asking non-theologians to step out of their own expertise in order to engage faith with their field of inquiry. These faculty members should be encouraged to acquire a sufficiently sophisticated intellectual account of their faith as preparation for an engagement that does justice to their secular expertise. Following this opportunity for general theological education, more specialized courses in the school's particular tradition of thought ought to be offered to interested faculty. When such theological education reaches more and more faculty, the possibilities for exciting faith and learning engagement will multiply exponentially.

Fourth, the animating religious vision of the college or university can be bolstered by funding institutes, centers, endowed professorships, and staff positions that deal with the themes and practices of its sponsoring tradition. Notre Dame is a master of such a strategy, but all six of our schools have exerted their own efforts in that direction. Creating such agencies to carry the vision in a special way not only gives additional luster and flair to Christian schools, it also can partially compensate for failures in the general practice of the school to bear the vision adequately. Indeed, there is a bit of a danger in allowing such instruments to carry too much of the load. As either the finishing touch or compensation, however, these agencies are very significant in conveying the particular characteristics of the sponsoring religious heritage. An additional advantage is that they are permanent if adequately endowed.

While neither orthodox schools nor critical-mass schools should in principle need faith and learning groups, there are in fact reasons why they should be maintained. By "faith and learning groups," I mean those organizations that devote themselves to strengthening the interaction of faith and learning on both the personal and institutional fronts. They keep track of the burgeoning literature on Christian higher education, they find ways to encourage faith and learning interaction in the programs, conferences, and curricula of the school, and they encourage faculty to do their own faith and learning engagement. Another of their important tasks is to help the school maintain its involvement in intercollegiate conversations and networks, such as the Lilly Program in Humanities and the Arts or the Rhodes Consultation.

In principle, each college or university should itself be performing the tasks listed above. However, the manifold challenges of higher education can push these tasks to the back burner. An active faith and learning group, even in orthodox and critical-mass schools, can serve as a kind of conscience for such schools. It can monitor their performance, remind them of their current commitments, and raise the horizon toward which such schools might strive in the future.

The careful attention given to persons, ethos, and vision has made our six schools identifiably Christian in all the major facets of their lives. The strategies they have employed have flowed from the fundamental conviction that the Christian religious account is comprehensive, unsurpassable, and central. From those strategies I have tried to distill the essential ones that will be useful for those schools who want to "keep the faith" in their institutions as well as for those who want to strengthen and extend it. Perhaps it is not necessary for Christian schools to follow them all; it is probably impossible for them to do so. But each is worth consideration for those interested in keeping or restoring the faith in colleges and universities whose histories are bound up with the Christian story.

8 | *The Long Road Back*

What follows is directed toward those colleges and universities that have experienced the darkening trends I outlined in Chapter One. Their numbers are legion. For many and various reasons the Christian vision and ethos no longer shape their identity and mission. The communicants of the sponsoring traditions are present in only a haphazard way and have no special influence as communicants on the life of the schools. The mission statement of the colleges is obviously shaped by secular academic or civic concerns. Religion, if it figures in it at all, is relegated to the founding of the institutions or to vague talk of "values" or "atmosphere." Religious concerns are so marginal to these schools that a public discussion of their role is almost impossible. Faculty cannot see their relevance. The ethos of the schools is by this time highly secular. Piety is tucked into minor interstices of college life.

Yet in many cases, the relationship between a school and its sponsoring tradition is not one of hostility but rather of affable distance. What can be done to make that relationship stronger and richer? If what I have argued throughout the book is at all persuasive, I need not go into the reasons for reconnecting with that sponsoring heritage here. What can be done and how to proceed are the relevant issues here.

First, there have to be "true believers" somewhere in the major constituencies of a school that are willing to act in concert as agents of change. They must believe that the tradition to which the college is related should be publicly relevant to its life. But such true believers must also have the prudence to realize that their school may be quite impervious to their efforts to make its religious heritage more relevant. The inertia of institutional life is an awesome thing. After all, the vast majority of current participants in the life of most colleges were probably not around during the days of religious influence and may well be befuddled or alarmed when it is re-introduced. Except in highly unusual circumstances — the near collapse of a school necessitating a radical new beginning, for example — there can be no simple leap from "affable distance" or "accidental pluralism" to a critical-mass college. Prudence dictates that goals be more feasible. The intermediate stage between affable distance and critical mass is "intentional pluralism," a more realistic goal. It is that toward which the agents of change should strive.

While initiatives might come from cohorts of true believers in any of the college constituencies, it is unlikely that they will get off the ground without strong commitment to them by the president. The president might arrive on the job with such a commitment or might be persuaded to it by board or faculty members, but he or she must be "on board" if anything is to happen. It will be the president who will convince the board to go along with plans to reconnect to a religious heritage, not faculty members or the dean. By this time only a few, if any, on the board will understand why reconnection should be attempted or what it might mean. The president will have to do the explaining and persuading. He or she will also have to acquire a dean that understands and supports such a purpose. The president will also have to begin introducing Christian rhetoric into key addresses to and materials for the various constituencies of the college. Such overt references have probably long since departed and therefore must be slowly and carefully re-introduced.

Faculty members are crucial in getting initiatives off the ground. A small group of faculty communicants of the parent tradition might be the initiators of the move to reconnect meaningfully, but they will have to convince the president that it is an important move. Then they can provide indispensable support for the president as moves are made to reconnect. In fact, one of the most important things for such a faculty group to do is to get a faith and learning organization started. The organization may begin with only a few persons, but if proper educational enticements are offered, other supporters may well be found. The growth of such an organization might be slow and painful, though, because in such a college the faculty members currently in place were certainly not selected for their interest in or commitment to the engagement of faith and learning. As the group grows, it is important to invite administrators and staff to the group's meetings. It is especially important to invite the president and other top officials.

Once going, the faith and learning group can study the copious materials on the secularization of American colleges and universities. When persons see what has indeed happened, they often have a kind of revelatory experience. They begin to wonder why religion has been so marginalized, and they can at that point become open to the possibility of its more meaningful role in college life. After all, the school is still related to a religious tradition. Why shouldn't that relation mean something? Later the group can invite speakers who can analyze both the secularization process and the efforts of schools that have maintained a robust relation to their heritage. They can read books about their own tradition's approach to Christian higher education. As trust builds, members of the faith and learning group can reflect on strategies for their school to make stronger connections with its heritage. They might serve as mentors in a voluntary program to acquaint new faculty with the tradition of the school. Somewhere along the way they can also take their cause to a broader audience by sponsoring events that address the subject of faith and learning and also make specific proposals for change in the life of the school.

A very important function of such a group is to encourage the president to apply for school membership in networks like the Lilly Fellows Program in Humanities and the Arts or the Rhodes Consultation on the Future of the Church-Related College, which exist to stimulate conversation about what it means to be a church-related institution. If the sponsoring denomination supports such an ongoing conversation among its network of schools, it is important to participate in that conversation. These networks supply important opportunities to encourage the group already engaged in faith and learning initiatives, but perhaps even more importantly, to send possible comrades in the cause to events that will spur them on and broaden their horizons. As membership in the faith and learning group is expanded, it can also sponsor national or regional events in conjunction with those networks. These strategies can create real momentum.

A committed president supported by a faculty faith and learning group can then begin to move toward a program of intentional pluralism, though that program may yet be only that of a concerted group of persons within the school rather than the broad majority. They will have to articulate the meaning of such a program and convince some members of the board, donors, administrators, and faculty members of its desirability. They will have to explain what this "intentional pluralism" really is.

First of all, intentional pluralism flows from the conviction that the sponsoring tradition has elements of vision and ethos that should be relevant in some significant way to a school's life if there is to be any real meaning in the school's ongoing connection to that tradition. But since the time likely has long passed when the Christian account as vision and ethos was the organizing principle of the school, it must have some other kind of relation to the school. That other kind of relation is not one of preeminence or privilege, but one of *assured voice*. If the Christian account is not and cannot be the organizing paradigm, it can at least provide one voice in the larger array of voices that inhabit any college or university. Furthermore, that voice can be assured a role by intentionally placing it amid the key facets of the school's life — faculty, administration, board, and student body.

Under the conditions of postmodernism in which the Enlightenment paradigm has been deposed or at least fractured, it has become increasingly attractive and imperative to represent a diversity of voices and perspectives in the ongoing life of a college or university. Certainly a college related to a religious tradition should find space for the voice or perspective of that sponsoring tradition to be represented amid the many others. If feminists, Marxists, utilitarians, and skeptics can offer their perspectives in college affairs, it certainly seems reasonable to suggest that Christians should be able to so in a school their tradition founded. Indeed, some public colleges and universities have provided space for Christian perspectives among all the others. Private colleges and universities should be able systematically to provide space for their own sponsoring traditions.

The best place to begin the program of intentional pluralism is to garner the necessary resources from sympathetic donors to endow centers or institutes or programs that lift up the Christian perspective on relevant matters. In some cases, it may be important as a first step to endow centers that create a place for the particular tradition's perspective. In other cases, it may be advantageous simply to focus on the broader Christian perspective. For example, a Presbyterian college could endow a center for religion and society, or a Baptist college an institute for religious freedom, or a Lutheran college a program in Christian bioethics. Such a strategy not only offers high-visibility positions to serious Christians but also interjects the Christian perspective into many discussions where it would not normally appear. The latter is especially important because it may persuade various constituencies that Christianity bears an intellectual and moral tradition that can be employed in serious discussions. It prepares the way for the provision of yet more places for a Christian perspective.

Beyond these "strategic hamlets," the agents of reconnection might try to persuade others to return the Christian voice in the chaplaincy, in student religious organizations, and in the religion department. Endowments for denominational chaplaincies and professorships in Lutheran or Catholic or other denominational studies assure Christian presence in the college in perpetuity. What's more, if these positions are endowed, they do not draw resources from the general budget and therefore are likely to be less controversial. Such gifts are hard to refuse, even by prickly faculty, though careful consultation with key faculty should always be the order of the day.

Other proposals will present much more difficult challenges. One will be in "non-religious" academic appointments. An effective intentional pluralism will seek to insure the presence of Christian public intellectuals in most every department. In every department there should be at least one professor who is willing and able publicly to exhibit the engagement of faith and learning in a persuasive way. Students can then be given a model for relating their Christian convictions to their studies. But many department chairs will naturally be unconvinced that such a model is necessary; most department chairs in such schools believe that religious conviction or outlook should have no role in faculty hiring. It is helpful, of course, if the dean can select department chairs that are sympathetic to this intentional pluralism. Further, it is a great aid to the cause if the dean is able to offer incentives to a department for hiring such persons. The best incentive would be to offer an endowed position, one that stipulates that the occupant represent Christian themes in his or her work. But another incentive might be to fund either partially or fully another position in the department if it pays attention to the Christian tradition in that department. The religion department in particular should have at least one communicant of the sponsoring tradition who is well versed in it and willing to articulate its perspective in broader discussions. While most religion departments currently are committed to "religious studies," there should be at least one person who speaks *for* the tradition as well as *about* it.

As this intentionally pluralist approach gains momentum, it will be important to hire faculty who do not simply tolerate this sort of pluralism but support it. Such faculty understand that the sponsoring tradition deserves some affirmative-action strategies on its behalf, if only to keep a Christian voice audible in the larger conversation. As the argument for a Christian presence in higher education gains credibility, more and more potential faculty members who support this approach will become available.

In due time such intentional pluralism might well show up in the mission statement of the school and then be reflected in its curricular offerings, especially in its general education requirements. This intentional pluralism should find its way into the school's admissions materials and other public presentations of itself. A careful statement of this sort of pluralism will not frighten "non-religious" students away but may well attract more serious Christian students in general and more communicants of the sponsoring tradition in particular. Students of this sort likely will contribute positively to the ethos of the school. This approach will have the added feature of assuring the sponsoring tradition that the school is taking its heritage seriously. Donors from the sponsoring tradition will then more likely be willing to support the religious dimensions of the school's life.

In student affairs and the college's service activities, Christian perspectives and rationales should be included along with those coming from non-religious sources. For example, student affairs might well include Christian arguments for pre-marital sexual abstinence ("true love waits") along with the more utilitarian arguments ("you might catch a terrible disease") favored by various secular establishments (if they even argue for abstinence at all). Likewise, Christian arguments for service to others ("all are created in the image of God and worthy of respect and care") as well as civic ("you should pay back the community for the opportunities it has given you") might well be included. Why should the school be embarrassed about articulating its founding tradition's rationale for community life and service, especially if it is part of a non-exclusive approach? There will no doubt be serious Christians among the students of such a church-related college, and there is good reason to inspire them with their own tradition's rhetoric.

Even more than critical-mass schools, intentionally pluralist schools will see themselves as assuring voice for broadly Christian views, but yet under the auspices of the particular denominational leadership. While there will be only a small minority of communicants of the sponsoring heritage, they will have a special responsibility to lead the efforts at effecting intentional pluralism for reasons I outlined in Chapter Seven. But the Christian "slots" at these schools will be filled with many kinds of Christians, not just members of the sponsoring tradition.

Changing the ethos of a school moving toward intentional pluralism is a great challenge, perhaps greater even than changing the character of the faculty. Student culture in secularized schools is invariably resistant to any limits on freedom, especially if those limits are religiously inspired. Fraternities and sororities shape a good deal of the ethos in many such schools, and they too resist incursions from outside. If a school has not touted itself as beholden to Christian religious or moral commitments, it has not created a very fertile ground for Christian ethos, to say the least. The Christian perspective will be seen as simply an arbitrary power move.

In such a situation, it is best to work from the bottom up. Partly secularized schools often have active interdenominational groups working within them, such as InterVarsity Christian Fellowship or Campus Crusade for Christ. There may even be some small denominational groups. The school's chaplain, who generally belongs to the sponsoring tradition, may also have an ecumenical ministry going on. There probably will be strong service groups. The administration and faculty, who might well serve as advisors for these various groups, should encourage all of this. If these groups flourish and multiply, they can change the ethos for the better.

The school can also recruit students on the basis of religion, among other criteria. Students who have high civic and religious involvement in high school are likely to make good citizens of a college. Church-related colleges should overcome their embarrassment about considering religious criteria for entrance. They should even make systematic efforts to recruit students of the sponsoring tradition. It is remarkable how much a small minority of good students from the sponsoring tradition can positively influence a school through their leadership capacities. These two recruitment strategies together can also help to improve the school's ethos.

When Christian religious presence becomes more visible on campus, it may be time to bring chapel into a public place and fixed time. Though it will take a long time to establish chapel as a central event in the life of this sort of school, chapel can become a realistic alternative for many persons of the college. Since administrators are generally in charge of the daily schedule, it may lie within the power of the president to carve out a time or two in the weekly schedule for chapel. Considerable attention and resources should be given to chapel so that it will be a high-quality, attractive experience for those who choose to attend. The support of the faith and learning group should be elicited, along with that of student religious organizations. If the chaplain can count on a decent number of people in the weekly or bi-weekly sessions, he or she will be encouraged to take even greater care for the quality of the worship. The school's musical resources should be employed as much as possible. Attractive faculty speakers and outside guests should be invited to speak. With such an approach, over time chapel can perhaps again become a habit for at least a portion of the school's participants.

These cumulative efforts may well succeed if carried out wisely by an organized and committed minority in the school. They may lead to an intentionally pluralist school in which the Christian account is assured a role among the other accounts that will no doubt be current in the school. Accomplishing this may well add flavor and differentiation to a school that might otherwise look exactly like the hundreds of generic private liberal arts colleges that once had strong relations to a religious tradition. It might well add healthy pluralism to a homogenizing world of higher education. It could add a bit more vitality to civil society. But the main reason for creating room for the Christian account is that it is the right thing to do. The Christian vision and ethos have indeed played a powerful role in the lives of the vast majority of people in America in particular and the West in general. They continue to play such a role; why shouldn't they have voice in a college? More pointedly, why shouldn't they have a role to play in a college that that was founded and nurtured by a particular tradition within that larger Christian account? A tradition, in the words of G. K. Chesterton, is a democracy in which the dead have a vote. Perhaps it is time for those partly secularized colleges to hear those ancient voices, take responsibility for the cause they championed, and reconnect with the heritage of those who have gone before and those who enliven that heritage today.

Index

Accidentally pluralist colleges, 49, 52-53, 207-14; public relevance and rhetoric of, 56-57; theology departments and courses in, 60-61; chapel and ethos of, 62; church support and governance of, 64

Add-on model of faith and learning, 36-37, 76, 81, 105, 112, 142. *See also* Two-spheres model of faith and learning

Adrian, William, ix-x

Armstrong, Anton, 157

Baylor University, 6, 141-42, 180; ethos, 165-69; persons, 80-82, 113-14, 117; sponsorship, 78-83; vision, 81-82, 112-17

Beaty, Michael, 80-81, 114, 117

Bebbington, David, 74

Becker, Carl, 25

Bellah, Robert, 23

Blanchard, Charles, 75

Blanchard, Jonathan, 75

Boe, Rev. L. W., 89

Bratt, James D., 69n.1

Buras, Todd, 81

Burtchaell, James T., ix-x, 3, 5-6, 9, 19, 29, 36, 40, 44-45, 65, 91, 126, 131, 133, 183

Buswell, J. Oliver, 75

Calvin College, 6, 77, 81, 111, 141-43, 154; ethos, 145-49; persons, 70, 72-73, 97-98; sponsorship, 69-73; vision, 71-72, 97-107

Christian account, 7, 15-17, 25-29, 32, 70, 72, 76-77, 81, 97-101, 105-6, 112-15, 127-28, 134-35, 140-44, 148, 152, 158-59, 163, 168, 173, 183-85, 196-206, 210-11, 213-14; centrality of, 15-17, 200-201; comprehensiveness of, 15-17, 197-99; unsurpassability of, 15-17, 199-200

Christian Reformed Church, 69-73, 97-98, 146, 180

Christiansen, F. Melius, 156

Colleges, Christian: accidentally pluralist, *see* Accidentally pluralist colleges; Baptist, 45, 78-83, 112-17, 165-69; Catholic, 21-22, 30, 83-87, 117-26, 143-44, 169-74, 180-81, 202-3; and church governance, 183-85; and church sponsorship, 63-64, 139-40, 164, 179-83; critical-mass, *see* Critical-mass colleges; evangelical, 73-78, 104-12, 149-54, 180; intentionally pluralist, *see* Inten-

215

LaVergne, TN USA
11 April 2010
178891LV00006B/11/A

QUALITY WITH SOUL